¶ LIFE IN ELIZABETHAN DAYS, A Picture of a
Typical English Community at the End of the
Sixteenth Century.

LIFE IN
ELIZABETHAN DAYS

*A Picture of a Typical English
Community at the End of the
Sixteenth Century*

By

WILLIAM STEARNS DAVIS
Author of "Life on a Mediæval Barony," *Etc.*

HARPER & ROW, PUBLISHERS
NEW YORK, EVANSTON, AND LONDON

¶ To my teacher, ROGER BIGELOW MERRIMAN, who taught me the vast significance of the Sixteenth Century.

¶ Preface

THIS book describes life in the England of Queen Elizabeth in terms of the concrete. Perhaps no Boroughport or Hollydean Hall can be discovered on the maps of the 1550's, but there were scores of towns and hundreds of rich manors in which the things discussed in this study were wholly typical. The Hollydeans were not wiser, more cultivated or better than a great many contemporaries among the wealthier gentry; the episodes laid in Boroughport could be duplicated in almost any chartered town near the seaboard.

The importance of understanding the civilization of the Elizabethan age needs no reassertion. Perhaps the present study may prove a little useful as a commentary upon the plays of Shakespeare and his associates, but the interest is always in the manners and the customs, not the literary lore and the background of the epoch.

To write a book like this, the first requisite should be a working knowledge of those authors who directly interpret the life of this age. William Harrison's *Description of England,* Philip Stubbes's *Anatomy of Abuses,* the various writings of Thomas Dekker and Thomas Nash, and of a great number of minor poets and pamphleteers, provide a large part of all the details herein presented. The very numerous quotations sprinkled through these pages usually indicate a direct quotation from a contemporary author, although the plan of the book permits very few cross references.

Very great is my indebtedness to many modern commentators. Particularly I would acknowledge the constant use of that great compendium *Shakespeare's England* (edited by Raleigh, Onions, and others, two volumes, Oxford; 2d edition, 1926). Almost equally valuable have been the two collections of Elizabethan social documents—J. D. Wilson's *Life in Shakespeare's England* (Cambridge, 1926), and G. B. Harrison's *England in Shakespeare's Day* (London and New York, 1928). Sir Sidney Lee's *Life of William Shakespeare* (new edition, New York, 1927) contains much interesting general matter. As for Miss M. St. Claire Byrne's *Elizabethan Life in Town and Country* (London, 1925), a volume of the highest scholarship and general excellence, it is enough to say that if it had been cast in a somewhat different form this present effort would have been useless. My indebtedness betrays itself on very many pages. Finally, in the chapter dealing with superstition and witchcraft, I gladly confess my use of the very curious material, presented with a rare combination of scholarly ability and genuine humor, in my friend Professor Wallace Notestein's *History of Witchcraft in England* (Washington, 1911).

Since the whole subject of Tudor London has been admirably treated by Sir Walter Besant, it has seemed wise to omit any direct discussion of the life of the metropolis.

This book, of course, was written in the twentieth century for twentieth-century readers; there is, therefore, no attempt to imitate the sixteenth-century diction except in the way of quotation or very occasional suggestion.

W. S. D.

Exeter, New Hampshire.
February 7, 1930.

T A B L E   o f   C o n t e n t s

[ix]

TABLE OF CONTENTS

I L L U S T R A T I O N S

ILLUSTRATIONS

¶ LIFE IN ELIZABETHAN DAYS.

¶ *Chapter* I: CONCERNING GLORIANA'S ENGLAND

IN the year 159– the famous town of Boroughport, situate in the county of Thorpshire, lay east of the sun and west of the moon upon the southern coast of England. If you ask its location more particularly, we may add it was not over twenty leagues from the Isle of Wight, and within one day's hard and two days' easy riding of London.

In this time of "the most high, mighty, and magnificent Empress, renowned for piety, virtue, and all gracious government, Elizabeth, by the grace of God, Queen of England, France and Ireland, and of Virginia, Defender of the faith"—the nearest important manor to Boroughport, spread on the thriving farmlands of Hollydean parish, was Hollydean Hall, seat of the landlord, rising some two miles from Hockley Bar, the northernmost of the city gates.

It is granted us to visit Boroughport and Hollydean Hall, to converse with the worshipful mayor of the royal city and the still more worshipful knight, the lord of the manor and their intimates, to observe the manner of their lives, their faults, their virtues, their views concerning the world. If it seems a marvelous thing to whisk ourselves back across such a span of time, of a surety it is not much more marvelous than the wonders granted to the men of the sixteenth century since Columbus set foot in San Salvador and Vasco da Gama in Calicut. The age has been crammed with marvels: a New World discovered, the Old World immeasurably expanded. Christian folk have rounded Africa, penetrated to the courts of the Emperor of China, the Grand Mogul and the Shogun of Japan. The globe has been circumnavigated repeatedly. Muscovy has been opened to Western travelers. The treasures of the East Indies, as well as of Montezuma and Atahualpa, have been poured into the lap of Europeans. New beasts, birds, plants, fruits, and manufactured products of the remotest parts of the earth have been imported into Christendom and passed into familiar use. No travelers' tales seem too marvelous. It is as if an entire new planet had been suddenly opened to human ken.

Equally great has been the revolution in the minds of men. That movement called the Renaissance, which shook Italy in the fourteenth century, has spread now all its potence over northern Europe. The effects of Gutenberg's printing-press, which began its clangor about 1450, is showing itself in every quarter of the Western World. Great as is still the illiteracy of the masses, the proportion of educated men has been enormously increased. Simultaneously has come that religious earthquake known as the Protestant Reformation. The unity of the mediæval Catholic Church has been shattered irrevocably. More than one third of the old followers of the Pope have renounced loyalty to him altogether. The process of finding a new religious allegiance has been indescribably unsettling and painful, and has carried with it new thoughts and viewpoints about very many non-theological subjects. In short, about everything affecting man, from his ideas of geography to his ideas of the sacraments has been brewed up in a kind of witch's caldron. The result has been an utterly changed world—the world of the end of the sixteenth century.

Nowhere has this great shaking in the habits and the hearts of men been more thorough than in England. The English Reformation has not yet worked itself out—it will not for another hundred years. The first effects of an incomparable expansion upon the seas are just showing themselves in the national character. Very many things, economic, social, and moral, are either crumbling survivals of the past or crude experiments soon to be abandoned. For all that, the England of the 1590's witnesses one of those epochs of transition in which words are written or spoken, and deeds are wrought which will echo down the centuries, and affect lands and peoples far enough from little Boroughport, or mightier London, or her Grace's royal court at Greenwich.

England is still a small country, the population probably under four millions. The King of England has seemed a humble rival indeed to his pretentious "brothers" of France and Spain. Her royal revenues have seemed contemptible, likewise her commerce, likewise her military power. When Mary Tudor's sorrowful life ebbed away in 1558 the fortunes of England were at the nadir, the realm was poor, ill-governed, and miserably torn by quarrels over religion. The one thing possibly that saved the country from becoming a Spanish satrapy was the inveterate jealousy of France toward Hapsburg expansion.

All that was true less than forty years before our visit to Boroughport and Hollydean Hall. What a transformation! England is becoming a great commercial country. Her navigators are circling the globe. Her seamen have worsted Spain in perhaps the greatest naval duel in history. Her subsidies and armed contingents are helping Henry of Navarre to become Henry IV of France, and the Dutch provinces in revolt against Spain to become the flourishing independent United Netherlands. England, in short, is a great power; a position which she will never abdicate.

Internally England is becoming rich and enjoying the cultivated luxuries which come with economic prosperity. The English language, which has made little progress as a literary tongue, has suddenly developed an enormous vigor and productivity. Every printing-press is active. A great mass of poetry is being written which will be treasured across the centuries; above all, the first part of the *Faerie Queene* has been published, and in London (where the new theaters are so popular) a young playwright from Stratford-upon-Avon is almost producing a series of dramas for which a vast library will provide the commentaries.

This age, then, is one of the cardinal epochs in the advance of civilization. Many things have brought this about; primarily, of course, the inherent stability, energy, and moral character of the English people, once the outlet for its abilities was fairly provided; but history will accord a very large part of the praise to one of the most remarkable monarchs who ever graced a throne.

Elizabeth has now reigned nearly forty years. She has seen her kingdom raised from being a mere shuttlecock between France and Spain to a position of unprecedented splendor. Prose-masters and poetasters rejoice to praise the felicity of the realm, as when John Speed describes his own country as "the Court of Queen Ceres, the Granary of the Western World, the Fortunate Island, the Paradise of Pleasure, and Garden of God."

Of course the great Queen has had great ministers, the astute, cautious but never feeble Burghley, the penetrating, indefatigable Walsingham, and others like him. She has been capricious, perverse, hesitant, and her defeated foes cry out, double-faced and unscrupulous. But for all her wavering policies, the favor of God and her own genius have fended off calamity. She has lived down danger after danger. Mary Stuart is dead and Philip II soon to be dying. She has surrounded herself with diplomats and admirals of incomparable ability. Above all, as with almost no monarch before or after her, she has commanded her people's devoted love.

The praises showered upon the Queen far transcend the

tinsel of courtly flattery. There is a passionate sincerity behind such lines as these: [1]

> She (Elizabeth) giveth laws of justice and of peace,
> And on her head as fits her fortune best
> She wears a wreath of laurel, gold and palm. . . .
> She giveth arms of happy victory
> And flowers to deck her lions crowned with gold—
> This peerless nymph, whom heaven and earth beloves,
> This paragon, this only, this is she,
> In whom are met so many gifts in one . . .
> As chaste as Dian in her chaste desires.

If the success of a monarch can be measured in terms of rewarding victory, prosperity of the people, deepening respect abroad, and intense popularity at home, no reign can be more fortunate than Elizabeth's. True, there are certain crabbed people (coming now to be called Puritans) who scold vehemently about the degeneracy of the times. To such a writer as Bernabe Rich (1581) you can only bewail "the miserable condition of this our present time . . . especially here in England. . . . No man is thought to be wise but that he is wealthy; no man is thought to speak a truth but such as can lie, flatter, and dissemble. . . . What fawning upon him that fortune doth advance! What little care of the poor and such as be in want! What feasting of the rich and such as be wealthy!" etc. And proven enough many of these charges will appear as we frequent Boroughport and Hollydean. Then other men will profess themselves bewildered by the violent changes of the times, sigh for the age before the country had cut loose from its moorings, and look back upon "Merrie England" as a non-existent era that always existed in the Good Old Times. Charges abound of prevalent gluttony, laziness,

[1] From Peale's "Arraignment of Paris," printed in 1584.

and luxury, increase of atheism, swearing and general impiety, general avarice and the swaggering self-confidence of young gallants "who think that they have God Almighty by the heel when in truth they hold the Devil by the toe."

But the majority of Englishmen are by no means precisian. There is an enormous joy in life, and satisfaction in the mere act of living. If the realm and epoch produce their full share of worldlings and scoundrels, they produce more than their share of those choicer spirits who can spring only from a healthy people in a healthy age. Omit the master-poets and admirals; take such a product as Sir Philip Sidney, who has perished in 1586 at only thirty-two. Though of mediocre fortune and no very exalted birth, from the Queen downward all England rejoiced to be his friend, and countless highly stationed youths took him for a model. He seemed the mirror of a perfect gentleman in his athletic address, his accomplishments in war, his training as a courtier and diplomat, his wide knowledge of the classics and modern literature, his own achievements as a poet; while, as for his character, writes an intimate (Fulke Greville), "His heart and his tongue went both one way, and so with every one that went with the truth, as knowing no other kindred, party or end." No evil epoch could have taken such a personage for a pattern. Far, far has the viewpoint of life traversed from feudal ages when the ideals of young manhood were the brutal Richard Cœur de Lions or the pale monastics shutting out the world from the cloister.

As stated already there has been a vast increase of material prosperity in England. A large part of this prosperity has come solely from the fact that Elizabeth has secured to her subjects long decades of peace. The fightings in Scotland have barely touched England; the naval struggle with Spain (unlike most wars) has brought enormous booty, not crippling debt; no invaders have ravaged the land; commerce has not been seriously interrupted; the Queen's notorious parsimony has had this great end—that taxes are very light; no battle now has been fought on English soil for many years, save near the Scottish border. France and the Netherlands have blazed, but as Walsingham sagely wrote in 1576, "Here at home we live in security as we were wont, grounding our quietness on others' harms." And the case has indeed been well put by Lord Burghley in one of his famous aphorisms, "A realm gaineth more by one year of peace than by ten years of (successful) war."

But not merely has England enjoyed the blessings of peace, she has been favored with a considerable return of prosperity to her most important class—the agriculturists. The acute miseries caused by "enclosing" (dividing privately) very much of the lands held in common among the villagers, which took place earlier in the century, have been considerably lived down; so, too, has the serious dislocation of the poor farmers following the confiscation and secularization of the vast estates of the abbeys, suppressed by Henry VIII. Some details of these troubles we can study later; the great healing fact now is that better relations of landlord and peasant begin to prevail; the price of wool is falling and that of wheat is rising—which means an end to the destructive process of turning good plowland into pasture land. Farm produce is bringing fair prices, to match the increasing activities of the towns. England, in short, is becoming peaceful, prosperous, contented. If there are wars they are usually glorious foreign adventures, neither costly nor very bloody.

So then there are the optimism, the material resources, the moral stimulus, the protected leisure for a great creative age. Brutality, crudity, uncouth mediæval survivals, there are, of course, a-plenty. New riches always spell excesses in dress and manners and a sorry deal of riotous living. Non-squeamish folk of the twentieth century can shudder at the unabashed animalism flaunted at every turn in sixteenth-century England; but it is an open, unsophisticated animalism, much coarseness but little glossing vice; evil living is not masked under a cant philosophy. The good, the bad in the Elizabethan world stand forth patent and unashamed.[1]

Enough now for moralizing. We can draw nearer to Boroughport and Hollydean.

[1] Wrote Sir Walter Raleigh's namesake of the twentieth century, "The Age of Elizabeth is the most glorious and in some ways the most significant period of English history."

ILLUSTRATIONS TO "SHEPHERD'S CALENDAR," 1597. JANUARY.

¶ *Chapter* II: CONCERNING BOROUGHPORT AND THE HOUSE OF HOLLYDEAN

T HE ancient town of Boroughport claims, or at least the antiquarian, Master Nicolas Thwacker, head of the grammar school claims for it, vast antiquity. Here the hero Brute, fleeing from Troy, first landed on British shores on his way to found London. Master Thwacker also affirms that Cæsar landed at its harbor on his second expedition to Britain. More confidently we are told that the town was required to provide some of those ships with which Alfred the Saxon founded the first regular English navy. Certain it is, however, that Boroughport only emerged as a pretentious community well after the Norman Conquest.

The town indeed was never one of the famous "Cinque Ports" obligated to provide ships and seamen to the Plantagenet kings, but as early as the twelfth century the harbor was used for embarking or disembarking the military expeditions constantly shuttling to and from France, and a little later foreign merchants—Normans, Flemings, and "Easterlings" from the German North Sea and Baltic—began to be seen on the streets. These outlanders were allowed for a time to maintain their "factories," enclosed trading posts, where they could deposit their merchandise and live under their own law. As for the natives, they gradually developed a tolerable commerce in wheat and wool—the two commodities of which England long had a surplus to export. Finally in the fourteenth century Boroughport was honored by being made one of the "Staple Towns," sharing with certain rivals from London downward in a practical monopoly of exporting wool, leather, tin, and lead, with special privileges for its merchants.

All this meant a steady growth in size and riches. During the Hundred Years' War the pious community had been proud to build the handsome perpendicular church of St. Michael's, whose soaring spire every sailor seeks eagerly as his ship lifts the harbor mouth faring homeward. A little later the equally elegant and ornate Gild Hall was erected where now the Mayor and the Corporation solemnly convene to ordain the fair town's welfare. Of the wharves, storehouses, shops, rich merchants' houses—enough here to say that they grew apace, just as in twenty other seaboard towns in mediæval England.

As for internal trade the town had long since had its weekly market and semi-annual fair, drawing in all the traffickers from half of Thorpshire. The center of the retail trade was of course around the fine Market Cross, built sometime in the thirteenth century; this was a stone monument covered by a low-tiled shed, round which ran benches for the listeners to the sermons sometimes preached there as at St. Paul's Cross in London; while hard by was the town-pump where housewives blithely washed their clothes, then hung them on the cross to dry—in steadfast defiance of the prohibitions voted by the Council. And close at hand stood the stocks, whipping post, and pillory—all of which civic ornaments seldom lacked their human sufferers about every other day.

Boroughport thus is proud and prosperous, yet one need not imagine its size to be imposing. Probably not more than six thousand of the Queen's lieges dwell within its "liberties," yet even so it ranks as one of the larger towns of England. Its streets are ill paved or more often are dirt alleys, unspeakably dusty in midsummer, unspeakably muddy the rest of the year. Sewerage is often attended to by simply hurling all filth into the middle of the streets, and trusting to the dogs, the pigs, the birds, and the rains to carry it away. This condition is felt to be somewhat undesirable. There are repeated entries on the town books of fines of even prominent burgesses for maintaining a *sterquinarium* at the front doors—otherwise a great dung heap. People say that the plague is promoted by such filth, and that it would be well to close up the open, fetid ditch (once the stream for an old mill) which runs straight across the town receiving all manner of sewerage. But the occasional fines go into the treasury; the constables and aldermen shrug their shoulders and speculate about the wars in France. Filthy streets like foul weather seem sent by God for men to endure, although if the stench becomes very bad it can be partly suppressed by burning fragrant woods in the streets.

The town of course has its royal charter and autonomous government. There was a personage calling himself "Mayor" as early as 1250. By 1300 the local landowners, the community of merchants, and the industrial classes were all united under a semi-free government confirmed by the king. We need not follow its vicissitudes. By 1500 this government has become a close corporation filling its own vacancies. There had been more displacements when Henry VIII dissolved the old gilds—hitherto of great local authority. Now Boroughport is ruled by a Corporation into which acceptable townsmen are admitted by the old members as there are gaps. These "burgesses" choose the council of a mayor, a recorder, and ten aldermen assisted by ten "chief burgesses." Usually, when once appointed, the old officers are reëlected year after year.

Master Edmund Gainful, a prosperous merchant, has been mayor now for over a decade. He began his career as a mere ale-tester, empowered to visit all the taverns and test the quality of their brews; then he became "petty constable"; after that he was one of the "chamberlains" having oversight of the town finances; next he was alderman, and a few years later he (and his wife still more) rejoiced in the glory of being first magistrate, uncapped to by even gentlemen and knights, and often asked to dinner by the Lord Lieutenant of Thorpshire. Master Gainful and all his juniors the aldermen wear scarlet gowns to proclaim their glory. In addition Master Gainful wears a hood of velvet and a heavy gold chain. At civic functions an imposing sword bearer walks before him, and, crowning honor, before his house two handsomely carved posts are set on either side of the doorway, proclaiming louder than words, "Here dwells the Worshipful, the Lord Mayor of Boroughport."

Boroughport, naturally has had its ups and downs of prosperity. It sent six ships to Edward III's fleet when it worsted the French in the battle of Sluys (1340 A.D.), the first great English naval victory. The place flourished during the Hundred Years' War, thanks to the constant intercourse with France. But the Wars of the Roses smote the good town heavily. It was repeatedly occupied, exploited, and partially plundered by Yorkist or Lancastrian. The dislocation of commerce during the fifteenth century was an even harder blow. Like many another small town in Henry VIII's time, there was bitter complaint of ruined houses, vacant spaces heaped with rubbish, and of tottering walls. The old craft gilds had decayed and ceased to control the industrialists; in the streets loitered swarms of idle, starving poor; nor had there been real improvement till the death of Mary Tudor.

Then came the blessed change under Elizabeth. Many things contributed. The agricultural improvement put new life into the shopkeepers, the markets, the fairs, the petty industrialists. The expansion of trade brought profitable adventures especially to the Baltic and the dominions of the Grand Turk. The Queen was officially at peace with France and until recently with Spain, but her Grace's subjects at Boroughport never ceased to spoil French and Spanish merchantmen they met on the narrow seas. In short, there were many profitable piracies. More notable still were certain raids to the Indies following Drake's exploits. All Boroughport remembers when they brought home the great carrack loaded at Nombre de Dios for Cadiz with enough pistoles and pieces of eight to pay forty earls' ransoms. When the Armada came in 1588 the town sent forth five stout ships which played their part well, as we shall see. In a word, Boroughport is one of the dozen ports of southern England which write their names across the seas, until the increased size of ships (demanding the deepest ports available) and the shifting tides of commerce must silence the humming in their streets, and bid them sink painlessly into an age-long sleep.

But Boroughport, despite its bare six thousand, is a town, and the great majority of Englishmen do not live in towns. England is most decidedly an agricultural country, and even great London would perish if it could not supply the needs of the great hinterland of farmsteads. The normal thing for the Queen's lieges is to dwell in little villages somewhere near a great manor house and a parish steeple, pursuing a laborious, very unscientific agriculture, and counting it a great adventure to journey twenty miles to some remote market. What we may say of farming methods and land tenure can wisely wait; the task now is to inspect Hollydean, two miles from the town, whither the good knight of the Manor is constantly resorting, to transact business or discuss a fat capon with his friend the Mayor.

The Hollydeans are really a very old family. Sir Walter Hollydean likes to talk of "Norman ancestors," but the oldest parchment in his strong chest seems to be merely a grant of certain lands under the seal of Henry III. Still it is certain that a Hollydean fought in Edward I's wars in Scotland, and that his grandson was knighted on the battle-field of Crécy by Edward III the evening after the victory. The Hollydeans shared the usual vicissitudes of the lesser nobility. Sometimes by royal favor and fortunate marriages their lands expanded, and under the weak Henry VI one scion of the house actually became an earl. His Lordship, however, was caught on the Lancastrian side when the Wars of the Roses broke out. He was captured at Towton, and ended his life and his peerage upon the scaffold. Under Edward IV and Richard III his heirs lost nearly all their lands and barely kept their ancestral manor near Borough-port. Then Bosworth Field brought a turn for the better. The grandfather of Sir Walter was knighted by Henry VII, and recovered a fair part of the old estates. His heir, Master Francis Hollydean, had some troubles in digesting the start-ling religious revolutions under Henry VIII, but being a very practical man at last adjusted his theology and made friends with government enough to become possessor of a fine strip of the lands of St. Michael's abbey, when that religious house was suppressed.

Once having changed his creed Francis Hollydean, un-like many contemporaries, was at least a steadfast Protes-tant. He was a staunch supporter of the extreme Reformers under Edward VI, and when Mary Tudor took back the old religion, he had an incriminating share in Wyatt's unlucky rebellion which tried to restore Protestantism. All this landed Master Hollydean in the Tower, and it was only the grace of God which saved him from the Tyburn gal-lows or even the heretic's bonfire at Smithfield. As it was, he languished piteously in durance through all the reign of Mary. Part of his property was confiscated, and the influence of powerful kinsmen barely managed again to save the old family estate.

When Elizabeth mounted the throne he was promptly set at liberty, but he was an enfeebled, broken man, and died in the early 1560's, leaving a shrunken, debt-laden heritage to his only son.

Young Walter Hollydean was barely a slim lad when his father died, but he fortunately had a maternal uncle who preferred trading profitably with Antwerp to vegetating as a rusty squireen. Despite family grumblings Walter had been articled to a rich "Turkey merchant" who soon became a London alderman. Thus the life of young Hollydean was far removed from that of common clerk or craftsman's helper, although he had to wear for the nonce the blue garb and other insignia of a London prentice. He frequented the exchanges; he accompanied his master on delicate business missions to Antwerp and Hamburg; later he went as supercargo on one of the alderman's ships to the Levant, visited Aleppo and Grand Cairo, and did his share in a shrewd brush with Algerine pirates. Thus he learned the ways of the world, and being honest, faithful, and very intelligent commended himself to his patron.

The end can soon be told. Alderman Rich had one child, the fair Mistress Catherine. That she should look favorably upon the handsome, high-born supercargo was written among the stars. Her parents smiled. Hollydean himself was quite practical enough not to let mercantile blood weigh against beauty and rose nobles. The wedding was solemnized. The good alderman soon went off in an apoplexy after an unusually heavy trading company dinner. The fortunes of Walter Hollydean were made.

Instantly the old summons in his blood from the ancestral meadows and wolds asserted itself. Walter might have become a power in the goldsmiths' shops in the city, but back to Thorpshire speedily he took his bride. Her portion promptly rebuilt the crazy old manor house in the most approved architecture. The young landlord's London connection soon made him a magnate among the Boroughport merchants. He bought back most of the lost fields and was promptly named Justice of the Peace. The country squires stifled their grumblings at "marrying into trade" when they saw the new mansion rising. Their wives (far more rigorous) forgot to snub the new Mistress Hollydean when they saw her marvelous ruffs, farthingales, stomachers, and jewels.

All this was nearly thirty years ago. A gallant son and two personable daughters have blessed the union. The Master of Hollydean became Sir Walter after great service to the Crown in 1569, while serving in the North during the abortive revolt of the Earls of Northumberland and Westmoreland. His lady is now a great stickler for ranks and pedigrees, and tries to make her children believe that her own grandfather was nothing less than a lordly royal cofferer and not merely a petty usurer as the malicious allege.

Sir Walter has prospered in his ventures. He is just back from a conference at London with his friend Raleigh arranging a new Colonial expedition to Virginia. The worthy knight has become ruddy and portly, but he is still stout and hale, blessed with a keen eye and a jolly wit. He has never been to the university, but is a tolerable Latinist and loves to collect books; which fact does not prevent him from carefully watching the state of the crops, the chances of a good lambing season, or the latest trading in wool, wines, and spices. He swears incessantly but is a devout churchgoer, and is sure that God is best pleased when he curses Papists in general and Spaniards in particular. Add that he is reasonably kindly to the poor and a great dispenser of hospitality to equals. There are very many country gentlemen much like him.

Lady Hollydean has found it much better to reign socially as a queen in Thorpshire, than to be merely one of a hundred rich merchants' dames in London. Despite a fondness for absurd fashions and gewgaws and her cultivation of pedigrees, she is a woman of much goodness of heart; compassionate, charitable, and worshiped by the tenantry. She is extraordinarily pious and spends long hours in her "closet" over books of religion, or else in the hall listening to the holy, long exhortations of her chaplain Master Crabtree, who sets forth foreordination and saving grace after the strictest gospel of Calvin. With it all she is a notable housekeeper and knows when to cuff the maids and get the maximum of work out of the man servants.

Just now the Hall is rejoicing in the safe and triumphant return from the French wars of his parents' prime treasure, Captain Andrew Hollydean. He is a "gallant" of the most approved garments and swagger, is reputed the hero of half a dozen affairs and almost as many duels, although probably fame has been a little unkind to him. His friends say that actually he is an honorable young gentleman, and that nine parts of his rakishness has been assumed for effect. Unlike his father he has been to the university, and he can write tolerable poetry, talk airily about the theory of the sonnet, and speak (when he chooses) with an affected foreign lisp, as if French or Italian were his native tongue. Of course he has been somewhat at court and seizes every excuse for telling how once he was flipped daintily with the glove of "the peerless Cynthia" when he bent to kiss her hand.

As for his sisters, Mistress Anne and younger Mistress

Arabella, they are healthy strapping girls in their teens; whereof the first has reached that age when she can be chosen May Queen at Boroughport and begin to attract the eyes of the young country gentlemen, the second is still at her mother's side learning "piety and discretion." The family is singularly united and affectionate. There have been plenty of small sorrows, but as yet no great ones. The manor house is of course the center for a small army of poor relations, dependents and servitors, and it is equally the focus for the entire life of the adjacent Hollydean village. Between Boroughport and Hollydean therefore we shall pass and repass; sometimes in the Hall, sometimes in the farmhouses, sometimes in the town market stalls or along the bustling quays. When we have finished our prying intimacies, perhaps we shall know a little better what is meant by "Elizabethan England."

ILLUSTRATIONS TO "SHEPHERD'S CALENDAR," 1597.   FEBRUARY.

¶ *Chapter* III: CONCERNING COUNTRY LIFE AND SOCIAL CLASSES

BEFORE we knock at the gates of the ornate porter's lodge of Hollydean Hall we shall fare the more wisely if certain facts about Elizabethan society become plain to us. We are treading a land which if far from being under an unrestrained despotism is equally far socially or politically from being a democracy.

One of the first lessons inculcated (and, if needs be, flogged) into a growing child is "to be contented with his lot in life." "Render unto Cæsar the things which are Cæsar's"; "The Powers that be are ordained of God"; "Let every soul be subject to the Higher Powers"—"Sir" [1] Charles Surplice, the parish vicar, preaches a sermon on one of these texts just as periodically as St. George's Day follows Easter. Sir Walter himself had not the least sense of degradation when he fell on his knees before the Queen the last time he met her at Hampton Court. It was all very proper—just as that he should be treated with almost groveling obsequiousness when he goes among his tenants in the village.

Master John Lyly has put the accepted theory well in the mouth of one of his characters: "We should not look at what we cannot reach, nor long for that we should not have. Things above us are not for us; and therefore princes are placed under the Gods that they should not see what they do, and we under princes that we might not enquire what *they* do." A country clown or a poor journeyman feels

---

[1] Parish clergymen and schoolmasters were called in courtesy "Sir," as equivalent for the Latin "Dominus."

no great injury when a great man addresses him in a tone not much different from that with which the magnate accosts his dogs, provided the harsh words are not followed by inhumane actions. It is clearly the intention of God that the greater part of His human creatures should toil hard and enjoy only a modicum of decent food, shelter, and raiment. To repine at this is sheer impiety punishable in the present world and the next. The acceptance of this undoubted fact makes for general social happiness and stability.

Furthermore, unfortunate is the man who does not have some one he can look down upon. Scolds Thomas Nashe (1593), "The courtier disdaineth the citizen; the citizen the countryman; the shoemaker the cobbler." The tailor who almost falls on his knees with joy when Captain Andrew deigns to visit his shop, is toplofty as a bashaw when he cuffs about his own prentices. Nevertheless there are limits to all this servility. The Queen herself owes half of her power to her uncanny knowledge of where to draw the line in enforcing it. The meanest clodhopper or pedlar has his rights and is perfectly aware of the fact. There are no serfs left in England. When Elizabeth mounted the throne there were a few poor folk, technically bondsmen, upon the royal domain land, but she has ordered them set free. England thus has escaped that grievous process of "emancipation," which will rack and torment so many Continental kingdoms. In theory at least the poorest journeyman can sue the richest merchant or proudest earl and obtain even justice at the law. This is something that ought to make Englishmen swell with pride as much as does the defeat of the Armada.

However, brushing legalities aside, England is a country of rank and privilege, and fortunate is he who stands near the social apex. First of all are those glittering magnates who boast themselves Peers of the Realm, and who are entitled to converse even with Gloriana on terms of something like equality. Few Englishmen dissent from an opinion like this: "Noblemen ought to be preferred in fees, honors, offices, and other dignities of command and government before the common people. We ought to give credit to a Noble before any of the inferior sort. His punishment (if guilty of offense) ought to be more favorable and honorable upon his trial and conviction; and that to be by his Peers of the same noble rank. He ought in all sittings, meetings and salutations to have the upper hand and the greatest respect." [1]

It is a relatively greater honor to be called "My lord" in 1590 than it will be four hundred years later. Across the centuries the number of "lay peers" will rise until some seven hundred and forty noblemen can sit in the House of Lords. In Elizabeth's time also neither Irish peers nor Scotch peers claim a place in the aristocracy. The Reformation has abolished the "mitred abbotts" who once elbowed into the upper branch of Parliament; the only lords spiritual are twenty-six somewhat discredited bishops. In the first year of the Queen there was one duke, one marquis, twelve earls, two viscounts, and twenty-seven barons— barely forty-three lay peers in all. Since 1558 the great title of "Duke" has temporarily lapsed following the death on the block of the Duke of Norfolk in 1572. The title of "Marquis" is also in abeyance; but the next rank, the "Earl" has increased. There will be twenty-five earls and eighty-one lay peers in all when the Queen passes away in 1603.

In any case it is a wonderful thing to be actually noblemen. The Queen feels it her duty to defend their honors

[1] Actually written by Henry Peacham about 1634, but even more true in the 1590's.

somewhat as being part of her own dignity. In 1573 the
Earl of Oxford, a most turbulent and ill-mannered young
scoundrel, called Sir Philip Sidney "a puppy" during a
tennis game. Sidney demanded an apology or the satisfaction of a duel. Her Grace at once sent for Sir Philip and
told him "there was a great difference in degree between
earls and private gentlemen, and that princes were bound
to support the nobility and to insist on their being treated
with proper respect." Sir Philip rejoined manfully that
"place was never intended to privilege wrong," and that
"although the earl was a great lord, yet was he no lord
over him, and that the difference of degrees between free
men entitled men of the highest rank to no other homage
than precedency." The Queen took this bold retort in good
part. Oxford neither fought nor apologized but he never
recovered his standing at court. Sidney nevertheless found
it wise to retire for a time into the country in order to
compose his "Arcadia."

However the peers of England have younger brothers,
younger sons, and a great swarm of other kinsmen who can
seldom hope to be noblemen. They are all "gentlemen," a
term which, like charity, covers a multitude of virtues and
sins. A peer's second son is mere "gentleman," but a
"gentleman" too is the shabby attorney at the law or even
the upstart linen draper's ex-prentice who has made his
fortune, sold his shop, bought a genteel estate, and lives
now upon his income. True it is that there is the somewhat
intermediate glory of "knight." Knighthood is merely an
honor; it conveys no direct legal privileges. Under Elizabeth it is a somewhat unusual honor bestowed directly by
the Queen or by some captain general or high admiral, her
deputy. Gloriana is justly jealous lest the award become
cheap. Ordinarily only the sons of great noblemen who
have won royal favor, or commoners who have rendered

high public service can feel the Queen's sword upon their shoulders. Walsingham was a privy councillor and joint secretary of state for four years before he was knighted in 1577. Everybody knows how Drake was knighted after his astonishing encirclement of the world. A man can live as a landed magnate of pedigree, influence, and wealth and remain a simple squire. Walter Hollydean, we have stated, was knighted for unusual services to the Crown. Captain Andrew will not inherit his title, but must win it for himself. There are no bantam noblemen, hereditary "baronets," lording it yet in England.[1]

In any case the "knights" represent only a select fraction of the "gentle" folk of the realm. "Gentlemen" form, as hinted, an extremely wide caste. Anybody in fact who can make lawful claims to coat armor can demand to be addressed as "Esquire," or "Gent," and feel insulted if the honor is denied. "As for gentlemen they be made good cheap in England," writes Sir Thomas Smith, "for whosoever studieth the laws of the realm, who studieth in the universities, who professeth liberal sciences, and, to be short, can live idly and without manual labor, and will bear the port, charge, and countenance of a gentleman, he shall be called 'master' and shall be taken for a gentleman."

The title of "Master" indeed is often given by courtesy to plenty of honest folk, who have never had their coat armor blazoned at the Herald's college, but who have risen a trifle in the world. Master craftsmen and active retailers are regularly "mastered" and their wives "mistressed." The real test for a gentleman is, "Do you have to work with your hands, or only with your tongue or pen or not at all?" And although upper schoolmasters, physi-

---

[1] The hereditary rank of baronet was of course created in 1611 by James I against the ignoble prime qualification of £1095, paid for by each recipient of the honor.

cians, and lawyers are undoubtedly gentlemen, social salvation is not really achieved until you can live in genteel idleness upon the income, not from ships or shops, but lands.

The country gentlemen of England, whereof the Hollydeans are slightly superior examples, are almost the warp and woof of the realm. Their families provide most of the governing class. They have the major share in naming and supplying members of Parliament. The squires are expected to relieve local want and furnish the rustics with steady employment. As a great army of unpaid justices of the peace they relieve the Queen's ministers of most of the burdens of local administration, and assure the loyalty of the masses. Many of them indeed have little that is "gentle" about them but their pedigrees; they can barely read, know just enough law to clap vagrants in the stocks, are sordid and swinish in their habits; but the best of them are alert, well-educated gentlemen in the truest sense of the word.

Under this very wide class of men of worship and coat armor comes the great mass of the commonalty; the people whom young Captain Andrew in his more arrogant moods loves to "thou" and teach their place. Even here, however, are plain distinctions. In Boroughport there are the "citizens" and "burgesses," prosperous tradespeople and master craftsmen who have substance enough to pay the charges to hold town office and serve on juries. Such folk are likely to be flattered as "masters" also, although Captain Andrew says this is sheer perversion of the title. Outside the town walls there are a goodly number of farmers whom even Sir Walter treats with a decided courtesy; they are the yeomen small land owners, and often the thrifty possessors of really valuable property. But (alas for their respectability) they work their acres with their own hands when your gentleman must touch nothing but his pen or his sword. The yeomen have supplied a great share of the brains and muscle that make England England. They have a certain part in parish government. No matter—they are to be called only "goodman" or "goodwife." By the plain ordinance of God, between them and the gentry there is a great gulf fixed.

Down at the bottom of the social scale are the petty traders, the common craftsmen and the great army of tenant farmers, the day laborers. Doubtless they have their own distinctions but their betters lump them together as "folk of the meanest class." Sometimes they can be ale-testers in the villages, constables, or even jurymen in absence of solid merchants or yeomen. Otherwise they share in the government of England no more than they do in the government of heaven. Inevitably very few of them can read. All that most of them ask for is plenty of rye bread, and bun ale, the year round; with occasional access to the great house feastings and abundance of holidays for coarse and uproarious junketings.

So much for the dry bones of society around Thorpshire. There are also certain other things to observe. One is that near as the Hollydean lands are to Boroughport, the manor is in no sense dependent upon the town for its everyday well-being. The grain and most of the meat consumed in the Hall is raised on the estate. All the beer comes from Sir Walter's brewhouse. Many of the servants' garments are of home wool and weaving. Lady Catherine has complete charge of the dairy, and will frequently walk out a mile to inspect her cows or urge on the reapers. If actual manual toil for a gentleman is derogatory, for even a gentlewoman to be too finical to inspect her estate leads to shrugs and comments about being "too clean-fingered." Of course the worst landlords are the upstart merchants, who have turned to purchased estates as a mere genteel speculation. Such base-born souls usually living still in London employ agents whom they drive on to rack-rent the tenantry and wring the last farthing out of their unfortunate dependents. They feel no responsibility for the poor, and are merely usurers turned land exploiters. The Hollydean folk count it a mercy that their landlord lives ordinarily at home, hates bailiffs, and every day makes a personal tour of his farms. If he curses idlers and often lays a stick on them that is very proper and quite within his prerogatives.

Life assuredly seems very pleasant around Hollydean even if another age will not call the country strikingly beautiful. There are no factory chimneys marring the landscape, although here and there above certain woods there rise lazy columns of clean, sweet smoke where they are burning charcoal. All through the spring and early summer wherever you go at the proper hours can be heard the bird song—the music of the throstle, of the lark, of the golden-billed ouzel, and especially in the mild evenings if you throw open the tall windows of the great gallery to watch the white moonlight slanting through the leafage of the park, there can come the tremulous strains of the poet's most honored minstrel, the nightingale.[1]

Start off along the ill-kept highroad, either the short way to Boroughport, or that far longer way where the finger-posts point "London"; at every turn you can strike off into pleasant little winding lanes, barely four feet wide —just enough for a horse with pack saddles. They meander like green ribbons across hill and dale, and all bordered by hawthorn hedges.

If you push Londonward, it is true that you can indeed soon cross stretches of unspoiled wilderness, where the lanes

---

[1] The nightingale seldom visits Wales and is never seen in Scotland, but is fairly abundant in the spring in southern England.

end in the merest sheep tracks. The amount of England that is sparsely populated or not populated at all can seem amazing. Although the "enclosing" policy has led to a fairly wide distribution of the old common lands to private owners, and these owners have promptly set picturesque hedges around their possessions, still a good many villages have stuck to the former ownership of the plowlands by the entire community; here there are no hedgerows, only long green balks of turf to show the strips of each temporary cultivator. In any case, "common" or "several," there are wide wastes of heath, turf, or marshland, where on the smoother parts a few cattle or even flocks of geese may be nipping the grass. Even where the land is fairly cleared there spread tracts of brushwood, or of enormous, venerable trees, survivors of the forest primeval.

Everywhere, go where you will, there is the friendly contact with nature. Buildings are of local stone, of big beams rough hewn, or of an artificial clay and wattles. Field is separated from field not by barbed wire but by the verdant hedgerows. Cow sheds and barns are not of corrugated iron or planed boards but of timber from the forest and thatch from the fields. Great trees and orchards help to frame in the farmsteads. The houses are æsthetic, not because the village masons are artists, but because their materials are varied and beautiful and the gables and windows in vogue are artistic in themselves. Buildings too are of no monotonous type. Each has its own special plan, material, individuality.

In short, once away from the murky town streets (and how small is Boroughport!) instantly your Englishman is out in a verdant land of thicket, lawn, and copse. He hears the purl of the mill-stream, the swish of the great water wheel, not the rasp of power-driven machinery. He trudges over a very poor road; but on either hand he can touch the buttercups. When Captain Andrew writes his conventional pastorals concerning Pan, and shepherds and shepherdesses, he never has to learn about his flocks, herds, green meadows, and bosky shades from books. What wonder that *some* of his class at least concoct sonnets and sing songs which shall last across the ages?

We have seen too that England, if in no sense an autocracy, is under a government which leaves the democrat much to desire. But the average Englishman seldom theorizes about his rights so long as things he counts his due are seldom trampled upon. The Queen is enormously powerful, largely, however, because her policies directly commend themselves to a large part of her subjects and because whatever their troubles they are one of the most lightly taxed and governed people in the world. Star Chamber and the Royal High Commission court can be harsh and arbitrary enough; but they are infinitely less tyrannous and interfering than such an engine as the Spanish Inquisition in Spain. The laws are comparatively simple, and usually administered by such justices as Sir Walter, anything but learned lawyers although gifted with great common sense. Even the severest statutes, furthermore, are often made tolerable by great laxity in enforcement. A Thorpshire man, therefore, seldom troubles himself about Queen and Parliament while the tods of wool fetch good prices.

Finally in this society there is the great factor that life has not yet been stripped of its claims to mystery. Sir Walter smiles and Captain Andrew almost laughs openly when the shepherds talk of seeing Jack-o'-Lantern whisking by night in the swamps. But neither of those gentlefolk is sure in his heart of hearts that there is no Jack-o'-Lantern. There is not the least doubt with either of them as to a personal devil and the evidence is sufficient that witches can ride on broomsticks. The world is not governed by immutable natural laws but by what the frivolous call "fortune," and the parsons "the inscrutable behests of God." Any number of great courtiers, the Captain reports, patronize alchemists, and Dr. John Dee, not merely an astrologer but a downright necromancer, is protected and subsidized by the Queen's Majesty herself.

All this makes life still more of a glorious adventure. We find plenty of quaint superstitions surviving around Hollydean, although only a few debasing ones. The Bible miracles nowhere present any difficulty save to a few deplorable scoffers. The unseen is still all around us and at intervals we can catch tantalizing glimpses of its mysteries. On the other hand, this unseen has ceased to be so very terrible. The devastating wars, famines, plagues of the early Middle Ages which bred so many horrid beliefs, seem dropping happily behind, and the world will lose as well as gain something when Reason decrees the abolition of lucky days and pixies.

Hark! The throstles in the beeches have already been proclaiming the July sunrise. On the buttery benches the maids are setting out the steaming porridge for the yawning cowherds who must be off to their task. The first red gleams of morning are glinting on the great broadside of windows of Hollydean Hall.

¶ *Chapter* IV: CONCERNING A STATELY MANSION AND ITS FURNISHINGS

FRAILTIES the folk of Elizabeth's England have, but usually not that of late rising. Even at two in the morning Sir Walter's gamekeepers have been out in the barely graying darkness to patrol for enterprising poachers, and Master Crabtree has slipped from his pallet to light a candle and con his *Errors of Popery Refuted*. By three the servants' quarters are really awake, the work horses are being coupled up, and yawning maids are going toward the dairy. By four Captain Andrew is out in the stable ordering the grooms who are rounding up the dogs for the day's hunt, and at five the road from Boroughport past Hollydean is fairly well covered with travelers who are making a long day to London. In the town Master Thwacker is waiting to see which scholar will creep in last and earn the oil of birch, and the prentices before the shops are all bawling their "What d'ye lack!"

Sir Walter and Lady Catherine have been about already, for like honest people they hold it best "to rise with the lark, and to go to bed with the lamb, so we have the break of day and the brightness of the sun to cheer our spirits"; while all this joyousness is missed by sluggish fools "who make night of day and day of night."

By five, in other words, Hollydean Hall, with all England, is alive and active on a summer morning. What better time for our visit?

When Walter Hollydean returned to his birthplace with his bride and married riches, the old manor house of his fathers was in a piteous state, almost surrendered to the

[30]

bats and rooks. Built in the days of Edward I, somewhat as a small castle capable of temporary defense, it had suffered all the ruin wrought by the Wars of the Roses (when it was taken with violence several times) and then by the poverty of the later heirs. At best it was a gray, forbidding place—its stone-lined chambers, small, dark, and clammy, and its great hall a cavernous void of sooted rafters hung with rusty armor. Its new London-bred mistress had shuddered when she entered it; and her father's pounds sterling in a few years provided a splendid successor—not a forbidding castle, but a mansion ornate, and elegant, proclaiming better than with words, "I belong to a new age."

The great period of Church building is over in England. The Reformation has ruined the beautiful monasteries. The Puritan element wishes to strip the old cathedrals of "the last vestiges of Rome," not to erect new ones. The Queen and courtiers spend their revenues on wars or pageants. Barring Sir Thomas Gresham's great Royal Exchange in London, scarcely one notable public building has risen anywhere in the country during the entire reign. But never have architects, masons, carpenters been busier; from Northumberland to Cornwall Englishmen are spending their new wealth on perhaps the most precious material things in the world—comfortable, dignified *homes*.

The needs for military defense practically ended with the Wars of the Roses. Baronial lawlessness has vanished from all but a few countries. Walter Hollydean required protection against only a few chance robbers, and having visited foreign parts he promptly fell in with the schemes of a popular architect, Master Sylvester, that he make him a mansion in the new "Italianate" style.

Sylvester talked much of long residence in Italy, although jealous rivals hinted he had only been as far as France or

Flanders. In any case his mouth was full of "Doric, Ionic, and Corinthian orders," and "the designs of Brunelleschi." For the "uncouth Gothic" architecture of the Middle Ages he had violent contempt and was happiest when pouring scorn on such creations as Salisbury or Canterbury cathedrals. Later ages will say that his own style was a curious mixture of old Greek motifs, altered by the Italian and German Renaissance, and not untinctured by the abhorred Gothic itself—but the result while jumbled and inconsistent is not unimposing. Hollydean Hall will remain a show place for visitors centuries after its first occupants are laid to rest.

The first impression of the Hall is of great arrays of square-headed, mullioned windows, so many that it is humorously complained "one cannot tell where to get out of the sun or out of the cold." Vanished forever are the massive castle walls with their slits for archers and frowning battlements. There is a vast expanse of glass intersected by narrow members of richly carved masonry. There is a small forest of light, soaring pinnacles. Everywhere there is an excess of ornamentation. There is also a regular battery of tall, widely scattered chimneys. As yet no ivy has been allowed to creep up along the mortar. The Hall stands bare, ornate, pretentious, confidently peaceful, the absolute symbol that the rough days of the feudal wars are ended forever.

The owner, being one of the most loyal of country gentlemen, was glad when Master Sylvester planned the mansion in the fashionable form of an inverted "E" in honor of the Queen's Majesty. You come up to Hollydean Hall along a stately avenue of oaks, survivors from the days of the old fortified manor. The porter's lodge is in the projecting porch of the central section of this "ℿ."

Even from the outside it is clear what is the general idea

of the interior arrangements. In the discarded castle there was really only one capacious room, the enormous hall where the inhabitants (or rather garrison) for the most part ate, talked, worked, and even slept. The chambers were few, small, and reserved only for the owner and his favored intimates. Now has intruded the revolutionary idea of *personal privacy*. The great hall is only one of several large rooms used for various social purposes. Every person of consequence must have a fairly commodious chamber to himself; hence two long tiers of separate windows.

Furthermore a remarkable convenience has been introduced—chimneys. True they are not strictly a new invention; during the Middle Ages the best palaces, the richer monasteries, and possibly some other fine buildings possessed them. But many lordly castles, not to name manor houses and lesser dwellings, did all their cooking and warming (little enough of the latter!) upon one or two unenclosed hearths smoking in the open halls and kitchens, and supposed to harden the timbers above them by their constant deposit of soot. Now not merely in the public rooms are great fireplaces under substantial chimneys, but every important chamber has its own fireplace, and Sir Walter or Lady Catherine actually will grumble at having to get out of bed in the winter until a big pile of twigs is merrily snapping in their bedrooms.

Since Boroughport is a harbor town, many snug merchants indulge in a luxury more far-fetched still. Coasting vessels bring down from Newcastle caldrons of a hard black substance known as "sea-coal." It is already a familiar fuel in London and gives a hot, lasting fire although a rather disagreeable smoke. Wherever water transport is easy this fuel is becoming cheap and abundant in England, but until roads and land transport improve, the sooty stuff will remain too expensive to displace the great roaring logs in the average fireplace.

Plenty of people shake their heads at these changes. The smoke from the old open hearths, we are assured, is an excellent remedy against "quacks and poses" (hoarseness and colds). Chimneys have actually become common upon poor farmers' houses and mean city lodgings. Is this not another sign of the degenerate times; of the advance of "Persian delicacy"? Scolds good Master Harrison, the Antiquary, "Now our tenderlings complain of rheums and catarrhs." [1] And again (viewing the innovations even in the cheaper dwellings), "See the change! For when our houses were built of willow, then had we oaken men, but now that our houses are come to be made of oak, our men are not only become willow, but a great many are altogether of straw—which is a sore alteration."

Who, however, can battle against the love for new-fangled ease and luxury? Already within and without, the Elizabethan home boasts many things at which the fifteenth century would have stared.[2] Even in the cheaper houses, brick and stone are driving out the picturesque old timber and "raddles" (wattles); while Hollydean Hall displays a number of magnificent turrets which are clearly enough intended to provide spacious bay windows or the wells for magnificent winding staircases. Furthermore the Hall is very large. The " ⋔ " encloses on three of its sides two spacious courts set out with formal flower gardens; and the long body of the mansion, if not as vast as Sir Christopher Hatton's new Holdenby House (where you can walk 410

---

[1] Writing originally in 1577.

[2] These changes came on the whole very suddenly; as late as the reign of Mary Tudor, visiting Spaniards are said to have commented, "These English have their houses made of sticks and dirt, but they fare (at table) commonly as well as the King."

feet in a straight line in the gallery), is of magnificent proportions.

Nevertheless the real glory of the building can only be
grasped by penetrating the interior. We go past the porter's
lodge at the gate house, under a turret where the martins
are flitting energetically in and out, and note the coat of
arms with the three griffins *passant* ("walking") of the
Hollydeans blazoned above the portal. Then, since we are
welcome guests, we are escorted through a kind of passage-
way of servants' and stewards' offices into what is still the
chief compartment of a mansion, the great hall of the
owner.

The hall is an apartment of noble dimensions even if it
is the only large public room in the mansion. The master's
family no longer dines there upon the dais, save upon grand
occasions; but here for dinner and supper gather all the
servants, lesser hangers-on and less preferred guests, all
under the hospitable presidency of Master Scanwell, the
proprietor's steward. There is a gallery for musicians over
against the dais, set up near the high ceiling of ornamental
plaster work. At the center of one side wall, raised upon
another low platform, is an enormous fireplace armed with
huge, iron firedogs.

Most of the walls, between the tall mullioned windows,
are hung with "painted cloths"—whereof more hereafter,
as well as concerning the deep pile of rushes which carpets
the floor—but the magnificent woodwork calls for immediate comment. The heavy roof timbers, the panels under and
around the windows, the chimney shelf molding, and many
other surfaces are covered with intricate carving of rich
and beautiful design. Everywhere are conspicuous the three
griffins of the Hollydean arms; these same griffins run out
their tongues harmlessly upon each of the great stained
glass windows. The master's dais itself is set before a huge

bay window above which is carved the gracious motto "Amicus fidelis putexio fortis." In niches here and there is a whole company of busts or small statues—*Justitia, Virtus,* and the learned *Arithmetica* and *Geometria,* not forgetting the band of Apollo and the Muses.

From one end of the hall ascends what is one of the most startling innovations in the new architecture—an elegant and impressive winding staircase. In the old castles you clamber from one clammy loft to another by narrow corkscrew steps of stone set in a tower. Here before us is a fine open *wooden* staircase rising by short flights from one generous landing to another, with treads, handrails, balusters, and all else made of fine woods tastefully carved. The mere sight of this noble mode of ascent gives a foretaste of the splendid apartments above; and it needs little imagination to picture the glittering pageantry when Hollydean is thrown open in high festival, and gentles, gallants, and their dames move upward and downward, their brave clothes shimmering and their bright scabbards twinkling.

In truth, color is the last thing lacking all around the mansion. The paneling has not aged down to sober tones as it will during coming centuries; either the fresh tintings of the woods stand out, or more often the stiles and rails have been painted a rich red, and the panels are traced around with designs in green or other colors. The tapestries, "painted cloths," needlework, and silk draperies are extremely bright; the furniture even in the common hall is painted brilliantly. Add such effects as the suits of armor and racks of arquebuses and spears set upon the walls, and the old pennon that a Hollydean carried at Flanders' Field, the newer standard that Sir Walter took when they spoiled a Spanish galleon off Calais—the result is vivid, almost startling.

The great hall is only the introduction to the vast and

complicated mansion. Most of the other rooms on the ground floor are abandoned to the servants, to the kitchens, the enormous pantries, to the butler, and other upper servants' quarters. The master lives on the upper floor, only sweeping down the grand staircase when he wishes to go out or to visit the hall. Very many of the upper apartments we must ignore, but some are important. A room sometimes placed on the ground floor is called the "winter parlor." It is really the private dining room for the family, a small but very handsomely appointed chamber, used by Sir Walter and his intimates when they do not wish to honor the great boisterous hall. Then there is the parlor proper, by no means a place of social leisure but practically the living room for the ladies of the mansion, their place for all kinds of housewifely tasks which formerly they had to do in the great hall or in their chambers; and next is the majestic gallery.[1]

The gallery, like the staircase, is peculiar to Elizabethan mansions. There is nothing like it in the old castles. The Hollydean gallery is small compared with some of its rivals, but it is ample and majestic enough. The first important gallery seems to have been in Hampton Court, the creation of Cardinal Wolsey, and the new style apartment was instantly found to minister to the elegance, the luxury, and the ostentation of the new age.

Imagine now an immense room with a length many times its breadth, and running well over two hundred feet almost the entire width of the house. In no sense is it a "living room." In bad weather one can promenade in the gallery and by a few turns around get very proper exercise. Ranged along the elaborate wainscoting or tapestried walls stands the finest furniture in the mansion, especially

[1] Of course the floor plans of Elizabethan mansions varied absolutely; the arrangements suggested are merely typical.

those stately buffets and cabinets of walnut, rosewood, and even silver mounted ebony. There lack not window seats, ponderous chests, and a sprinkling of stools and chairs. The cabinets shine with plate, rare majolica ware, china that sought Europe through Portugal, bronzes, and other curios. The square-paned windows, bearing the Hollydean arms in stained glass, break the oblique rays of the sun into golden pointers as it beams over the panels, the bric-a-brac, and the tapestry; but most glorious of all can be the gallery when hundreds of candles are gleaming, when the rebecs and viols are sounding, and half the gentility of Thorpshire is moving in or watching the pavan or the galliard.

Likewise it were a sin not to name the owner's "closet," really a fair-sized room blessed with a sizable library, with wall maps of the world, of England, Scotland, France, and the Low Countries, and a perpetual almanac in a frame. There are a couple of stiff, black, family portraits (which abound too in the gallery), a much-used calculating board with counters, and on the desk a pair of scales, scissors, knife, a foot rule, seals, and a huge pewter inkstand.

Finally we must glance into the numerous bedrooms, usually ranged along corridors so vast that the strange guest must always be lighted off to bed by a servant—he never could find his bedroom unaided. Although these bedrooms provide reasonable privacy and warmth, they will appear to another age bare and plain with little ornamentation, the only furnishings an oaken chest on which rests a silver basin, a hand-mirror (or more rarely a stand looking-glass), a stool, and last, but in no wise least, an enormous four-poster bed with its canopy and curtains dominating the entire room. Frequently too there is a truckle-bed tucked away under the four-poster to be drawn out for the use of a servant who will sleep at his master's feet.

Certain things, as we move about this truly magnificent

residence, impress us immediately—particularly the absence of carpets. Several blazing rugs straight from the Levant indeed are to be seen, but they are spread merely as coverings upon the chests, tables, and couches. The poorer folk count themselves lucky to have a bare stone or wooden floor in their houses, but in all the better homes up to the royal palaces themselves, the floors are strewn with thick layers of rushes. Enter her Majesty's presence chamber; the silken clad legs of lordly courtiers are pricked as they kneel in salutation upon the hay. Plaited mats are coming into a slight degree of use, but they are still a doubtful innovation.

Hollydean, like all contemporary mansions, has this deep crackly floor covering in all the better chambers. Just now in summer when grasses, rushes, and wild flowers are abundant, this natural carpet is not unpleasant. The rushes have just been changed, and the whole dwelling is permeated by the clean, sweet odor of new-mown hay. Especially in Lady Catherine's parlor where great heaps of fragrant herbs and wild flowers have been flung upon the tiling, the scent is really delightful. "A terrestrial paradise," beamed an unctuous curate, lately, after admiring the tapestries, while paying his devoir to the pious lady bountiful. In midwinter and early spring the case, alas, is very different; the old rushes have been allowed to remain since autumn. Dust, ale droppings, grease, and all manner of rubbish have sifted down through them. In many rooms there is constant eating; how easy to clear the plates and trenchers merely by flinging down the bones and crusts to hide themselves in the stalks, and, presumably, to be devoured by the numerous cats and dogs constantly ranging the apartments! Then in March when the meadows begin to supply a new crop, there is a tremendous bundling and sweeping.

The old rushes are cast out for the lads' bonfires, and are replaced with the fragrant layer of the new.

Qualmish people, however, complain that the hordes of vermin that breed happily all through the winter are never quite cleared out of a mansion. Not merely the floor rushes but the tapestries, hangings, and curtains are sure to be populous. Wherever there is a jolly young master (like Captain Andrew) who lets his dogs range everywhere, such conditions are always accented. What matter? An Englishman's skin should be tough; and if the odor from the rushes is sometimes a trifle strong, a fine gentleman can hold to his nose his ever-ready scent-ball or "pomander." As for the suggestion that stale rushes breed disease, Sir Walter simply wags his head and swears that the world is full of silly notions.

We have seen nevertheless that Hollydean is provided (in defiance of the Good Old Times) with a great array of fireplaces, and Captain Andrew has even brought back from the Low Countries a remarkable innovation—a tall tiled stove, and professes to enjoy its heat in his chamber in bitter weather. Most of his father's visitors shake their heads at this, and ask whether soon gentlemen will build their houses "not to work and feed in, but now and then to sweat in," and deplore the effeminacy of the rising generation.

The least satisfactory feature of the Hall is perhaps the lighting by night. The large rooms are illuminated by numerous iron "coronas," swinging from the ceiling and holding a number of candles. These candles no doubt are better than the old torches which were set on iron brackets along the walls of the ancient castles, but they afford an insufficient unsteady light. The best of them made of wax or white tallow with cotton wicks are fairly expensive, and in the ordinary rooms often enough there burn merely the cheap rush candles, made of kitchen fat, dark and ill-smelling with wicks made out of rushes. The cost of lighting a mansion like Hollydean is very serious, and the constant changing and snuffing of the candles lays a heavy burden upon the servants.

Mention has been made of the hangings which cover the walls. The great multiplication of windows and of fine paneling has reduced the broad blank surfaces which need to be masked. Where bare walls exist they are neither decorated with frescoes,[1] as with the Ancients, nor with the wall paper which will become common in later days. The walls of Hollydean are hung either with tapestries or their humbler substitutes, "painted cloths."

The latter, being much cheaper, are far more common. They are long strips of canvas painted in a kind of tempera, the scenes being sketched in broadly somewhat as will be the theater scenery of another age. No great artistic skill nor originality enters into them, yet the general effect is somewhat pleasing. Of course there are all manner of designs, especially conventionalized plants and beasts, but above all there are crude "histories"—scenes from the Bible or else from the old mythology. Around Hollydean they are hung without the least system—Abraham offering Isaac is cheek by jowl with The Labors of Hercules, followed by a procession of ferocious lions, unicorns, and dragons. No one is worried by such incongruities. Almost all the walls of the less important apartments are hung in this manner, and "painted cloths" are so cheap that every well-to-do merchant or farmer boasts a good number of them. They are the wall paper of the sixteenth century.

But the great hall, the parlors, and the great galleries are hung with really rich and beautiful tapestries imported

[1] Frescoes still survived in churches and public buildings dating from the Middle Ages but few of them seem to have existed in private dwellings.

from Flanders. Every person of wealth collects tapestries just as he might jewels. The Queen has a perfect treasure house of them; lesser dignitaries often possess a great store. They are elegant in themselves and have the additional merit of revealing the owner's riches and consequence.

Besides the painted cloths and tapestries, a fine mansion displays many excellent specimens of "Turkey work." These have in no sense been manufactured in the Orient. They are very handsome embroideries supposed to be made in imitation of Eastern carpets. They are used for window seats, chair cushions, table coverings, and the like. Very many have been made directly for Sir Walter with the Hollydean arms blazoned upon them. Quite as many display loyally the Queen's own cognizances and the royal "E. R." Between all these various forms of wall covering and draperies there are very few wooden surfaces left in the entire hall, except where there is elaborate paneling or carving.

Here and there about the mansion are scattered handsomely framed pictures. Almost none of them are landscape scenes or easel paintings, but personal portraits abound. Since the visit of the great Holbein to England in Henry VIII's time, for a lady or gentleman not to have a portrait painted has meant not to be in fashion. Unfortunately most of the artists (usually from the Low Countries) have been commonplace hackworkers employed by patrons who are very poor art critics. The actual portrait is often sketched in hurriedly with pencil or chalk, and the main stress has been laid on the costume. Lady Catherine's father who frowns with worshipful importance across the gallery is said to be hardly recognizable in his features, but his brilliant alderman's robes are decoratively magnificent. All the members of the Hollydean house are likewise represented, including of course Sir Walter at various ages.

The dining apartments are brave in their display of silver plate, but even more frequent is the soft sheen of pewter. This is becoming very common, and even prosperous farmers and traders are giving up their old wooden trenchers for an array of pewter dishes. Here is another extravagance which makes the champions of the Good Old Times shake their heads; were not "treen" (carved of wood) platters and great leather drinking cups quite good enough for everybody while Merrie England was still Merrie England?

As for the furniture of Hollydean, it is right to say it gives signs everywhere of the richer, more artificial age. For one thing armchairs are multiplying in the place of stools for all but the greatest luminaries; although it is a fact that there is nothing disreputable in sitting down plump upon the floor rushes, preferably with a soft cushion under you, and even at great banquets the guests usually sit on folding stools—it is always easy to bring in more and accommodate late comers. In any case to sit in ponderous, oak panel-back chairs at the head of the table is still the indispensable honor for the master and the mistress of the house, and for their more honored companions.

Buffets, cupboards, and cabinets, deeply carved, are fairly common. They are too heavy for some ideas of elegance, but their costly material—rosewood, fine oak, or walnut inlaid with marqueterie—gives an elaborate and massive effect. Especially there are the huge "court cupboards," practically movable closets, which answer the purposes of sideboards, and are covered with carpets on which rests the brave array of silver plate and pewter. As for chests of drawers, they are comparatively rare; the old mediæval custom of locking things away in solid chests still obtains, and no bedroom lacks its ponderous "coffer" in which good clothing and all other desirable articles can be kept safe from curious eyes and light-fingered servants.

Undoubtedly the most elaborate part of the furnishings of an Elizabethan home is the bed and bedding. In no other domestic matter has there been greater improvement. Harrison, the antiquary, descants upon this fact. "Our fathers were glad to sleep usually on straw pallets or rough mats, and covered themselves with coarse dagswain or hop-harlots" (very coarse material) with a "good round log for a pillow." Servants almost never had a sheet beneath them; they were lucky if they had one over them to keep off the pricking of the straw from "their hardened hides." Real pillows ordinarily were proper only for women in child-bed. When a man began to prosper, he proclaimed the fact by buying a mattress or "flock bed" and indulging in a sack of chaff for a pillow.

BEDSTEAD, A.D. 1593.
Wright, "Archæological Album."

Now fine bedding, sheets, blankets, and down pillows are fairly common even in pretty humble houses; and unfortunate is the dwelling that cannot boast at least one of the objects which stand in every bedroom in Hollydean—enormous four-poster beds. These are likely to be formidable structures with every inch of the high headboards and footboards a labyrinth of carving. The tall posts may imitate Ionic pillars, but most imposing of all are the curtains and canopy. The curtains have this decided excuse; many bedrooms have their only exit through another bedroom and you have no privacy unless you are thoroughly shut in. Besides, all physicians assure you that drafts and night air cause any amount of illness. The less fresh air while sleeping, the healthier—another reason for drawing curtains tightly.

Opened or closed these curtains with the bedspread, valance, and the great "tester" (canopy) represent some of the finest embroidery in the house, and the beds in the principal chambers are ample enough for giants, even if none of them rival the famous "Great Bed of Ware," wherein (according to one story) twelve people once actually lay down together. Visitors of another age might not indeed find comfort matching all this magnificence. Sir Walter's tremendous four-poster is springless with only a hard crisscross of ropes to hold up the straw under-pallet. This however is mitigated by two or three deep feather mattresses, in which one must literally "sink to rest." In any event the fine sheets of silver linen, the snow-white blankets, the tastefully patterned yellow and green coverlet would please any emperor.

A bed with rich silken canopy and curtains, and embroidery and linen to match can be worth a thousand pounds —and the Hollydeans are proud to possess several such lordly objects.[1] There is the more reason for owning them because every man of consequence frequently receives his morning visitors in bed; and a splendid bedstead is just as much one of the appurtenances of greatness as a couple of gentlemen-in-waiting and plenty of grooms in livery. At night in winter while the master is slipping into his furred damask dressing gown and nightcap, his valet warms the vast area of chilly sheets with the brass warming pan. The process is needful, for without a warming pan, the plunge into the recesses of such a bed resembles nothing but a voyage to Iceland.

So then we wander among the material glories of Hollydean, saying little as yet about its human inhabitants. One other feature of the mansion must be scrutinized before comment becomes more personal—it is needful to explore the garden. Probably the love of elaborate gardens has found its way north from Italy. All through the Middle Ages every monastery had its garden of medicinal herbs, and no doubt fine ladies with their knights enjoyed strolling out amid the bowers of roses. The coming of the Renaissance has accented all the natural human love for flowers and greenery. The great Lord Burghley, for example, is passionately fond of his garden and loves to ride about its paths on a favorite little mule; and Master Francis Bacon, who possesses perhaps the wisest head in England, soon will write "God Almighty first planted a garden, and indeed it is the purest of human pleasure, (and) the greatest refreshment to the spirits of man." Even in London there are many fine gardens; and in smaller places such as Boroughport, behind almost every

---

[1] Beds with their outfits could cost much more than this. In the next reign, James I visited the Earl of Dorset. The earl honored his royal guest with a bed hung entirely with cloth of gold. It cost his lordship £8000.

house there is a strip of land hemmed in by clay walls crowned with a row of thatch, giving space for the house-wife to cultivate a little flower garden, an herb garden, and a few choice fruit trees.

Master Sylvester, in laying out Hollydean, would have failed in his duty had he omitted not one garden but a whole system thereof, and to maintain these requires a head gardener who is almost as arrogant as the butler himself. The beds are arranged to lie in full view of the principal windows of the mansion, and now at the height of the summer they present a perfect maze of colors and greenery. Here are flower beds edged with trellises of painted woodwork, yonder arbors, and curving "galleries" or pergolas. Inevitably there are several fountains, and large masses of yew and box trimmed to the shape of un-couth monsters; while standing upon the broad patches of greensward are scattered amazing beasts—lions, leopards, unicorns, griffins, and dragons nearly life size (if there is a life size for dragons!), made of wood and brilliantly gilded and painted. The effect of this menagerie is some-what astonishing, but in connection with the flower beds not too garish. As for the flower beds themselves they are in the Italian style, strictly trained and artificial; but Master Sylvester was gifted with too much wit not to realize the beauty of the wilder bits of nature. Outside of the formal garden before you wander away into the park there is a good imitation of a fragrant heath with strawberries peep-ing beneath the sweet briar and the honeysuckle.[1] Also the patches of well-shorn lawn are most artfully disposed to bring out the full beauties of the flower beds and the trel-lises. Around the whole outer confines of the garden there runs a verdant hedge of holly and hornbeam, and nearest

[1] Bacon, in his famous discussion of gardens, lays down emphatically that there should be a fair compromise between the wild and the artificial.

the house there is an elaborate iron gate with lesser gates on the other sides.

Here in the cool of the day Sir Walter or Lady Catherine can walk at ease and discuss the fine gilliflowers. To have well-balanced beds, each coming on in season, is the aim of wise gardening. Your Elizabethan is fond of strong odors, and the scent from beds of flowers growing is counted much superior to that from any bouquet. The result is sometimes a fragrance that is almost overpowering. In their time there is special delight in the white double violets, then in the intoxicating musk roses, and also in the grateful odor of strawberry leaves. The sweetbriar, pink, gilliflower, and honeysuckle are desired as much to please the eye as the nostrils, but Sir Walter especially favors the wild thyme and the water mints for the fragrance they give off when you tread on them. Damask roses, rosemary, and sweet marjoram are fair to look upon, but to get their real odor they have to be plucked. As for the flowers common in every Boroughport home garden, their list is long—"pale" primroses, "saffron" crocuses, "azured" harebells, "pied" daisies, "freckled" cowslips, orchids, columbines, carnations, peonies, poppies, oxslips, anemones, eglantine, pansies ("Cupid's flower"), sweet william, hollyhocks, lilies of the valley—these are only some of them. But one flower is conspicuous by its absence—the tulip; already known in Holland, it will hardly reach England before 1600. There lack not too in the Hollydean garden numerous exotic flowers from the Levant, or even from the Indies and the Americas; but such imports go mainly to the vegetable garden or the orchard.

These adjuncts however do not fail. Sir Walter would be ashamed to eat ordinary fruits and vegetables which were not grown on the estate. The kitchen garden is indeed set at some distance from the house and carefully walled off, because, as the writers of herbals will say, "The many different scents from such herbs as cabbages and onions are scarce pleasing as perfumes." But there is a great abundance not merely of such standard vegetables as pumpkins, carrots, turnips, broad beans, parsnips, and the salad plants, but also such recent importations into England as artichokes and peas, though one will look in vain as yet for asparagus, kidney beans, and above all the white potato. The gardener will point "potatoes" out to you, but they are only the sweet potatoes, adopted into England very soon after the discovery of America.

As for the orchard, it lies carefully set on the northeast side of the flower garden to give protection from the wind. Through it run graveled paths gratefully arbored over with "pleached" cherry or apple trees. All the old English fruits —apples, pears, quinces, plums, and cherries—are in abundance, as well as a few walnuts, hazelnuts, and filberts. The gardener has also had fair success with a few trees of the new imported fruits—apricots, peaches, and almonds; but he admits that such exotics as wild olives, lemons, and oranges can only be rarities in the great establishments of the greatest noblemen.

Hollydean, it is needless to say, is a great mansion, the abode of a wealthy magnate. Its thousand and one humbler contemporaries in country and town must pass with little comment save to observe that even down to the poorer cottages the age has witnessed a great increase in comforts and luxuries. For example, all but the meanest hovels boast now not merely chimneys but windows of glass, albeit often of cheap glass full of "bulls' eyes" and barely transparent.

Around the Thorpshire country are scattered any number of fine substantial squires' or yeomens' houses, very likely built in the loyal " m " plan, with their great halls, great staircases, parlors, bedrooms, and modest long galleries. In

Boroughport most of the houses are still of beamed frame-work with the spaces filled with lath and plaster. Usually they are two stories high with dormer windows and steep gables, and with their doors shaded by porch or "pent house"—a narrow sloping roof extending a little into the street and giving protection in a drizzle to the people outside. But the better dwellings of the citizens have brick substituted for the plaster, and tiles are replacing the dangerous thatch. In fact as soon as a townsman prospers he is likely to rebuild his old house with walls of brick or even stone; so that without quitting his ancestral hall and parlor, he has a handsome modern residence.[1]

The homes of the very poor (alas!) need detain us little; poverty seldom has much to say for itself. In the towns they are likely to be crazy old houses deserted by the prosperous, and ranged along such noisome byways as that significantly called "Offal Lane." In the country the cheapest cottages are made by driving timbers upright in the ground and filling in the spaces with straw splints on which is spread thick clay. The roof is the commonest thatch; the floor merely of well-trampled earth, and the furniture a few straw pallets, low stools, and battered old chests.

Thus ends our survey of the dwellings of the age of Gloriana. We have moved about Hollydean as if its human inhabitants did not exist, or as if wrapped in our Cloak of Invisibility they completely ignored us. It is time now to become more personal—to turn to the great and eternally vital subjects of wherewith a man must clothe himself, and what he must eat and drink.

[1] Of course Shakespeare thus rebuilt the greater part of his Stratford-upon-Avon house with stone.

¶ *Chapter* V: CONCERNING RAIMENT, SOBER AND GAY

HAD we visited Thorpshire in another era, reason would tell us that most of what we say pertaining to costume and garments should begin when we pry into the mysteries of Lady Catherine's chamber, but truth compels us to say that her son, Captain Andrew, is almost as much concerned about the eternal question of dress as his elder sister, the fair Mistress Anne.

Never was there an age when the sterner sex gave more heed to its garments, when fashions were more artificial, when men as well as women could clap a fortune on their backs. Up through Henry VIII's time English costume was reasonably natural and withal handsome. Men wore a long tunic cut open at the throat, and filled in with pleated linen, set off with ample puffed sleeves. Then these "gothic features" gave way to the æsthetic close-fitting doublet with tight sleeves, and a high collar edged with lace. Add to these round upper hose or breeches above the long stockings and you have the fundamentals of the costume of the courtiers around her Majesty in the earlier part of her reign.

Grave folk mutter under breath that they fear the Queen herself is not without blame for the extravagances which will become ever more pronounced until almost the end of the reign. Elizabeth undeniably is garish in her own tastes, and loves to see her courtiers push their brilliance even to absurdity. The result is a riot of barbaric gorgeousness and a perfect heyday for all favored tailors. At least it can be said that if the sedate and standardized masculine costume of a later age saves its wearers infinite time and trouble, it does not permit that expression of personal moods and tastes open to even a very discreet gentleman of the sixteenth century.

Complaints, nevertheless, are not confined to the strict Puritans. It is alleged that English costumes are borrowed slavishly and indiscriminately from foreign lands; that the mere fact that a mode is imported is enough to commend it; that your well-dressed man indulges in "the Spanish guise today; in French toys tomorrow," and next in the "high Almain (German) fashion" or even "the Turkish manner." He must have his "Morisco gowns and his short French breeches" and so "except it were a dog in a doublet you shall not see any creatures so disguised as are our countrymen of England."

Worse still, all means of telling a man's rank by his costume have been abandoned. Mere yeomen or even hirelings think nothing of flaunting silks, velvets, damasks, and taffetas if they can find the pelf or credit to obtain them. The spendthrift gallant who is at length starving himself on three-penny dinners in order to make an astonishing show with his cloak, ruff, and doublet, is a stock character in the London theaters; while a lucky heir like Captain Andrew thinks himself meanly clad if he appears in a gala costume worth less than £100, not counting jewels.[1]

Besides his regular dress, for every gentleman some kind of weapon is still a normal accompaniment, although peaceful burghers can get along with merely a large knife at their girdles, never used except at table or for nibbing their pens. But men of the Hollydean class belt around a walking-sword almost as frequently as they swing on a

---

[1] To appreciate such a figure, it must be remembered that the purchasing power of money was then at least *six times* that of the same nominal amount at the present day.

cloak. A long Toledo slapping its silvered scabbard at his thigh certainly adds to the rakish appearance of many a gaudily dressed fellow, and as certainly provides a prompt implement for brawls. It also helps to heap up the expense of these costumes against which even non-Puritans rage incessantly. "Never was England merrier," runs their plaint, "than when men wore simple garments with some pretty furniture of velvet or furs without such cuts and garish colors as are brought in but by the consent of the French."

What profit scoldings? Sooner can monarchs change their subjects' religions than their fashions. The long dictatorship of the tailor and the costumer is only at its beginning! . . .

. . . When Sir Walter rises in the morning, his very important body-servant, "Master Ambrose," as he insists upon being called by the turnspits, first aids his worshipful master to put on an undershirt, then a kind of short breeches, then a snugly fitted jacket-bodice to which the long close tights or trunk hose are laced by numerous points; after that a coat-jacket which extends below the waist with a lower skirt which covers completely the line of points sustaining the nether garments. Finally the good knight suffers some kind of ruff or lace collar (the ampler the better in Master Ambrose's opinion) to be fastened about his neck, and he is ready to begin the day.

This costume of course varies with the occasion, whether Sir Walter plans to ride out hunting or to make a call in the borough upon Master Markham, the Lord Mayor. There is not a great deal of change between winter garments and summer garments; underwear has not yet been invented although lambskin jackets exist for invalids. All you can do is to pull one shirt on top of another until you perhaps waddle about with a very awkward and bulgy appearance. Also in winter there is likely to be a much greater wearing of fur on cloaks and jackets both for trimmings and linings. Old sumptuary laws stand on the books against the use of fur by anybody under the rank of knight or dame, but prosperous drapers and butchers and their wives flaunt their sables unhindered.

One innovation indeed has not yet touched the plebeian classes. Since the days of Adam and Eve honest mortals have gone to bed just as naked as God made them. Now among the very rich and fastidious since about 1550 has come in the luxury of donning "night rails"—garments actually worn to bed. Sir Walter says that he is too old-fashioned for such an absurd luxury, but Captain Andrew professes to sleep better in a night rail and adds that it gives a certain protection against those invaders from which even the cleanliest bedding cannot be always free.

The list of everyday garments, therefore, is not a long one; but what elaborations are possible with each article! For example, shirts can be of cambric or lawn, and wrought with such splendid silk needlework that they can cost the amazing sum of ten pounds apiece. The short "Spanish" cloak which gallants like to have swinging down to their hips can be made of the softest and costliest variety of perfumed leather. The good old cloth breeches will never do on great occasions; they must be of velvet, although velvet breeches have been lately denounced in Master Robert Greene's pamphlet as "an upstart came out of Italy, begot by Pride, nursed by Self-Love, and brought into this country by New Fangledness." As for the trunk-hose, some come only to the knees, some called "Venetian hose" rise to mid-thigh. These are cut very full at the top, then narrowed at the knee and alleged to give the wearer a decidedly "melon-shaped" appearance. If the cloaks are not of leather they can be of the most costly of all fabrics, faced with gold or silver lace or even with pearl embroideries, with high fur collars and extravagant linings. The doublets and hose, whatever their material, are likely to be ornamented with fantastic ribbings, spots and stripes, suggestive (especially after the winged triangular cloaks have been donned) of enormous insects, so that her Majesty's courtiers have been likened to the "court drones who hum and buzz around their Queen."

No other articles of dress can, however, usurp the place of the ruff. Merely seeing an Englishman wearing one places him instantly in the age of Gloriana. Her father, Henry VIII, is said once to have given the example to his subjects by one day appearing before them wearing a white band about his not small neck—very plain, very narrow, and without lace. Instantly loyal gallants and costumers caught up the idea which was also filtering over from France. Speedily "ruffs proper," large pleated collars standing out from the neck, were all the rage. Early in her present Majesty's reign, a certain Master Higgins, a tailor near London,[1] swept in riches by producing ruffs finer and more elaborate than any rival could supply.

Unfortunately these embellishments, as they grew larger and with ever more deeply pleated embroideries, were so limp they had to be propped out by a narrow framework. Then appeared an invention more revolutionary (for the hour) than gunpowder or printing. In 1564 a Mistress Dinghen, daughter of a Dutch refugee, appeared in London. She brought with her the great mystery of *starching*. For five pounds she would teach any one how to make starch and how to cause lace ruffs made of the flimsiest lace to stand out like spider webs. Mistress Dinghen soon was wealthy; and all the drapers' shops were full of ever-

[1] He lived on a road presently called Piccadilly, from his famous "picardels" or ruffs.

expanding lawn and cambric ruffs until they became of astonishing size. Now by the 1590's ruffs a foot deep are very usual, and a gallant's head sticking out of them looks "like John the Baptist's head upon the platter." Even the Queen, extravagant enough in her own fashions, is trying in vain to control these masterpieces of absurdity.

Sir Walter counts himself grave and proper in all matters of costume; Captain Andrew merely dresses "in concord with his station and fortune," but some of Captain Andrew's friends are unconscionable. For example, a young master of Norfolkshire, Eustace Fortesque, has just quitted Hollydean after a visit in which he almost wore out his welcome. He has lately come into a small estate which he is running through as rapidly as possible. He horsewhipped the grooms, kicked Sir Walter's favorite hound, and snored aloud during Master Crabtree's godly exhortations while Captain Andrew was especially outraged at his extravagant clothes.

Master Fortesque's ruff "rose so high and sharp it was nigh to cut his throat;" and his breeches were "full as deep as the middle of the winter." Worse still, these breeches, to make them keep their shape, were carefully stuffed with bran. One day at dinner something scratched through them; instantly, when their owner rose, the bran tumbled out of him all in a heap upon the floor, to the infinite merriment of young Mistresses Anne and Arabella, toward the former of whom Master Eustace had been making languishing eyes.

True, none could deny that his best doublet was a triumph of the sartor. It was of deep turquoise Genoa velvet worth three pounds per yard. It was fronted with numerous rows of silk buttons placed very close together, and the embroidery and gold lace was all to match. To stiffen the front of this wonderful doublet there had been worked a triangular piece of wood as thin as cardboard. Altogether Master Eustace had seemed completely sheathed in his garments, as if they were a suit of armor, and the effect was enhanced by his expensive earrings, the string of pearls about his neck, a jeweled ring on either thumb, and long hair tied with a bunch of ribbons. His beard of course was of fantastic cut, and he kept opening a case of golden toothpicks merely to show that their handles were set with gems as well as was the hilt of his dagger.

Such men who "turn five hundred acres of good land into two or three trunks of apparel" are the most vulnerable targets for the Puritans. Their anathemas increase when they deal with the sex through which, as the preachers eternally remind their listeners, "iniquity first entered the Garden of Eden." If masculine costume is astonishing, what shall be said of the women's? In 1560 female dress was relatively sensible and economical. Even a gentlewoman was usually content with simple cloth gowns. Then, as luxury increased, simplicity flew out of the window. Feminine ruffs exceed if anything masculine ruffs, and to these are added the amazing farthingale. The new fashions have penetrated to all classes. Rails Master Philip Stubbes, the censor, "Every artificer's wife will not stick to go in her hat of velvet every day, every merchant's wife and 'mean gentlewoman' in her French hood, and every cottage daughter in her taffeta hat. But how they come by this they care not. Who payeth for it they regard not!" [1]

Now the details of all these mysteries are not lightly to be pried into. In a few words, when Mistress Anne's pert tirewoman, Goody Agatha, helps her into her clothes at five o'clock in the morning, first the young lady dons a

---

[1] Stubbes's *Anatomy of Abuses* (1583) is of course one of our prime sources of information for very many phases of Elizabethan life.

fairly ample chemise. Next come stockings of cloth or often of knitted silk, gartered at the knee. There follows corsets, a perfect coat of leather armor, stiffly encasing the figure and vigorously laced in; over that goes a fitted bodice on which are to be tied the sleeves of the gown, below which is slung the astonishing farthingale. This is succeeded by a petticoat cut very full and bunched over the stiff side projections of the corset. Superimposed thereon is the gown, cut open on the breast and showing the frontlet of the upper petticoat. Lastly there comes the ruff and the stomacher, a taut belt holding in the waist tightly at the back. Mistress Anne thus faces the world with a stiff, stilted figure, walking indeed with free hips but almost immovable at the back. Being very much a fine lady of fashion she only pities the humble dames who wear softer corsets and in general a much freer and simpler costume.

These garments are capable of infinite luxury and elaboration. The two most formidable to masculine eyes are undoubtedly the farthingale and the ruff. The farthingale began its tyranny about 1580. It is a monstrous-wheeled invention which holds the skirts out stiffly all around the figure; in fact it is a kind of projecting shelf of whalebone and leather dexterously slung at the bottom from the corset. To drape the petticoats and gown over this enormous fabric calls for all the skill of Goody Agatha. She counts it lucky (if young gentlemen are visiting) if her impatient mistress does not box her ears before the great task is over.

As for the ladies' ruffs, they are if anything more outrageous than those of the gentlemen. The pleats become ever more complicated; there can be two or three layers of cambric each starched to stand up stiffly from the head unless caught in a breeze when "they strike sail and flutter like dishcloths about their owners' necks." Snow-white ruffs can provide sufficient vanity, but what of the advancing rage for colored starches? There is a launderer in Bor-oughport who has just learned the high mystery of making and using *yellow starch,* the greatest rage now at court. Of course he commands the vastly profitable patronage of the Hollydean ladies.

Yellow starch, to be sure, in the eyes of many grave persons savors of straight impiety. Influential clergymen, even deans, have vainly endeavored to bar all ladies with the accursed "yellow ruffs" from their services. The com-plete failure of such prohibitions proclaims the folly of mere parsons in defying the whims of the more powerful sex. Of course the men never keep back their flings at the foibles of their wives and daughters. Only the other day Sir Walter gravely repeated the current story that the masculine half of England affects to believe to be true. "It took place (runs the report) on the 27th of March, 1582," in the Flemish city of Antwerp. A young woman, a rich merchant's daughter, was getting ready for a great wedding. Like all fashionable damsels, having dyed her hair, painted her face, and put on most of her armor, she came to her great yellow ruff. It gave more than the usual amount of trouble. At last in her impatience she wished aloud that "the devil might take her if she ever wore a ruff again." Instantly there appeared a pleasant and courteous young man, possibly a tailor's prentice. "May I assist the gracious lady?"—But the moment he had the ruff fairly about her, he twisted her neck and disappeared in a whiff of sulphur, leaving her dead. At her funeral her coffin seemed amazingly heavy. The bearers opened it. Inside was discovered a lean and deformed black cat sit-ting upon a great pile of ruffs and frizzings of hair.

Sir Walter and all his male guests laugh approval at Master Stubbes's denunciation of starch as "the devil's liquor," and starching houses as "consecrate to Beelzebub and Cerberus, arch-devils of ruffs"—and go on wearing their own ruffs along with the ladies!

Inevitably the catalog of female specialties or absurdities is very long. For example, all unmarried women, including the Virgin Queen herself, show their bosoms decidedly exposed; despite all the cavilings of the preachers about "gross immodesty." All ladies rejoice in such innocencies as fine silk stockings (a very proper gift for New Years), and enjoy handsome gloves often gauntleted and embroidered on the backs with silk tassels and gold thread, much perfumed and lined with fur. Any quantity of small jewels can be sewn upon the bodice; and as for gowns, they can be made of silk, velvet, grosgrain, and taffeta up to forty shillings and more per yard, can be decorated with lace two fingers broad or with velvet edged with lace, while the petticoat can become a kirtle, a jacket with skirt attached, made of fine stuff or silk.

One necessity in the attire of other days many high ladies indeed go without. Foreign visitors are astonished at the extent to which Englishwomen, and especially the young and unmarried, go without hats or even hoods. Indeed in mild weather it is permissible to sally forth without mantle, hood, or veil—merely with the vast farthingale bellying out around the wearer, making her look "like a trussed-up chicken set upon a bell." This custom, of course, puts an extra stress upon hair dressing, and curiously enough, although it is very proper to appear hatless or bonnetless, coquettish dames have discovered the advantage of wearing small masques of colored cloth, covering the upper cheeks and nose with the eye-holes filled with glass. These are commonly worn while traveling. They are grotesque and ugly enough, but every one assures us they pique the curiosity of the men—and is not that five parts the object of all feminine attire?

Now concerning many other niceties which we must investigate. Of course Lady Catherine and Mistress Anne, like all their compeers, carry small silver mirrors dangling at their girdles—and consult them very often. Also they often have their fans of gay feathers with silver or ivory handles. They would surpass their sex if they did not possess each a small arsenal of face paints and hair washes—and many dames blithely change the color of their tresses from year to year.[1] Few gentle dames fail to use strong perfumes copiously, and almost as many have private knowledge of some "wise woman" who teaches them how to beautify their complexions, brighten their eyes, give a gloss to their hair, and otherwise make themselves more perilous to the men.

So much for various matters wherein the sexes separate, but Mistress Anne is little ahead of her brother in her devotion to jewelry. Captain Andrew on occasions imitates his friend Fortesque in wearing pearl earrings, although he has not followed the partial custom of having his ears pierced for carrying some love tokens of the lady of his heart. Rings are worn in profusion. Every gentleman has his big signet ring, graven with his coat of arms or some identifying emblem, and often enough fits it on his thumb. A great courtier will wear a large diamond, turquoise, or fine cameo upon nearly all of his fingers. Even a poor man will wear bands of silver, brass, or even pewter rather than go without any ring at all. Every person of property also displays his gold chain, sometimes plain, sometimes intricate and enameled in striking black and white combinations. The gift of a chain to an inferior is a familiar and

---

[1] The portraits of Queen Mary Tudor show hers in different colors. Elizabeth with all her vanities at least stuck to her original red.

gracious act. Rich men give gold chains frequently to their retainers, and her Majesty often presents chains worth fifty or even one hundred pounds to her favorite noblemen. From these chains the fashionable dangle pendants set with jewels or costly cameos: or a true lover causes the miniature of his mistress to be set in the back of the pendant so he can press it frequently to his heart. Ladies rejoice in their long chains of pearls or precious stones strung together, but the wearing of these by men is counted effeminate—even among dandies.

One luxury carries a certain excuse of utility. Since the time of Henry VIII there has been a kind of portable clock known as a watch. They are still too costly for any but the very rich. They seem large affairs, sometimes octagonal or oval instead of round, and the outer case is pierced with elaborate open work to enable the strike within to be heard. Gradually they are becoming smaller, and when set with diamonds and hung from a long gold chain make very effective pendants indeed. Captain Andrew does not possess one yet, but is resolved to boast one as soon as he can make certain payments to his tailor.

It remains to consider how the inhabitants of Hollydean cover their hands, their feet, and their heads. Persons of fashion of either sex have been known to wear two or even three pairs of gloves, one above the other. In any case they ought to be handsomely embroidered, with lace or fur edges. The foppish Master Fortesque wore a pair of brightly painted leather gauntlets sewn with small jewels, and when Captain Andrew was last admitted to the Queen he appeared with gloves of fine goatskin plentifully perfumed with ambergris. Shoes are comparatively simple. They can be of leather or velvet, are preferably pointed and often perforated for embroidery and decorated with buckles of gold, silver, or copper gilt. Usually they match in color (both for gentlemen and ladies) the color of the general dress, and it may be said that they average less extreme and fantastical (to the eye from another age) than most articles in the Elizabethan wardrobe.

No such praise can be bestowed upon the treatment men and women vouchsafe their heads. True the run of men's hats are not so startling. Not merely are prentices bound to wear round cloth caps with low flat crowns, but very many of their elders and betters do likewise. By act of Parliament in 1571 every male subject of the Queen unless of the highest rank is bound to wear a cloth cap Sundays and holidays in order to help the woolen trade. These "statute caps" are not unpleasing especially when made up in agreeable green, blue, and red. On other days, however, many men of coat armor rejoice in *tall* hats, "perking up like the spire of a steeple," rising high above the head and when of velvet, silk, or fine imported beaver costing up to forty shillings and betraying "the fantasies of inconstant minds." As for the ladies we have stated that often they go hatless. When needing protection from wind and weather a veil or hood more or less elegant can be thrown on, although many fine dames will appear in feathered bonnets or cloth caps of such varied and freakish style that this headgear is likened to "a sow's maw," although the astonishing "lattice caps" with horns seem passing out of vogue.

Hatted or hatless, however, men and women pay the uttermost attention to hair-dressing, and the men to the cut of their beards. Mighty is the sartor, but almost equally potent are his brothers the tonsor and the hairdresser. As might be expected the fashions for ladies' hair are endless. Mistress Anne and her friends appear one day curled with innumerable curls, another tightly crisped, and on some great occasions with their tresses built out over a cushion, spread well over the forehead, ornamented with jewels, small wreaths of silver and gold, and held in place with hairpins. Over such a structure it is quite proper to set a stiff caul made of net wire and cloth of gold or tinsel.

False hair unavoidably is in eternal request. From London come stories of poor little girls with fine tresses who are enticed into solitary courts and then shorn of their long hair before they are allowed to run screaming away. Does blonde hair command the greatest favor with the men? The women affect to believe so, although up in London that rising playwright Master Shakespeare says in his sonnets that he prefers dark hair, complexion, and eyes, although admitting that the fair hue is more often associated in romance with beauty. Blonde or dark, a woman counts herself more irresistible if her crowning glory has plenty of jeweled pins worked into it, and if to these can be added such a rich ornament as a little ship made of mother-of-pearl garnished with rubies, here is an excellent way of saying, "I am a great lady."

But masculine customs with the hair are almost as varied. Hearken again to the worthy Master Harrison: "Sometimes our heads are polled, sometimes curled, or suffered to grow at length like woman's locks; and many times the hair is cut off above or under the ears, round as by a wooden dish." In general it is already true to say that your gallant wears his long love-locks, while the grave citizen of Puritanical cast is rather closely cropped. Up at court some young noblemen, like my Lord the Earl of Southampton,[1] wear long heavy tresses falling over their shoulders, and not a few duels have begun by pulling a companion's long hair during the heat of some bowling or tennis game.

---

[1] Well known is the portrait of this patron of Shakespeare, with a long heavy tress of walnut hair descending upon his breast.

Being a soldier, Captain Andrew considers such a custom inconvenient, but he like his father wears his hair much longer than will the men of another epoch.

The gallant captain, in any case, thinks less of the cut of his hair than of his beard. Not many men go clean shaven, but the trim of the whiskers can be infinite. When Captain Andrew enters the shop of Master Giles Snipper, the most favored barber of Boroughport, the latter beams and begins a patter he inflicts on every worshipful customer: "How, sir, will you be trimmed? Will you have your beard like a spade or a bodkin? A pent house on your upper lip or an alley (forked beard) on your chin? Your mustaches sharp at the ends like shoemaker's awls, or hanging down to your mouth like goats' flakes?" And so onward in a torrent, until his patron has vouchsafed his commands.[1]

Master Snipper provides all the accomplishments of his art. He has "the French cut, the Spanish cut, and the Dutch cut"; also "the bravado cut, the gentleman's cut, and the court cut." A customer with a lean straight face is handsomely broadened out with a "Marquis Otto's cut," but a platter-like countenance is narrowed down by a long slender beard. If you are likely to meet the Queen, you are reminded that her Majesty likes ample beards and has lately scolded a bishop for trimming his too short.

Then there are the cuts for the duelist. Some time since, young Master Aikenside, a neighbor to Hollydean, had a quarrel on his hands. After he sent his challenge he visited Master Snipper. The latter peaked his beard to the style of a Don Desperado, trained his mustachios so that they turned up to his ears like horns, and finally dyed all the hair on his face a devilish red. The result was so ferocious

[1] Master Snipper's talk is extremely like that of the barber in John Lyly's *Midas* (1592).

an appearance that the courage of his rather feeble adversary perceptibly froze and friends were permitted to compound the quarrel.

Certain questions must arise ere we turn from men's outer garb to other things. Is your Elizabethan cleanly? The answer is yes—within somewhat modest limits.[1] Almost every one bathes once a week in a large wooden tub set before the fire. Much soap is consumed, mostly home-made although balls of "sweet soap" are bought by the gentility and there are regular soap factories in London. Clothes are regularly laundered in the rivers and wells —to no advantage to the drinking water; but poor families "wash their bucks" (dirty clothes) in the "street streams"; that is to say, the gutters just after rainy days. Toothbrushes are hardly in use, but it is usual to rub the teeth and gums with a bit of fine cloth dipped in some soft powder, and it is a sign of superiority to pick your teeth ostentatiously in public. Better still, however, you can produce a pomander, an ornamented gold and silver ball much perforated and hung about the neck. Inside is hidden a quantity of rich perfume-ambergris, musk, or clove, with disinfectants against the plague. To lift this often delicately to your nose is excellent. It shows you are a man of birth and leisure, exempt from plebeian bustle, and disgusted with the vulgar smells which forever offend aristocratic nostrils.[2]

Finally may be asked, what of the dress of the innumer-

---

[1] There are on the other side such stories as that by the Countess of Dorset who in 1603 with her mother visited the court and "were all lousy by sitting in Sir Thomas Erskine's chambers."

[2] Certain usages do not permit of easy classification, yet cannot be omitted; for example, the general employment of *scratch backs*. These were almost as indispensable to a dame of quality as her fan and were always ready about her toilet. The tight uncomfortable dresses made them very desirable. Often they were handsomely carved with silver handles and ivory claws shaped into a delicate hand.

able sober decent folk not gifted with the wealth and the grandeur of the Hollydeans? Plain garments unfortunately provide few racy stories. Around Thorpshire stout yeomen and all the gamekeepers and forest rangers like to go about in neat Kendal green, although the common rustics are usually in doublets of "mutton taffeta"; that is, sheep skins. They may display filthy greasy hats very likely gnawed with a rat-hole, carry a plain leather pouch, and wear knitted hose, kersey stockings, and big shoes full of hob-nails. Quiet elderly people flaunt no ruffs nor farthingales; elderly men wear long gowns with hanging sleeves over their doublet and hose, all in very modest colors. In Bor-oughport all the lawyers and clergymen of course have their black, and you can tell sheriffs or aldermen by the fur on their gowns and sleeves. The plain citizens show cloaks of brown or chocolate; the craftsmen have doublets of heavy cloth or leather, and in winter overcoats going down to the ankles. The numerous prentices are instantly discoverable by their cloaks of blue. As for the humbler women folk in general, they dress soberly like their husbands if they are wise, extravagantly like fine ladies if they are foolish.

So much then for the great question of raiment for the subjects of the dread Virginia; turn now to the equally vital question of food and drink.

¶ *Chapter* VI: CONCERNING FOOD AND FEASTING

HOLLYDEAN rejoices in its brilliant clothes, but Hollydean rejoices in its hearty appetites and the means God provides for satisfying them.

Visiting Frenchmen and Spaniards are astonished at the ability of Englishmen to devour great quantities of very heavy food. Above all Englishmen are meat eaters: this they explain by saying "our region lying near unto the North doth cause the heat of our stomachs to be of somewhat greater force than with our neighbors of warmer countries." They go on to argue that a hearty meat diet is really more healthful than the meals of bread and herbs favored by the Italians, for "all fulness is ill, but that of bread is worst."

Nevertheless the time has brought certain changes in the eating customs of Thorpshire; especially the old usage of many repasts at odd times is disappearing. Formerly people had "beverages or nuncheons" after dinner, and "rear suppers" after supper. Now almost everybody is content with dinner and supper alone. Only two meals are the rule, for breakfast is still a very trifling affair, although, be it confessed, these two meals are so hearty that only St. George's dragon could desire anything additional.

When the day begins, at first dawn the field hands and under servants have their porridge. About half-past six their masters take a light breakfast—usually not more than a little bread and butter washed down with a pot of ale.[1]

---

[1] The heartier "English" breakfast was, however, coming in. Queen Elizabeth, we know, sometimes began her day with mutton stew, beef, veal, rabbits, or chickens.

People of leisure and quality usually assemble at eleven o'clock for the great meal of the day—dinner; and again for supper a little after five, although merchants and busy folk generally wait until noon for dinner and six for supper. Farmers seldom sup until after seven when the evening chores have been disposed of.

In general the diet of Englishmen has been improving. Not merely, as prosperity has increased, are there fewer starving poor, but more of the population is able to afford flesh and fish, and depends less upon mere "white meats" (milk, butter, and cheese). Fine tablecloths are common; we have seen how silver and pewter are replacing the old wooden trenchers, and napkins are now very usual. The Reformation of course has played havoc with the old Catholic fast days. It is no use for a strict churchman like Archbishop Grindal to try to make Wednesday a day of abstinence, on which "only one sober competent meal" ought to be eaten. But Friday has been saved by Parliamentary statute as strictly a fish day—not, as it carefully explains, from any religious reason but in order to encourage the great fishing industry.

Englishmen love eating and drinking; they love these most when accompanied by profuse hospitality. Foreigners allege that the Queen's subjects are always glad of the least excuse for "giving a feast to a stranger." They would rather (wrote a Venetian ambassador) give five or six ducats to provide an entertainment for a person, than give a groat to assist him in any distress. In the country every one, high or low, is forever asking in guests to his table. Humble-folk are constantly exchanging little presents of eatables—a cake, a pudding, and the like. Sir Walter is one of these landed magnates who tries to live up to the ideal of a good squire —"a man who loves an open cellar, a full hall, and a sweating cook"; and he regularly provides three dinners—

[69]

for his family, for his servants, and the poor of the neighborhood. At Hollydean as at Sir Christopher Hatton's great Holdenby House, any stranger coming on the most trifling business is pressed to stay to dinner, and practically any needy person living within six or seven miles of the hall has only to show himself and be sure of a tolerable meal.

Sir Walter, it is true, does not quite imitate the profusion of Sir William Holles, that very wealthy squire in Nottinghamshire who has a sheer passion for hospitality. Sir William begins his Christmas on All Hallows' Eve (October 31-November 1), and continues it until Candlemas (February 2), during which interval any man is permitted to stay and feast for three days without being asked "whence he came or what he is." For each of the twelve days before Christmas Sir William allows his guests a fat ox and other provisions in proportion; and he never will dine before one o'clock lest some belated friend may be on his way to see him.

Constantly, indeed, will we be assured "hospitality is not what it was,"—another sign the Good Old Times are behind us. Ballad mongers hawk about such laments as

> The Country's causes did (once) require
> Each nobleman to keep his house,
> The Blue coats had what they require
> Good cheer and many a full carouse:
> But now it's not as it used to be,
> For dead is Liberality.

No stranger, however, will count hospitality a general vice of England, and undoubtedly this ease with which certain folk can get free dinners puts a premium upon those beggars and other rogues who are the curse of the countryside.

Concerning Food and Feasting

Hospitality comes easily to gentry of means because of the abundance of servants. They are very cheap and a great house like Hollydean swarms with them. To have an abundance of servitors, wearing your arms on their short blue cloaks and doublets, is one of the promptest methods of showing your own importance. My Lord Burghley, the great Lord Treasurer, keeps eighty ordinary servants constantly in his livery in addition to twenty gentlemen-in-waiting. Sir Walter cannot compete with this but besides the chaplain, and several poor relations who live in the hall, he keeps three or four sons of shabby-genteel squires, who call themselves his "gentlemen ushers" and run on his less menial errands. Below these are perhaps forty servants of varying importance, who make a brave appearance in their spruce livery coats and swords and buckles when they march behind their master on occasions of ceremony.

Every duty is carefully distributed and no castes are more sharply marked than those that separate the upper servants from the under menials. Highest of all consider themselves the valets of the master and the young master. They condescend to warm their employer's bed for him, to draw his curtains, to arrange his fire and candle, and "avoid the dogs" when he retires. In the morning they help him on with his clothing and above all "truss up his points"; the rest of the day (save when he changes his dress) they have most of their time for busy idleness. But the butler is almost as consequential and lays out the "high table" with all the dignity of a chief justice at a grand assize. There is a special carver who feels insulted if he is commanded to do anything but "unlace a coney (rabbit) or raise a capon" with superb professional artistry. The cellarer disputes precedence with the butler. The cooks form almost as perfect a hierarchy as surrounds the Pope at Rome. No one reckons up the sweepers, turnspits, brewers, and scullions, the smartly dressed lackeys who frisk open the doors and set the candles, or the tall "yeomen," who are not yeomen at all, but pages who pass the dishes at table. In the out-building can be mustered a second small army of upper grooms, under grooms, falconers, gamekeepers, and hardy boys who hold the horses and get most of the knocks.

In Lady Catherine's dominions there is still another galaxy of lady's maids, laundresses, needlewomen, and dairy maids—all under the high direction of "Mistress" Sharply, the housekeeper. Her precedence nevertheless is disputed by Lady Catherine's two ladies-in-waiting. These "decayed gentlewomen," poor, proud, and homely, carry her prayer book and wimple for her, read aloud pious works while she is dressing, and in general enable this patroness to feel that she is such a great lady that she requires ladies to wait on her.

Over all this regiment there commands as colonel-in-chief the steward or, as he likes to be called, the Major-domo, Master Simon Scanwell, who (as you learn quickly enough) is no servant at all but "the son of an old house," who for some unannounced reason finds it to his advantage to live at Hollydean, rule Sir Walter's household, and condescend very privately to receive a few rose nobles per month for his genteel services.

The lower servants find such lords as the butler, head cook, and head groom tyrannous enough, but inasmuch as rank and condition are perfectly understood between even the lackeys and their actual masters there is a genuine camaraderie and even familiarity at first a trifle surprising. Sir Walter is not slow to cane an idle rascal with his own hands; a box on the ear from Captain Andrew is all in the day's work, but the more favored servants never hesitate to talk freely when guests are not present, to make pointed suggestions about household matters, or even, sometimes, to throw in remarks while waiting on table.

The servants indeed are real members of the household, humble members who "must know their place," but not without their privileges and above all the Englishman's inveterate right of incessant grumbling. Lady Catherine gossips continually with her maids, and is genuinely attentive if even a scullion or kitchen wench falls ill. In fine, Hollydean is simply a great family in which the members squabble and bicker often enough, but in which fundamentally they are loyally fond of one another. It would be the height of impiety for any of the older servants to betray Sir Walter's interests; it would be a family disgrace for him to fail to assist one of them most heartily in any real hour of need.

The owner of Hollydean, as we have discovered, rises early. His first task is to see that all the servants are at work and to cast an eye over the nearer parts of his estate. Then he retires to his closet, being a religious man, "to serve God and read the Holy Scriptures," although after devotions and meditations are done he attacks a quantity of business correspondence—documents to be signed as Justice of the Peace—and listens to a report by the steward about some new calves and another report by Master Nibpen, his lawyer-clerk, about six sturdy beggars caught last night by the constables and the need of interrogating them later in the day. During this pious-busy interval one of the lackeys brings in the breakfast tray with bread, butter, and small ale—and, since there is much work this morning, a good dish of pottage.

As the time drifts on a great savor of roasting meats begins to drift from the kitchen, and all the numerous household and toilers begin to feel hungry. Sir Walter usually dines in his winter parlor, but graciousness and policy require that once a week he should join his retainers in the great hall, and this is the day. The butler and his deputy the pantler have made sure there are to be no guests of honor, and have decided the great question of the position of the salt.

The very long table beginning upon the dais and descending thence nearly the entire length of the hall has been spread with a fine damask cloth. The half dozen seats on the dais are of course reserved for the knightly family, but a step below, within reach of loud conversation with Sir Walter, sit the steward, the chaplain, the gentleman-ushers, and the ladies-in-waiting. Directly below this gentility is a large silver dish full of salt. Like a disposing angel at the Day of Judgment this dish separates the social sheep from the social goats. Below the salt are all the house servants not concerned with serving the dinner, half a dozen tenants who have come to see the steward, and two or three honest wayfarers who have claimed hospitality. Their humbler condition is patent to all men. They cannot presume to talk with those on the other side of the magic salt dish. Let a stranger enter the hall—all the menials watch to discover "is he above or below the salt?" If above he must be treated with utter obsequiousness; if anywhere below "he is one of us," to be jested with, elbowed, and perhaps pushed around or even sent out flying.

On the dais there are great armchairs for Sir Walter and Lady Catherine, also, as becomes the heir of the house, for Captain Andrew. All the other gentlefolk sit on stools. Below the salt the noisy throng nudges about upon long benches. Inevitably there will be a difference in the viands served above and below the salt-dish. Sir Walter will be drinking malmsey, while the lackeys are quaffing small ale, but there will be abundance of solid food for every one.

Concerning Food and Feasting

Nobody admitted to the board of Hollydean can be allowed to rise hungry.

As eleven o'clock approaches the vigor of the preparations increases. The pewter for the gentles and the trenchers for the meaner folk have been scraped; the stools arranged, the knives scoured, the napkins folded. Then a hand bell clanged vigorously brings an enormous scurrying and shuffling from all parts of the building. The mass of servitors and tenants jostle in from the lower entrance and they take their places amid shouting and banging. The worshipful owner and his "gentle" companions come in more quietly by a small door near the dais. If there were honored guests Sir Walter would present them to his wife and daughters, if they had not met already, then give the conventional, "Kate, Anne, 'Bella, bid the gentleman welcome." Whereupon, without the slightest hesitation or embarrassment, first Lady Catherine, then Mistress Anne, then dainty little Mistress Arabella would each give a smacking buss upon the visitor's cheek, who would unconcernedly put down his head to receive the good old English salutation.

There being no guests today the hungry hall is not kept waiting for this ceremony. Suddenly the steward rises from his stool and taps resoundingly with a long white wand. Silence is instantaneous. Master Crabtree the chaplain rises with more dignity, and his dry voice sounds out the Grace which all England is repeating at every dinner table, "God save our Queen and Realm and send us peace in Christ, Amen!" Immediately arises a clatter unspeakable. Below the salt every one has seized a knife and is hacking off huge pieces of the bread standing on trenchers, hewing off slices of meat the moment the platters are thrust on the table, or making darts for the big wooden spoons in the steaming kettles of cabbage and carrots.

Above the salt proceedings are much more decorous. Sir Walter does not claim to imitate certain pretentious noblemen, who would never touch food until their yeoman ushers had solemnly laid the cloth before them, and set down knife, spoon, and silver dish, bowing reverently as they placed each article. Nor does he require the whole of the rest of the company to stand attentively while a gentleman usher leads the carver up to the dais, both stopping twice to bow profoundly as they advance across the hall. Still less does Sir Walter insist upon "taking the say," that is, causing the chief yeoman solemnly to take a taste in his master's presence from every dish and a sip from every cup to prove it is not poisoned—a rather common practice even for non-royal personages. However, the waiters never fail with a graceful bow each time they proffer a dish to their master or to his lady. The expert carver, who officiates upon the meat and poultry set upon the upper table, makes a regular salaam before he begins his mystery of "rearing a goose, spoiling a hen, breaking a deer, or chining a salmon." Before the eating begins silver bowls and napkins are passed to all the better guests, and (since there are no forks) again at the end just as the fruit and cheese are cleared away. The last ceremony will be sweeping the crumbs carefully from the table—we fear directly upon the rushes of the floor—and with an unusually deep bow to the master the butler will remove the great saltcellar. Silence again. Master Crabtree will solemnly proffer thanks; then the banging of benches, the rushing of feet. Dinner is over.

This being an ordinary day of work one hour suffices for dinner. If Sir Walter had dined with only his family in the parlor they might have sat idling over their wine and talk for two or three hours. Before the company has dispersed certain manners and sights in the hall deserve our comment. The gentlefolk above the salt are all truly well bred and avoid those gaucheries common enough in the gorging, guzzling company along the lower benches. Ladies and gentlemen carry their food delicately to their mouths in their fingers; they do not use their knives. Neither do they pick their teeth with their knives at the table. They do not return to their plates food they have already put in their mouths, nor dip their meat in the general saltcellar but spread the salt on with their knives; they do not roll their napkins up into cords nor tie them into knots. Finally no person of quality should imitate a very disorderly squire who was guest the other day, who blew his nose with the hand with which he took his meat. Handkerchiefs are still fairly rare. If without one, you should lay down your knife and blow decorously with the hand used for holding that.

All the gentlefolk too sit at table uncovered, but not a few of the tenants and under servants sit on the benches still wearing their hats. This is only a decent precaution. Many an honest man has his hair dense, dirty, and disorderly, and he ought to keep on his hat at mealtimes lest something offensive should fall into a common dish. Had we visited Thorpshire a century earlier one other "good old custom" might have plagued the squeamish— that of rinsing out the mouth with water or ale and spewing the liquid out again, often upon the table. Even the grosser yokels understand now that this is impossible, or that at worst the liquid must be spat upon the floor.

Hollydean being a very well-ordered household there is a regular routine for everyday dinners. On Sundays, Tuesdays, and Thursdays there is beef, mutton, and at least one kind of poultry or game; on Mondays and Wednesdays only boiled beef and mutton; on Fridays salt fish and two kinds of fresh fish; on Saturdays salt fish again, eggs, and probably whatever "leavings" the cook may not wish to carry over to Sunday. In the summer-time the family and guests adjourn to the garden to top off with choice drinks and sweetmeats; if it is winter they all go to some separate room for the same dessert.

Dinner in any event carries the household well into the afternoon. After his meal is once settled Sir Walter makes another survey of his property, more extended than in the morning, and discusses the pastures, corn, and cattle most intelligently with his farm servants. After that there is time to gallop to Boroughport for a matter with the mayor or (as today) to sit in judgment upon the six sturdy beggars snapped up by the constables. About five in the afternoon work begins to lag all over the estate, although there are no set hours of labor. The schoolboys will be running exultantly home from the village school; from the green begins to come the knock of the balls in the bowling. But there is no real pleasure until the household has assembled for supper—the menials once more in the hall, their betters this time in the winter parlor. Supper is not a solemnity like dinner; it is merely a light repast to prepare for bedtime. Sir Walter counts himself very moderate when they set before him a shoulder of mutton, some fried rabbits, bread, ale, or beer unlimited, and, for each guest present, a pint of mild claret.

After supper good order requires that after an hour or so of viol squeaking in the hall, or bowling and like sports outside on the green, the working part of the household should be commanded to bed—properly enough as they must rise so early. Mistress Arabella kneels for her parents' blessing as they stroll in the great gallery, then she disappears with one of the gentlewomen. Mistress Anne has reached the glory of being allowed to sit up with the others. Master Crabtree emerges from his study, and

while his master and mistress sit in their stiff armchairs
reads at length from Foxe's *Book of Martyrs*. Captain Andrew somewhat distresses his mother, but sinfully delights
his father and sister by some amazingly stilted passages
from Lyly's *Euphues and His England*. After that perhaps
there is time for an innocent half hour of primero, or of
tinkling Mistress Anne's virginals. It is now fully nine
o'clock. Master Crabtree promptly says prayers, all of the
upper servants silently coming in to kneel near their master. That dispatched, Captain Andrew and Mistress Anne
—grown persons as they are—kneel also for their parents'
blessing. Half an hour later all Hollydean is tight asleep
amid its feather beds, and with only the awkward watchman rattling about with his staff and lantern and muttering his sing-song about "cover the fires and look to your
locks."

What has Hollydean to eat and drink during this most
ordinary of routine days? What does it eat and drink when
it rejoices in high festival? The answer promptly is that
no Englishman by choice refrains from a great variety of
heavy meats. When the season permits great platters of
flesh are the chief part of every dinner. Beef and mutton,
veal and lamb, kid and pig, red deer and fallow, capon and
coney—these are proffered every day. The woods and
wastes are full of fowl, the seas are full of fish. The prices
of all this flesh (if you do not raise or capture it yourself)
will seem to a later day decidedly reasonable.[1]

Unfortunately this fresh-meat diet is sadly interrupted in
winter. It is almost impossible to put down enough fodder
to keep cattle fat and desirable from November until

[1] London food prices, as reported between 1500 and 1600, show that
meats were very much cheaper than they are today, even allowing for the
difference in the purchasing power of money. Outside of London they
would be cheaper still.

spring. Martinmas day (November 11) regularly witnesses a perfect massacre of innocent kine, whereof the beef is salted and smoke-dried in the farmhouse chimneys for winter use. Between Halloween (November 1) and Christmas there is another steady slaughter of the pigs that have been fattening in the woods upon acorns and beech-nuts. When Christmas holidays are over even the lucky of Hollydean will have to live on smoked salt meat until well into the spring except when they can supplement this diet with venison, fish, and a needful plenty of wild fowl.

Hollydean does not have to depend too much upon salt fish, although it is everywhere a favorite diet, and after harvest farmers regularly lay in a supply of salt ling and herring to carry them through Lent.

Fortunately for your hearty eater poultry fails not all through the year. Eggs are almost fabulously cheap—120 for two shillings sixpence, although the small-sized fowl makes the eggs small also. Besides the ordinary hens and fat capons geese are numerous and popular; ducks (although common enough) are less in demand. Also there are a good many swans; a large flotilla of these elegant birds spreads its sails on the little river near Hollydean, but the fact is they are bred not so much for beauty as for eating. Peacocks parading upon the lawns exist not merely for display while living but to form gala dishes when brought in cooked, with all their plumage to grace the board at great banquets. Another bird that is coming into favor is a large fowl really brought into Europe in 1518 from Mexico, but which by a vulgar error was assumed to come from the Levant; turkeys are now decidedly common in all large barnyards and "to swell like a turkey cock" has become a common expression. As for wild birds many and desirable, time fails to talk of them. Quail,

partridges, woodcock and plover can be had plentifully
within easy range of Hollydean.

Being near a seaport there is likewise no lack of fish,
but they are so much a compulsory diet during the winter
and early spring that the rest of the year the Hall gladly
goes without them, except when Captain Andrew or his
father has come back with a heavy basket after a long
and lucky morning along the trout streams. With poor
folk, however, to whom flesh meat is a great luxury, fish
is eaten readily all the year long; and "poor John" (salted
hake) and "stockfish" (dried codfish) furnish a standard diet in numberless cottages. The plowmen and artisans
indeed by custom have if possible the cheap "necks and
points" of beef on their tables every Thursday and Sunday
night; but the rest of the time must stick to their fish,
"white meat," and a little bacon.

When so much flesh is eaten it stands to reason that
our Englishmen are not great vegetarians. The main use
of vegetables at Hollydean seems to be merely to supplement and bring out the variety of the meats, although the
use of "herbs" has increased since the days of Henry VIII
when vegetables were "supposed to be a food more fit for
hogs and savage beasts" than for Christian men. Sir Walter
like other fine gentlemen is glad enough to eat his messes
of carrots, cabbages, turnips, parsnips, cucumbers, radishes,
and pumpkins. Beans are decidedly plentiful. Lettuce,
watercress, and similar salads are regularly served as a
separate dish before the meat at supper. Mistress Anne
especially eats heartily of the watercress, because (as her
brother sarcastically tells her) "she has heard that this herb
brings out the bloom in young ladies' complexions." Green
peas are common but taken more as a salad than a hearty
vegetable. Artichokes are in request as being excellent for
invalids. We have seen that England already knows the

sweet potato. The white potato is just coming into Europe from its native region around Quito in South America; a very few are being cultivated in England as "Virginia potatoes," but until well after 1600 they will remain a decided rarity.

As for fruits, Hollydean knows all the ordinary kinds and loves them. Plums and cherries are common enough, as well as native apricots and musk melons, and even a few figs. Grapes are raised but not on a large scale. It is impossible to have vineyards in Southern England that can produce wines worthy to compete with those of France and Spain. What people really rejoice in is their apples and pears. Apples abound in many favorite varieties. Sir Walter talks about his own and his neighbors' fine crops of Pomewaters, Bitter Sweetings, Golden and Easter Pippins, and Leathercoats. Pears are in at least equal request, perhaps more popular than they can be at another day; especially people enjoy the fine Poperin pears for table eating, while the famous Warden pears are best for stewing and making those great "Warden pies" which are one of the popular dishes of the realm.[1]

Concerning the high art of cookery and all its varied products Heaven forfend that we should have to expand. Sir Walter has a competent chief cook, a despotic fellow who of course rules his underlings, down to the wretched dogs who work the turnspits, with a rod of iron. He is not however an affected coxcomb like some London master cooks who pretend to "know the influence of the stars upon their meats," and talk in a jargon of astrology, astronomy, and medicine. Tom Bakewell can of course evolve his triumphs in jellies (coming now to greater favor with the increased use of sugar)—"flowers, herbs,

---

[1] Pears were put to another use also. Their pulp mixed with lard and rosemary was one of the most common forms of pomatum!

trees, forms of beasts, fish, fowl, and fruit." He can turn out all manner of wonderful marchpane castles and dragons; and any quantity of simple "tarts, conserves of fruits, suckets, marmalades, sugar breads, and ginger breads."

Sugar is now cheap and common enough to use in cooking in wealthy families, but there is still a great demand for honey, and sugar candy is still in the future. In the farmhouses there is great pride in the enormous mince pies, which are charged with so many Orient spices that people declare "the first mince pie must have been presented by the Three Wise Men to the Christ Child." During Lent, when fish becomes tiresome, it is a jolly practice for a party of friends to gather before the fire logs with long-handled frying pans and fry hearty fritters.

As for the "staff of life," the poorer you are the more likely you are to live mostly on bread. Hollydean of course prides itself on serving nothing but white wheaten bread to every diner in the Hall; but in the cottages and artisans' houses there is not much but loaves of barley and especially rye, and in hard times this bread is likely to contain a great deal of beans, peas, and oats. Cheese is common with high and low, and made in every country district, although the Banbury cheeses and the Cheshire cheeses already enjoy great fame and favor.

One or two innovations at mealtimes remain for comment. First of all Sir Walter follows the custom of discarding the good old silver cups of his ancestors for the handsome new drinking vessels of glass. These elegant goblets come from Venice, and much is the grumbling about the good money drained out of the kingdom for this new-fangled luxury. Even poorer folk are replacing the stone and leather drinking jacks of their fathers with crude jorums made cheaply in the English glass works.

[83]

Hollydean, however, is as yet barely touched by that delicacy which makes a few outlandish exquisites hesitate to take up tasty bits of meat with their own genteel fingers. About a month ago Captain Andrew brought to dinner a young Sir Henry Wanderfar just back from Italy. A delightful, easy-talking gentleman he was, but when the roast was served butler, pantler, and yeoman-ushers almost dropped their trays in astonishment. Sir Henry drew forth a leather case and produced a steel fork—such as the cook used while seething meat in kettles, only this was very small and with a beautifully carved silver handle. With this implement he conveyed all his meat in small morsels to his mouth, explaining that he had lived so long in Venice that he had acquired the Italian prejudice against having his dish touched by the fingers, "seeing that men's hands cannot be always clean." Certainly he ate his meal dexterously and neatly, but when he was gone Sir Walter fumed his "What are we coming to!" and Lady Catherine feared it was a "Popish custom savoring of sheer impiety." But Mistress Anne was much less scandalized and Captain Andrew said he had seen the like usage somewhat in France, and that at court her Gracious Majesty had lately accepted several of these forks with crystal or gold handles as New Year's gifts from certain favorite courtiers.[1]

The employment of small spoons at table has come down from time immemorial, and every Englishman carries at his belt a knife ready for cutting his bread and meat in case, as sometimes happens in respectable houses, the host fails to provide one for the use of each guest.

The Hollydean males may be still lifting their meat to their mouths with the implements used in the Garden of

---

[1] The use of forks won its way only slowly into England; probably it was not until nearly 1700 that eating meat with one's fingers had completely disappeared from the country districts.

Eden, but they have promptly succumbed to a custom
spreading with rapidity over England. The delight of "taking the smoke of the Indian herb called tobacco" is understood completely. Probably tobacco was first introduced
about 1565 by that doughty voyager Sir John Hawkins.
Since that time it has become astonishingly popular. To use
the weed you employ "an instrument formed like a little
ladle whereby the smoke passeth from the mouth into the
head and stomach." Tobacco is said to be excellent for
"rheums and other diseases of the lungs." Its devotees
swear that it is even an antidote for "green wounds," and
will clear "raw humors, obstructions, and crudities out of
the system." In London it is all the rage; you can get a
pinch of it and the use of a pipe in thousands of apothecaries and ordinaries. Women as well as men are beginning to smoke it around the family hearth after supper,
and schoolmasters are teaching their pupils the fashionable
way of bringing the smoke through their nostrils.

Assuredly this, like every other new custom, has its
critics. The probable heir to the English throne, King
James of Scotland, detests the habit. Perhaps already he
has written out his scathing denunciation of the "filthy novelty," whereby "men's breaths are corrupted by a stinking
smoke," and the general custom "loathsome to the age,
hateful to the nose, harmful to the brain, and in the black
stinking fume thereof nearest resembling the horrible
Stygian smoke of the Pit that is bottomless." Others echo
his Majesty and abominate the new tobacco shops, "the rendezvous of spitting, where men dialog with their noses
and their communication is smoke." [1] Do such diatribes
avail? Apparently not one whit. The constant tobacco
clouds floating around hall, parlor, and tavern room announce again, "We move in an altered age."

[1] Actually written by John Earle in 1628.

If tobacco has its opponents, you will find almost no one to run down the use of strong drink though you search all Christendom. Gross drunkenness is indeed not commendable. Grave English gentlemen deplore the swinish custom of "large carousing" which has drifted across the channel since the Dutch wars began. Among vulgar artisans and farmers "large and intemperate drinking" is a matter of course, and no one expects to be ready for work the mornings after the numerous holidays. Among gentle folk it is a fine thing to know how to drink a round of healths and keep your sobriety, and to become drunk every day at ordinary dinners shows the worst of ill-breeding. However, three or four times a year Sir Walter has to be helped off to bed, and Captain Andrew being young and a soldier has this happen very much oftener. Lady Catherine does not let such a commonplace event trouble her greatly; but she takes pains (if her guests are likely to sit over their sack for some time) that each is proffered a good large draught of salad oil, for the doctors say "that will float upon the wine and suppress the spirits from ascending to the brain."

Drinking healths at a dinner is a regular ceremony. The person leading off rises, uncovers, and those sitting on either side of him do the same. The great loving cup goes always to the right, but with three people (the drinker, the one before him, and the one after him) standing all the time. If your own health is being drunk the drinker bows to you and kisses his fingers. You must then rise, bow, and kiss your fingers back to him.

What will be found in the old blackjacks and silver cups or the new goblets and glasses? Almost invariably wine or ale. Distilled liquors are pretty rare although not unknown. Up in Scotland there is a fiery *usquebaugh* (which will later be refined into more delicate whiskey). Another potable spirit, distilled from grape wine, and just coming to a certain popularity in the Continent, will be known as brandy ("brand" or "burnt-wine"). But Englishmen still sharpen or muddle their wits upon either brewed or fermented liquors.

The great drink of the Queen's subjects is ale made from malt, although since early in the century when the use of hops was introduced from Flanders—adding a tang and flavor unknown earlier—the improved liquor is sometimes known as beer. Hops or no hops ale is drunk as freely as water. Tea and coffee are unknown; ale is consumed at breakfast and is offered the small children although these are rigorously kept from wine. The Puritans scowl at riotous public feasts and banquets but they never think of clamping down upon the everyday consumption of ale.[1]

Brewing ale is almost as common an activity as baking bread. It goes on in every house. Master Harrison, a modest country parson, tells how his good wife brewed two hundred gallons of ale per year at the cost of only twenty shillings—about three halfpence per gallon. What need at that price for any Englishman to go thirsty! The Boroughport Corporation like all its fellows takes pains that all ale put on sale shall be sweet and satisfying. It is a fine thing for a burgess to be appointed ale tester; he can go into every brew house, test copiously, wipe his lips, and levy his fee one gallon of strong ale and two gallons of small (common) ale out of every tun (250 gallons). At such an establishment as Hollydean the brew house sometimes in the year is the scene of intense activity. The number of tuns of good ale stowed all winter in the cellar is enormous.

Gentlefolk, nevertheless, must have their wine. It is wine

[1] Water drinking was not unknown but it was treated as at best a necessary evil. Milk drinking was a little more in favor.

that goes around in the loving cups at the great banquets, wine that loosens the tongues and sets the tavern rooms roaring when tall gallants troll such verses as

> And let me the canikin, clink, clink:
> And let me the canikin clink.

England has need of exporting much wool and wheat merely to pay for the enormous importation of foreign vintages.

There are over a hundred varieties of wine on the market—Greek, Italian, Canary, Rhenish—but the greater part comes from France with Spain as a decided second. At the corporation banquets in London the worshipful guests sometimes can have fifty-six different wines offered them. Alicante, claret, muscadine, charneco (a kind of port) are very popular. Bastard is a common wine sold in the cheaper taverns. But the Hollydean gentry, like all their rivals, never fail to lay in a full season's supply of sack—the favorite drink of all honest masters.

Sack properly is a dry sweet wine from Spain or the Canaries, but probably a great deal of it really comes from France. The true way to serve it is in a cup nearly half full of sugar, so that one really partakes of a kind of heady syrup. Heated and perhaps flavored with a few spices, the poets swear it makes a drink for the gods. Many a mellowing soul waxes eloquent over its praises. Good sack drives the vapors out of the brain, makes the tongue utter excellent wit, warms the blood, illumines the face, and makes men hot and valiant. Whoever argues that "thin potations" can excel sack conveys that he is lacking in decent sanity.[1] It is sack that inspires Master Edmund Spenser's poetry, Sir Walter Raleigh's courtier wit, Drake's

[1] Falstaff's praise of sherris (sherry) sack is too familiar to need further paraphrasing.

and Howard's naval valor, Lord Burghley's sage counsel, nay, very likely Gloriana's royal intelligence itself. Without sack for the gentles and ale for the commons, where in God's name would be England!

A few other drinks are perhaps worth sampling. In the autumn Hollydean is glad to turn down much good cider and perry (made of pears), and every good tavern serves metheglin made of honey, and cups of hippocras (cordial loaded with spices) or of pleasantly bitter wormwood.

The great banquets on high festival days with their incredibly lengthy bills of fare we can omit until we come to some of the actual festivals (see Chapter XVIII). We have now advanced our survey to the point of learning how the inhabitants of Hollydean are housed and clothed, how they are clad, how they stay their hunger and their thirst. Now we are ready to discover what they are as men and women themselves.

ILLUSTRATIONS TO "SHEPHERD'S CALENDAR," 1597. MARCH.

[89]

¶ *Chapter* VII: Concerning Maids, Matrons, and Matrimony

BEGIN we then with the greatest, as is only meet and proper.

Women rule the world, and undoubtedly, nowhere more than in Elizabethan England. This is in nowise solely because a chivalrous devotion to a great and extraordinarily popular Queen adds luster, importance, and command to her entire sex. The long centuries of Christianity, the adoration of the Virgin in the mediæval church, the passionate romance of the retreating days of chivalry all have had their influence, as had the general growth of reason, humanity, and fair play in the English people. Women may be far enough from winning their "rights." Probably not one of them dreams of making speeches in Parliament or storming one of the learned professions. What matter as yet! They are completely possessed of their "privileges," and most puissantly have they learned to use them.

True the legal status of women is such as will make their champions in another age cry out with horror. Unmarried, a woman is almost completely in the power of her father, elder brother, or other guardian. Married, she is as completely in the power of her husband, "her life only excepted." Her property is for practical purposes at his entire disposal. She is lawfully in a state of perpetual tutelage and minority. Husbands have kept their wives locked for years. If they use the lash or rod on them it is hard to find a legal remedy. All this is simply saying that every age has its share of tyrants and of brutes. However the power of a wife to make her husband's life one torment is understood to perfection. Under the old Catholic régime regular divorce was out of the question, although great folks sometimes procured annulments upon most surprising grounds. Under the new Protestantism, divorce by the bishops' courts is technically possible, but it is seldom granted and second marriages after it are of dubious validity—a great hardship for the women, but perhaps equally severe upon the consorts.

No society, however, ever existed simply on the strength of legalities. Foreigners, especially observant Dutchmen, visiting England are amazed at the freedom allowed the women. "They are not shut up as they are in Spain"; they have "free management of the house," go to market when they list and do the shopping, and leave the household drudgery to their servants. The women (these visitors also declare) "sit before the doors decked out in fine clothes, in order to see and be seen by the passers-by." At all banquets and feasts they have the greatest honor and the best places, and are served before the men. Upper-class women spend the rest of the time "visiting their gossips, playing cards, and making merry." At all such affairs as "christenings, churchings, and funerals," they have the leading part.

Young girls are perhaps more strictly brought up than in the Low Countries but marriage confers an astonishing degree of liberty; "England is called the Paradise of married women." These same travelers praise the women of England as being "beautiful, fair, well dressed, and modest" despite the fact that they usually parade about the streets "without mantle, hood, or veil." The unpopularity of hats has already been remarked upon. In upper circles it is common enough for fine ladies to spend much of their time in the escort of fine gentlemen who are anything but their husbands. In lower circles plenty of dames foregather at taverns, tipple and gossip, and presently glide home again, telling their husbands the transparent fable—"I have been to church."

Hollydean is an average and normal household. Very normally then Lady Catherine is a more potent dominator than Sir Walter, and all the servitors understand it is safer to take orders from the mistress than from the master, if they are pushed to a discreet choice.

Be it granted that in education the women are far less favored than their brothers. The proportion of women even in fair circumstances who cannot sign their names is deplorable.[1] Many a daughter of a wealthy mansion is put to it if she is forced to write a long letter. The great duty of a girl to to learn how to manage a home; everything else is secondary and for this there is no schoolmistress like her mother.

While Mistress Anne was little she used to kneel down every evening beside her mother, say her prayers, and bid dutifully her "Good night and good rest"; to which her Ladyship answered lovingly, "I pray God that so it be with you always—God be with you." As Anne grew older she was taught her letters and a few other mysteries of learning by one of the "decayed gentlewomen," it not being quite the proper thing to send her to dame-school in the village. After that her book learning largely was left to take care of itself until, reaching an age when she was likely to appear at court, her parents decided that a smattering of French would be useful, and a dapper smiling fellow, Monsieur Lebabillard, would ride up from Boroughport, where he was teaching "the Parisian accent" to sundry other young masters and mistresses who were expected to make a show in the world. Anne's French

---

[1] Shakespeare's daughter Susannah apparently could barely sign her name. His second daughter Judith it seems could only "make her mark."

knowledge is not extensive, but it has at least opened to her various romances and broadened her view of life. She has browsed plenteously in her father's library and has perhaps a better knowledge of his "collections of poems, plays, merry tales, and surprising adventures" than her brother the captain.

All this time her real education is continuing. Master Crabtree has drilled the catechism and the Bible stories into her, and grounded her well in all the essentials of Protestant piety. She has been taught to take a graceful part in all the popular dances and to play the virginals and lute. In general her mother tries to seek a golden mean between that training which teaches girls nothing but "working in curious Italian pearls and French borders," and that austere tuition in nothing but "plain, open seaming." Mistress Anne is carefully instructed in all the details of household management, especially the doings of the kitchen, laundry and dairy. She has learned to ride, sometimes by herself, but quite as often upon a pillion behind some relative or serving man. This is proper enough, for does not her Majesty herself sometimes gallop into London from Greenwich perched upon a pillion behind her lord chancellor? Anne can gallop out with the hawks or after the hounds and is a tolerable shot with the crossbow.

By the time she is fifteen she has assisted in manufacturing numerous fine curtains, quilts and "Turkey-work" coverings, and has learned quite sufficient to warrant her parents in saying, "We must look for a husband"; but this does not imply that she is beyond that correction which God-fearing mothers ought never to spare their beloved daughters. Mistress Anne does not undergo those constant reproofs and blows with which the unfortunate Lady Jane Grey was brought up, but Lady Catherine has never hesitated with the slipper or the switch for any serious fault, and even now (with marriage in the clear horizon) there can be deeds very painful to her young ladyship's feelings and pride in the safe recesses of her mother's closet.

Mistress Anne has had it bred in her bones that, however handsomely she may wed, her first duty is to become a good housewife. Is not half of the Queen's popularity due to the fact that she is such a thrifty housewife for her great mansion called England? Master Crabtree dins it into her first of all that time spent in prayer and "exercises" "will prove no lost time at the week end," and that her comely garments should preserve her health as well as "adorn her person." Mistress Sharpley initiates her into the mysteries of preserve and cordial making, of making quince and damson marmalade, syrups from roses and violets, candied flowers, and such delicacies as almond butter and marchpane. A competent lady of a manor must be a little of an apothecary; Lady Catherine herself is always passing out salves, medical herbs, and lotions to the servants and tenants. Her daughter receives constant examples of how to keep a whole retinue of maids cheerfully busy at all their multitudinous household tasks from dipping the candle wicks to boiling sea-water to extract the salt. Also the great army of beggars must be sifted out, the needy succored, the undeserving chased away; and above all Anne soon learns, however great her station, that too much must not be left to deputies. Lady Catherine never trusts even Mistress Sharpley too implicitly; and many an evening pries about to make sure that no cats have been left in the dairy, that no clothes, left out on the hedges to dry, have been forgotten for roving vagabonds, and that every candle in the barn and servants' quarters has been safely quenched.

Nothing else, however, consumes the time like that of preparing wool. If Lady Catherine kept a diary it might read like her contemporary Lady Hoby's—"Busy to dye wool"; "Wound yarn"; "Bought a little spinning wheel and span of that." Most of the garments of the servants have in fact been woven from wool clipped and spun on the estate, and then made under their energetic employer's personal direction. Mistress Anne of course is initiated into all this.

What of her pleasures? They seem limited enough to another age. Anne continues to play at dolls with her younger sister until she is a great girl indeed. They have a large collection of really handsome, lifelike dolls, mostly brought by their father from the great Bartholomew Fair, which is such a center for playthings that dolls are often called "Bartholomew's babies." Anne has only rarely been to London with her parents, but through the circuit of some thirty miles around she has a perfect coterie of "dearest friends" of like age and condition. These she is constantly visiting, perched on a pillion behind a trusted groom. Thus she knows not merely many likely girls, but (much to the point) their brothers, and understands all the nice details about various young men whom her parents might consider as son-in-law. In the constant round of holiday festivals her young ladyship takes a conspicuous part, and has plenty of assurance when dancing in public.

When all else fails there is always in summer the resource of the gardens, where she already loves the flowers and helps the gardeners with no small skill; and in the winter evenings if her elders are away or occupied, she sits with her sister and the better servants and (so the verses run)

> Then is it pleasure the young maids among,
> To watch by the fire the long nights long:
> And in the ashes some plays for to mark,

And cover words [1] for fault of other work:
To taste white shivers, to make prophet rôles,
And, after talk, at times to fill the bowls.

Dull, circumscribed, intolerable this life and training?
Doubtless it will seem so to the daughters of a vastly altered
age. But Mistress Anne has never known anything else.
Despite her parents' wealth she accepts implicitly the dictum, "Simplicity is best for maids." She is in no sense
unhappy. She gains keen enjoyment from insignificant
things. She is a lady born and will not lack dignity, grace,
and high command at all times. Lucky the man who gets
her. It is women reared to be such as she that make possible the great Virginia's England.

Of course there fail not many worse women high and
low. Omitting those who live by iniquity the realm contains a woeful number who provide fair targets for all
the darts of the Puritans. The charges amazingly resemble
those launched against womankind since the days of Sesos-
tris. Rich dames often "lie in bed three days together."
When they do get up it is only to think of an approaching
banquet. Then they spend "half a day practicing before
the glass how to look alluringly amiable." Thus Thomas
Dekker, adding, "Their heads they make a puppet show
of, with their top and topgallant lawn baby caps," while
their joy is all in "pinches, purls, flowery jaggings, super-
fluous interlacings and puffings up."

At dinners such women get "their heads prettily mizzled
with wine." When they walk abroad or sit conspicuously
by the open doors it is only "to show their braveries." If
they have a garden in the fields they walk thither with a
boy and a basket—not really to cull the flowers but only
to meet their lovers. Such women of course never are con-

[1] Play a word-guessing game.

tent with the beauty God has given them. They "diet their faces" to correct God's workmanship, then "ensparkle their eyes with spiritualized distillations," "fill up age's frets with fresh colors," and are always buying gallipots of such ointments and washes as "Water of Gourds," "Fat of Swans," "Turpentine of Abezzo," "Soap of Cyprus," and all other weapons of Venus calculated "to keep a woman of seventy as bright and smooth as any looking-glass."

As for boldness in dress, even the cautious Master Harrison admits that although once "staring attire" was the plain mark of "light housewives," it is now all too common with "chaste and sober matrons." Being only a man, he then unburdens himself concerning their "doublets with pendent cod-pieces on the breast, full of jags and cuts," and their "farthingales, galligaskins, and particolored nether socks," whereby their "bodies are rather deformed than commended."

Lady Catherine and Mistress Anne are neither better nor worse than the more honest members of their sex in these particulars; but they have not surrendered to the custom of their rivals in London and at Court of cultivating Melitei (Malta) lapdogs. It is quite the passion there for knights' ladies and countesses to cherish "sybaritical puppies," to hold them in their bosoms, to let them sleep on their beds, lie in their laps, and continually to dandle these creatures supposed to satisfy the nice delicacy of dainty classes.

The Hollydean women are pious, but certainly they do not carry their religion to the extent of many gentlewomen of extreme cast, who make their chaplains read sermons to them three times per day, discourage any singing but that of psalms, and confine their reading strictly to the Bible, books of homilies, Foxe's *Martyrs,* and some *Herbal* (book on gardening). Much less are they numbered among those extravagantly learned gentlewomen—like Sidney's sister the Countess of Pembroke—who add Italian and Spanish to their smattering of French, claim to have a sound knowledge of Greek and Latin, patronize the poets, and descant with erudition on all nice points of poetry, legend, and mythology.[1]

Women have a great part in nearly all the elaborate festivals which abound throughout the year, but naturally two fall into their peculiar empire—christenings and churchings.

When Mistress Anne entered this world her wealthy mother made it a great state ceremony. The lying-in bed was hung with white satin embroidered with silver lace and seed pearls.[2] The moment the mother and child were out of danger a prodigious rush of visitors began; card parties were held in the chamber and all the dames of the region showered Lady Catherine with valuable presents. Then came the christening held in the room also, in order that the mother might be present. The three sponsors each brought the standard gift of the twelve silver "apostle" spoons—so called because the ends of the handles form the figures of the twelve Apostles; although in poorer christenings four spoons—for the four Evangelists—might have answered. Young Mistress Anne was brought to the font wrapped in a splendidly embroidered "bearing cloth," but with a white "chrisom cloth" put under her tiny head. After the ceremony Hollydean gave itself up to an enormous feast in which every friend of the family honored the event by devouring just as much sugar, biscuits, comfits and

[1] Queen Elizabeth was undoubtedly a distinctly learned woman, making every allowance for courtly flattering. She apparently had some real knowledge of Greek and could deliver short impromptu orations in Latin.

[2] The lying-in bed of the Countess of Salisbury used in 1612, plus the Elizabethan hangings around the chamber, was worth £14,000.

carraways, marmalet and marchpane with all kinds of "sweet suckets" as was physically possible.

Yet how can even the most gladsome christening compare with the excitement and revelry of a wedding! Mistress Anne has learned to look forward to a wedding as almost the climax of her life. Spinsterhood (outside of Catholic nunneries) is extremely rare throughout Christendom; the worst a girl of good family has ordinarily to fear is that she may get a husband old, or poor, or ugly. If she is unwedded at twenty, it is a sign not so much that she is unattractive as that her family suffers under some disgrace and is niggardly with the dowry. Verses make such extraordinarily unlucky damsels lament

> Twenty winters have I seen,
>   And as many summers green:
> 'Tis long enough to breed despair,
>   So long maidenhead to wear
> Woe, alas! I am afraid
> I shall live and die a maid.

Among youths to be sure you hear the praises sung of bachelorhood:

> Ho for the Bachelor! Merry doth he live
> All the day long he can dance, sing and play!
>   His troubles are like to water within a sieve,
> The more it floweth in, the more it will away!
> Married men for him may sit and groan!
> He is well content, and letteth well alone!

That is all very fine, and many a man (more independent generally and less under parental control than his sisters) fends off matrimony until he is thirty. There are very few men left above that age who have not submitted to the common lot.

[99]

England has moved considerably away from the time when children (and especially daughters) can be married off by their parents without the least heed to the young people's wishes. Such cases occur, and their pros and cons debated in pamphlets. Has not a father the right to bestow a child at will, "for children are the goods of the parents"? "Not so," comes the rejoinder, "children are not obliged to obey parents if forced into wedlock out of sordid motives; and to match a lively young woman unwillingly with 'an infirm and decrepit person' is most unwise and a great occasion for incontinency." There has just been a pitiful case at Tavistock where a young Mistress Glandfield was forced to marry a rich old widower named Page. The young wife loved a certain steward named Strawbridge. The lovers and two servants strangled old Page in his bed. The crime leaked out; the wife and stewards were all hanged; but the woeful ballad hawked about this tragedy winds up with the pithy sentiment:

> Lord! Give all parents wisdom to foresee,
> The match is marred where minds do not agree.

The abuses are worst when the parents are dead and selfish guardians compel their wards to take most unwelcome consorts; but often enough such marriages can be upset later by "disparagement"—by proving in the courts that the other party is not of equal social rank with the ward; but protection is very imperfect and the evils of wardship surely are great.

Inasmuch however as most parents love their daughters and truly desire their happiness most marriages come to pass as doubtless Mistress Anne's will be arranged; a number of likely young gentlemen (the sons probably of Thorpshire land owners) will be often at Hollydean, and she will be allowed to visit their sisters. Her likes and dislikes will be quietly noted. Her parents will form their own estimate of potential sons-in-law. If any one youth seems particularly desirable his good points will be tactfully stressed. The young lady is keenly aware of the delights of a grand wedding. She knows that matrimony means the end of parental switchings and dictation, and an astonishing amount of freedom. When she is told that handsome young Master Stockwood of Thornpark has asked his father to ask Sir Walter for her hand, she is very much in a mood to be pleased if her parents seem willing.

Inevitably there are far less prearranged romances. Elopements figure in real life as well as in stage plays; although such are parental rights that many a runaway match can be set aside, and still more can turn out unhappily. A widow is likely to be able to "marry for love," or at least strictly according to her personal inclination, and no desolated female is expected to remain in widowhood very long.

What is the standard of social morality in Elizabethan England? Of course in London, Boroughport, and doubtless in every petty village there is an abundance of Doll Tearsheets and Mol Light o' loves, concerning whose easy virtues the least said the soonest mended. The customs of very many traders' and poor farmers' daughters are astonishingly lax. But among the yeomen's, merchants', and gentlemen's families the standard for the women is commendably high. English girls are famed for their discretion and modesty—they deserve the honor.

Regarding their brothers, of course the praise must be more stinted. The age has never bothered its head about "the double and the single standards." Right around Hollydean in several good houses there are children about whom folk shake their heads cunningly if you ask of the parents.

The girls are kept out of sight as much as possible and presently married out of the neighborhood. The boys are often allowed to hang around the hall with the other poor relations, and given hopes of a small post in the army or a still smaller living in the Church. Nobody thinks a great deal the worse of the fathers of these bastards, though it is certainly not a matter to their credit.

However, compared with France, Spain, and still more with Italy the morality of Englishmen is undoubtedly high. Plenty of gallant gentlemen are as honest as their sisters. Captain Andrew will swear ribald oaths, tell stories full of dirt, smear his talk with expressions utterly gross, but he scorns to corrupt a scullery maid. If his speech is amazingly free, be it remembered that his pious mother often uses phrases that ought to bring the blush to a sea captain.

Mistress Anne is now fifteen and perfectly willing to talk about "when my wedding comes." Her parents deprecate very early marriages. Plenty of girls are given away at thirteen and fourteen, but Sir Ralph Stockwood is already talking with Sir Walter about certain business matters "if we should agree to the match," and young Master Stockwood certainly wears his short cloak swingingly. Mistress Anne therefore views life with considerable expectation. She is the more excited because her bosom friend Mistress Mary Whitefield has just become Mistress Mary Ashwood.

Mary is four months younger than Anne, but her betrothal took place when she was only twelve. At that time a joint family council decided that she was destined to marry her old neighbor and playfellow Richard Ashwood. The young people knew and liked each other and made no resistance, but Dick was still a student at Cambridge and the wedding was postponed until he had taken his degree and then had been polished off by the very customary tour in France and Italy under a discreet tutor.

Concerning Maids, Matrons, and Matrimony

The betrothal at Whitefield House was quite a ceremony; all manner of guests, a great feast, and then under the eyes of all the contracting pair were brought together. With juvenile formality they approached each other, joined hands, and very diffidently exchanged kisses; then a curious ring was produced. It was in three hoops cleverly fitted together; and when taken apart one went on the finger of the maid, one to the lover, and one was kept as evidence of the pact by a pompous uncle. At the final bridal all three of these hoops were to be again united into the regular wedding ring. Besides this Mary and Richard broke a gold coin and each retained a half, and various small gifts were exchanged. Henceforth for either party to have withdrawn from the pact would have seemed an outrageous insult to the other's family.

However at last the solemnization is at hand. Sir Arthur Whitefield is obligated half to beggar himself by making all Thorpshire welcome to the bridal of his daughter. Besides the regiment of invited guests a perfect swarm of vagabonds of all conditions descends on the place confident of plenty of broken meats and probably an indiscriminate dole of lawful pennies.

The parsons try to maintain the old Catholic custom of discouraging marriages during the forty days of Lent. In 1587 the Puritan parliament deliberately passed an act permitting weddings in all seasons of the year, but one of the Ashwood relatives is a cathedral dean—invited now to bless the ceremony—and by general consent it is put late in April, a favorite month for weddings, the other great month being November.

Bridal customs keep a certain sameness from age to age. There is the inevitable mustering of all possible relatives, the pompous conferences between the solicitors of the two families about the settlement for the young couple, the indiscriminate hospitality. Enough beef, cakes, and ale are wasted around Whitefield house to carry half the worthy poor of Thorpshire during the coming winter. The bride and her mother order the males about with all the accustomed tyranny. Master Richard presents all the men guests with scarves, gloves, and garters of the favorite colors of the Whitefield and Ashwood families. An affected young gentleman who calls Masters Edmund Spenser and John Lyly "dear friends" recites "Prothalamion," composed for the occasion, which certainly ought to deserve immortality.

Everybody is already a trifle set up with liquor when the parish bell begins clanging on the fragrant springtime morning and the procession sets forth for the church. Nothing naturally counts in the affair but the appearance of the bride—not the garish costumes of the men, not the jeweled stomachers of the dames. Mistress Mary has been at her toilet since gray dawn. Like every English girl, wedding for the first time, she appears with her bosom decidedly exposed, and with her long golden brown hair combed out straight and falling almost down to her waist. Upon her head is set a garland of wheat ears laced with spring flowers. Her white dress of course is of the finest silk, lawn, lace, and embroidery which Whitefield riches can command.[1]

Prettily flushed she advances between the long lanes of uncapping tenants and courtesy bobbing women, led along as she is by two chubby boy cousins holding the "bride's laces," numerous white ribbons which tie her sleeves, bodice, and skirt. In front of her walks an older lad carrying a large silver cup filled with spiced wine and trimmed with a large branch of gilded rosemary. Next follow the musicians—a braying platoon of lutes, flutes, and viols—

---

[1] A bride's dress was not always white. Colors and especially russet could be worn without impropriety.

then the half dozen bridesmaids dressed in gayest colors and some carrying great "bride cakes" and some huge garlands of gilded wheat; but their real task is to convoy with appropriate gurgling Master Richard Ashwood himself, led along in splendiferous garments to his appointed doom, and not looking more helpless than befits the occasion. He carries stuck in his belt a large bunch of rosemary (token of manly qualities) tied up with ribbons and the special gift of the bride. After him, follow in all gala brilliance, the parents of the bride and groom with all the Whitefields and Ashwoods, greater and lesser, trailing behind them— and so to the parish church.

The ceremony before the visiting dean and the local vicar differs little from that which will solemnize Church of England weddings for many a year to come. The bride repeats the "obey" unhesitatingly, with as much and as little intention of keeping her vow as any other bride. The ring is put upon her finger—not upon her thumb as in a good many weddings.[1] Then follows an astonishing rush toward the altar. The young men are all scrambling and clutching for the "bride's laces"—all the numerous ribbons fluttering from the young lady's sleeves, bodice, and skirt. These are plucked off as trophies with very little gentleness. Audacious hands even tear away her ribbon garters. The successful youths hasten to pin their trophies in their hats and will wear them there for weeks. Utterly disheveled Mary is at last rescued by her husband and her mother, while a kind of order is restored to permit the two fathers to distribute brooches of considerable value to all the younger guests present, while there will be more scarves

[1] The triple ring, mentioned as used at the betrothal, was perhaps less common than one made with two hands clasping a heart made out of a jewel. Various other varieties were usual, but the plain hoop ring only came in with Puritan times in the seventeenth century.

and gloves for their elders. Nor, even in the church, can eating and drinking be dispensed with. The great bride cakes are broken and handed about. The huge cup is held to the lips of bride and groom who drink "prosperity to the marriage," then circulated through the entire company; this is the famous "knitting" or "contracting cup," everybody partaking of it certifying that the ceremony is properly performed.

Were Mistress Mary of less honorable degree a strange enough usage would be added. A cask of ale would be placed in the nave of the church and the bride unhesitatingly would sell flagons thereof to all guests present, every recipient paying for this "bride ale" with a good piece of silver—to help the new couple's housekeeping. As it is, at last the screaming, laughing flurry in the church is over, and Mistress Mary (sans ribbons and with her hair in complete disarray) on her husband's arm walks back to the Hall, the bell tumbling like mad, all the folk shouting, and the countryside getting ready for a feast and revel that will stop hard work for at least a week.

Master and Mistress Ashwood never think of departing for their new home with the groom's parents until all the dancing, feasting, and headaches are over, and the clowns have slept off their liquor. On the Sunday after the ceremony they must go back to the parish church, sit in an especially conspicuous pew, and listen to the vicar's discourse on "The Wedding Garment Beautiful." At all events they are now tightly married, and the romancers already assert that after that they ought to "live happily forever after."

"But," says Mistress Anne to Lady Catherine, "when *I* am married we will order things thus and so."

MISTRESS ANNE may have had her fearful hours with mother, but she looks back upon no such discipline as marked that of her brother Andrew along with every other normal boy in England.

Education is no part of the duties of government. The potent lords of her Majesty's Council never add to their heavy cares that of seeing that each lad and lass goes properly to school. As suggested, probably only about three adult persons in ten, the kingdom over, can read and write, the proportion of literate women being very much smaller than of the men. Deplorable; but a vast improvement doubtless since three centuries earlier, when book learning was a mystery only for clerics and the more favored part of the gentry and merchants.

When young Andrew ("Captain" not yet) came into this life he was at once put in swaddling bands, and in his next mortal stage dressed in a little coat of changeable taffeta, and provided with bibs, tiny petticoats, "biggins" (small caps), and a gold chain hung with corals to cut his teeth upon. It was the usual family event when he could say "Dad-dad"—calling his father, and "din"—meaning "drink." As soon as possible the son of so prosperous a house lacked not his ample supply of drums, hobby horses, pop-guns, kites, lambs of white wool with heads of plaster, and horns of tin. He was made happy with battledores and shuttlecocks, trumpets made of cows' horns, pipes from elder stems. From the fairs his father brought home a perilous amount of gilt ginger bread and peppermint cakes, already sold twenty for the penny.

Soon he could repeat after his nurse all the old fairy tales, the heritage of English childhood "from the days of King Arthur"—"Beauty and the Beast" (probably an old Anglo-Saxon story), "Jack the Giant Killer," "Tom Thumb," and all their companions.[1] Among the children of the upper servants and tenants he was presently a little tyrant, with always the leading part in hood-man-blind (blindman's buff), prisoner's base, hide-and-seek (also called hoop-and-hide), stool ball (an easy variety of cricket), hot cockles, and in quieter moods nine-mens-morris (a very simple form of checkers, played on squares marked on the grass turf). He delighted in "wild-mare" (see-saw), and when he grew older in such sports as pitching the bar and the violent scramble called football. His loving parents took pains that all these pleasures should not interfere with his true progress in life. He was not indeed like some children, constantly subjected to "pinches, nips, and bibs," but Sir Walter was too affectionate not to recall the plain Scripture "Chasten thy son, and let not thy soul spare for his crying," although he always applied the rod with his own hands and did not depute the task to servants. Andrew, however, was a tolerably amenable child and did not have to go sore to bed unreasonably often.[2]

At an early age the boy knew what was expected of him. He had to rise very early, carefully say a prayer, wash his hands, and comb his hair. Then he went down to his parents and dutifully knelt before each one, remaining until he was bidden to rise. If he met older people when he was

[1] But not yet the Arabian Nights' tales. What treasure-caves Sinbad and Ali Baba would have opened for Shakespeare!

[2] Some parental severities became famous. When Sir Peter Carew (later a distinguished soldier) ran away from school, his father caught him, had him coupled to a hound, and chained him up in a dog kennel.

out of doors, he was always "free with his cap." After he reached a certain size he joined the family meals, where he never ventured to begin eating until his parents had been served and was careful not to spill food upon his clothes.

Whatever the habits of the common folk below the salt, he soon learned that he must eat what was set before him, that the table was no place to pare his nails. He must not blow on his soup to cool it, cram his mouth too full, lean his elbows on the table, nor stare about impolitely:

> Not smacking thy lips as commonly do hogs,
> Nor gnawing thy bones as it were dogs.

Being a young person of quality he was initiated into the use of the handkerchief; especially he was warned at table, "Blow not your nose on the napkin, where you should wipe your hand."

As he grew older he was taught to wait on table himself. This was always a gracious service by the heir of the family to a distinguished guest and was not in the least degrading. Also when the chaplain was absent he was often expected to say Grace instead of his father; repeating:

> Give thanks to God with one accord
> For all that's set upon this board.

In a word he acquired, not too painfully, the manners of a proper gentleman, but unfortunately when his father chastised him once his schoolmaster applied the rod ten times; and between the two, after Andrew grew up, he could hardly look back upon boyhood with unmixed pleasure.

As the son of wealthy parents Andrew might have been put under the care of a tutor (usually a poor "bachelor" just out of the university) and never sent to school. Such was the practice with the nobility and very many of the upper gentry. But Sir Walter and his lady wisely considered the sound discipline of a competent Latin master to be an essential part of a boy's training; Boroughport was proud of its grammar school, and it was in no wise derogatory to send the heir of Hollydean thither.

Before, however, little Andrew could go to the grammar school he had to be taught at least reading and writing. When he had gained even these modest accomplishments he would be ahead of the majority of the tenants around the Manor. Teaching poor peasant and craftsmen to become literate was (serious pamphlets argued) simply doing them more harm than good. They were likely to read books that filled them with crazy notions, and had better spend their time learning some good "mystery." You can rise considerably in the world, become a thrifty yeoman, town burgess, or even town alderman, and never have need to do more than make your mark.[1] There are plenty of cheap letter writers and scriveners to help out with any occasional difficulty.

Nevertheless the number of schools is increasing; the fall of the old religious system almost ruined the numerous Church schools, but they have been mostly revived under more secular auspices. Plenty of money is being left for educational foundations, and charitable people think it a most public-spirited thing "to bring forth some young imps and buds of learning." This encouragement, however, seldom reaches down to the lowest schools. These have to be provided somehow by the parents of the young children, and the expedients are often deplorable enough. The cheapest admission to the gate of learning is by sending a little

[1] John Shakespeare the poet's father found it convenient to make his mark at a time he was Alderman of Stratford-upon-Avon, although probably he was not absolutely illiterate.

boy to the dame school. In the village of Hollydean there was (as in about every English parish) a poor old woman, barely literate herself, who, to fend off beggary, received children in her cottage and taught them their letters and a trifle beyond. The best that could be said for Dame Short-temper's pedagogy was that her abler pupils in later days could spell out the Bible, Foxe's *Martyrs,* and keep their farm accounts.

Master Andrew could not be submitted to any such vulgar tuition, but there was an elementary school in the parish receiving children of a gentler condition—sons of land owners, upper stewards, and the like. Master Swisher, its genius, had labored through Oxford some years before as a menial servitor and drifted to Hollydean village, where he had stagnated and grown lean and rusty. Unable to get a post in a grammar school he had set up for himself a less pretending reading and writing school, and struggled along on very small fees.

He was not more harsh than his envied betters at the grammar school, only he had to deal with much younger children. Under his stripes and admonition, little Andrew learned his letters from the *hornbook;* this was a printed sheet framed in wood and covered with a thin plate of transparent horn. On the sheet were printed the alphabet both in small letters and in capitals, with combinations of the five vowels with *b, c,* and *d,* and the Lord's Prayer done into English. A very short catechism was added sometimes to this document, which was often known as the "Absey" ("A B C") book.[1]

The contents of the hornbook Master Andrew presently had literally dinned into him. He was also taught the beginnings of writing in the crabbed "Old English" hand—a

---

[1] Quite as often the "Absey" book was a kind of separate "first reader," following the hornbook.

style very like the later "German script"; although the clearer more elegant "Italian" script, familiar through subsequent ages, came as a later accomplishment.

As soon as possible the heir of Hollydean was started for the grammar school, every morning being routed out of his warm bed, very often before gray twilight, and riding over to Boroughport on a pillion behind a trustworthy groom. Boys were received very young at the grammar school, for the entrance requirements were not heavy. Andrew had simply to be able to read his lesson and write with modest proficiency. It was to his credit that he was able to say off by rote certain of the Psalms, the Lord's Prayer, the Gloria, and part of the Nicene Creed in Latin, although hardly understanding a word of what he was repeating.

Boroughport grammar school was one of those numerous endowed schools which multiplied especially during the reign of Edward VI and the entire reign of Elizabeth. A public-spirited merchant had given most of the money to the corporation after an unusually successful venture to the Baltic, and one of Drake's companions had added generously after the return of the *Golden Hind*. The sons of inhabitants of Boroughport were entitled to enter this school without fee, although neighboring squires like the Hollydeans were expected to make a reasonable contribution if their offspring attended.

The grammar school was a sufficiently democratic institution in its customs. The mere fact that a father could give his boys a training in Latin would stamp him genuinely "Master," if not actually "worshipful." Andrew soon forgot that he was heir of Hollydean when he was out among his playfellows; and the headmaster, "Sir" Nicholas Thwacker (appointed by the town council and licensed by the Bishop), did not discriminate when he dealt out his blows. Under this vigorous tutelage Andrew was fated to continue until he was nearly ready for the university.

So season after season, year after year, the life of the lad was much the same—to be roused by one of the maids at gray dawn or before it, eat a hurried breakfast of porridge, kneel for the paternal blessing, take his satchel containing his ink horn, quill-pen, knife for sharpening pens, a few sheets of paper, mount behind the groom, and pound off to Boroughport. His companions from the town might rise a little later and crawl reluctantly through the streets. Once at the school each boy was expected not to loiter and play in the yard, but go straight to the schoolroom, bow respectfully to the master already sitting solemnly on his throne, take out his books quietly, and be ready promptly for study or recitation.

"Sir" Nicholas Thwacker is counted a superior schoolmaster. He is one of those "discreet and able teachers" who really impart knowledge to their pupils; not one of that great tribe of the "ignorant and careless" who "while they make one scholar mar ten." He holds a good degree from a Cambridge college; he has a real knowledge of the Latin authors, is far from being a mere pedant, and actually has the liberality to admit that the study of the correct writing of English is worthy of the efforts of a man of true learning. Being prosperous in his calling and often invited to wealthy dinners, he does not look a "hungry lean-faced villain" like so many of his brethren, but is red and round, and sometimes can even seem benevolent. Be it added that he takes a serious interest in the progress of his boys, and never flogs them save out of a genuine sense of Christian duty.

This fact does not prevent him from appearing to his schoolroom a veritable Xerxes or Tamerlane when he sits in his high seat, turning up his huge mustachios and tenderly fingering his birchen scepter which lies in plain view on the table before him. In ruling his empire he is assisted by a more meager deputy known as the "teacher," and two heavy-handed, unacademic individuals known as "ushers" who are more janitors and general watchmen than coadjutors in learned instruction.

The grammar school occupies part of the old gild hall building down on the market square, now otherwise used as a kind of city hall. The scholars all meet in a large hall upstairs, with oaken ceiling, wainscoted walls, and small windows high above the floor. The boys dangle their feet from high benches and lean their elbows on rude sloping desks. The master's desk is on a very high platform indeed so that his eagle eye can detect the first promptings of iniquity; the teacher occupies a lower coign of vantage on another side of the room.

In this hall at six every morning, except when it is absolutely too dark, the boys begin work by rising in a body, bowing toward Master Thwacker, and their shrill voices chorusing in Latin, *"Salve, magister!"* *"Salvete, pueri"*; he solemnly answers back *"Estote salvi!"* Then darting his eye along the anxious files before him: "Stand forth, Stripedwell—say now your lesson without your book." All of Stripedwell's companions heave sighs of relief, and rattle back upon their benches, while that unlucky lad begins his struggle to save his hide by conjugating *venio* without a blunder.

Latin, Latin, and yet more Latin; it is for that the grammar school and Master Thwacker absolutely exist. Latin is the language of the learned. To read it opens innumerable books ancient and recent which have never been translated. To speak it after a fashion, to interlard one's speech with phrases of it, above all to be able to write orations and even verses in it is the hall mark of a scholar. But the basis for this Latin knowledge is not a full vocabulary and easy power to use it, but an absolute memorizing of Latin "accidence" learned by rote. Since many boys fail to remain more than a few years at the grammar school, it follows that a large part of Master Thwacker's pupils never get to the point of actually opening a Latin text and making a smooth translation thereof, much less reading its pages with any kind of pleasure. In vain a few very enlightened pedagogues like great Roger Ascham (Queen Elizabeth's tutor) have deplored the extreme amount of time devoted to Latin grammar, as "tedious for the master, hard for the scholar, cold and uncomfortable for them both." Master Thwacker is confident that a painful memorizing of "accidence," with years spent on every rule and declension, is the only means of scholastic salvation. Almost all the educators of England agree with him.

The grammar or accidence that the Boroughport pupils are expected to know almost as well as their Lord's Prayer is probably William Lily's—an instrument of torture from which very few educated Englishmen have been able to escape. After it has been conned, memorized, and faultlessly recited down to the last exception and paradigm—a matter of two or three years—at last the lads are permitted to get some inkling that all this toil may have a practical value. They are started upon an elementary conversation book the *Sententias Pueriles,* made up of short sentences conveying high moral lessons. Then they can attempt the easy Eclogues of Baptista Mantuanus, an Italian Renaissance writer, supposed to be excellent as a textbook; or as they advance the *Zodiacus Vitae,* a long Latin poem by a Palingenius of Ferrara, giving a very popular summary of the current morals and philosophy from the days of Seneca to Ariosto. Finally if the boys remain still under Master Thwacker's mercies, they are actually allowed to read

[115]

understandingly certain parts of Seneca, Terence, Cicero, Vergil, Plautus, Ovid, and Horace.

Do the Boroughport scholars also study Greek? The fact seems to be that all the boys soon gather the firm conviction that there really is such a language as Greek, and they actually learn the Greek alphabet. Also a very few of Master Thwacker's brightest and least castigated pupils are taken by him somewhat privately and taught to translate a little of the original text of Homer and Xenophon. At such great and famous schools as Eton, Shrewsbury, and Harrow there is indeed a real attempt to teach Greek grammar and a few of the major authors of Hellas. For more than this the classically minded must wait until they go up to the university.

Does Latin (with this bare tracing of Greek) represent all that is taught in the Boroughport grammar school? Almost, but not absolutely. There are schoolmasters like Master Richard Mulcaster, who in 1582 was so enlightened as to urge the teaching of music and drawing along with the unescapable grammar. This great headmaster of a London school went so far as to risk the heresy of urging that writing good English must be taught as well as Latin. Such radical notions make little progress. However, the practical value of a good handwriting is appreciated, and at intervals certain writing masters come in to teach especially the rich merchants' sons a fine "secretary" hand. Also a little history and geography is counted desirable for the sons of gentlemen. The boys are mildly encouraged to a certain desultory reading at odd moments in the not very numerous history books: but geography (really a kind of mixture of geography, astronomy, and natural history as now understood) receives more formal treatment. There are maps upon the school walls, a big globe stands by the master's desk; and from time to time Master Thwacker unbends and gives his more advanced pupils informal talks about the countries of Europe, the wonderful East and West Indies opened by the Portuguese and Spaniards, the Empires of Turkey and Muscovy, and the art of finding places on maps. Alas! that such talks command better attention than the long hours of Latin composition and the verse of "The Mantuan."

Andrew Hollydean, besides this modicum of knowledge, also received certain instruction in French, Italian, and music. But this was away from the schoolroom, and under special teachers hired by his parents in their zeal to train him up as a fine gentleman. Master Thwacker scorns all such frivolities as wholly unnecessary for a scholar.

Such was the class work of Andrew and his fellows for nearly ten hours of each working day. At nine there was rather meager recess; at noon about an hour in which the boys obtained dinner. At three another recess. At five the blessed hour of release—release, that is, for all the boys not so unhappy as to be detained after school in way of punishment. Fortunately or unfortunately Master Thwacker prefers to inflict most of his punishments during school hours by the method approved by Holy Writ and immemorial usage. Write the pedagogues, "God hath sanctified the rod" to drive out from pupils "the folly which is bound up in their hearts. . . . To spare (your pupils) is to hate them, to love them is to correct them betimes." No doubt in this increasingly skeptical world even the need of castigating schoolboys has come under serious questioning. Wrote again Roger Ascham, that by the excessive use of the rod boys carry from school "a perpetual hatred of their masters and a continued contempt for learning." But Master Thwacker like most of his compeers considers such views sheer educational blasphemy. Sound Latinity rests almost as much upon the rod as sound Christianity upon the catechism.

Undoubtedly the rod should be used with discretion. Inferior pedagogues keep laying on for every trifle; and "Untruss your points!" snaps from their mouths twice per hour. Parents usually sustain any harshness; boys are counted incorrigible little animals, and the teacher who does not flog once in so often is put down as weak-armed and negligent. Still the thing should be done circumspectly. Master Thwacker disapproves of those teachers who whip their boys on cold mornings "for no other purpose than to get themselves into a heat," and he is glad none of his pupils can complain as do contemporary sufferers at Eton that they sometimes receive fifty or more stripes "for fault but small or none at all." Indeed he approves the theory that it is best to begin his animadversions with light admonitions, demotions in class, and bad marks—"black bills" —formally noted in a book.

Unfortunately the boys are often so unruly and calloused that nothing but acute dermal pain can really control them. They are alleged to steal from one another, lie, swear like sailors, fight among themselves incessantly, and play truant; furthermore the larger reduce the smaller ones to abject slavery as their fags—in return for a modicum of protection from other oppressors and for a certain boldly whispered prompting when they recite their lessons. With such pupils "three or four jerks with a birch or small red willow where birch cannot be had" seems usually the quickest way of inculcating prompt obedience and proper learning.

Often enough, however, as Andrew soon learned to his sorrow, such summary correction by no means suffices. Master Thwacker wholly subscribes to the dictum that a teacher must never administer a real flogging unless he is ready to make thorough work of it. Often the major beatings are reserved till Friday morning when the master holds grand assize, with all the little boys white and quivering upon their benches as one after another arch criminal is summoned to the desk. When a thorough beating is administered it is beneath a master's dignity to "strive and struggle" with a reluctant lad. The task of holding him firmly is given over to three or four favored scholars "honest and strong" enough to grasp him firmly and turn him over so he cannot escape the full force of the rod. Master Thwacker always administers the blows himself and does not depute this delicate task to an usher. He never smites a boy over the back with the risk of inflicting permanent injuries, although when extremely exasperated the squalling offender's skin is well worn off, before the blessed formula "Let him go!" In a phrase Master Thwacker counts himself (and is counted) a moderate and humane schoolteacher.

Under such treatment Andrew Hollydean unavoidably looked back upon Boroughport grammar school as a House of Bondage, or a downright purgatory. His plaints to his parents were sometimes pitiful but they never interfered. Discipline was discipline and the master was only discharging his clear professional duty, although once when Andrew was setting forth very late his kind-hearted father bade him ask the schoolmaster to the Hall for next Sunday's dinner—as an implied bribe to refrain from an extra severe beating.

In this sorrowful routine there is a fair scattering of single holidays, but no regular long vacation; especially none in summer. Like the famous grammar school at Shrewsbury, Boroughport allows eighteen days at Christmas, twelve at Easter, and nine at Whitsuntide (around June first). Otherwise Master Thwacker's arm continues as limber as ever.

As Andrew grows older he comes to view his school days philosophically, just as he looks back upon his more recent hardships upon the battlefield. He realizes that nineteen out of every twenty parents in England hesitate to "anoint the limbs of the laggard with the juice of the birch"; and that Master Thwacker is a leader among his kind. Indeed he will later praise him as did the former pupils of the famous pedagogue, Nicolas Udall, that truly humorous author of the earliest English comedy "Ralph Roister Doister," as being "the best schoolmaster and the greatest beater of his time." The world is full of hard knocks, and are not the years in the grammar school an admirable training for them? Could England ever have coped with the Armada and flung back the colossal power of Spain, if Devon and Thorpshire schoolmasters had failed in their duty?

When Captain Andrew has sons he will love them passionately, and place them under the direct successor of Master Thwacker.

ILLUSTRATIONS TO "SHEPHERD'S CALENDAR," 1597. APRIL.

[120]

¶ *Chapter* IX: Concerning the Politer Learning

NOT all of Captain Andrew Hollydean's education was inculcated by the rod and admonitions of his regular schoolmaster. It has been stated that he acquired from special tutors a smattering of French and Italian, and the art of writing in a fine Italian hand. He also was taught fencing as a necessary accomplishment by a fencing master whose powers will be discussed in another chapter.

Furthermore along with his sisters he was given considerable training in the unacademic subject of music.

Sixteenth-century England is an intensely musical nation. In Hollydean Hall, as in any other well-ordered mansion, books of music and instruments are lying about the rooms for the solace of any unoccupied guest. In the barber shop a lute is handy near the bench where customers await the ministrations of Master Snipper. In a cheap ordinary another lute is always ready to strum the minute some guest has finished his dinner. In the better taverns probably several fiddlers keep sawing away all through mealtime, or (if you order a private dining room) the door soon opens for a man with a viol and a boy with a lute, who bow and announce, "Doubtless your worships require music?"

In the very highest circles men and women are a bit ashamed if they cannot take their part singing a madrigal, or accompanying their songs upon some instrument. Professional skill is not expected, but to "sing your part at first sight" is almost as ordinary as to be a good rider.

This fondness for music has increased with the religious

tendencies of the age. Austere Protestants deprecate worldly music but heed well the Bible commandment: "Is any merry? Let him sing psalms." The Flemish weavers fleeing from Alva's persecution have spread the habit. Cloth workers stand hours before their looms droning the Songs of David. It will be reckoned that between 1560 and 1600 some ninety editions of metrical psalms with music will be published in England—an enormous number for the book trade.

In "gentle" circles such things as psalm singing are usually ignored with a shrug, although at Hollydean Master Crabtree sometimes leads off with the Twenty-First or Forty-Second before bedtime Sunday evenings.

Captain Andrew and Mistress Anne also can take their parts in more secular lyrics at a simple home banquet. The instruments on which they accompany themselves are simpler than in a later age but not unpleasing. Commonest of all is the lute, a mandolin with a pear-shaped body and a finger board divided by catgut or brass frets. You play it with your fingers without a plectrum. A lute is a charming instrument indeed, and Sir Walter himself, like many hearty gentlemen, keeps one close by his bedside in case he wishes to tinkle it a little if lazy and indisposed in the morning. The only trouble with the lute is the great difficulty of keeping it in tune; it is said of a certain lutist that "when he was eighty years old he had spent sixty in tuning his instrument."

Almost as popular is the viol, like a violin, but with a flat back and deeper ribs. Viols are of four sizes—treble, tenor, bass, and double bass. The bass, called the *viola da gamba,* is the most popular of all and usually played while held against the knees. Then there is the cittern, a very small lute and the rebec, a squeaking kind of fiddle with only three strings—very popular at rustic dances. As for

wind instruments (not so much in favor with gentlefolk)
there are the big clarions, the high-sounding trumpets, the
sackbuts—otherwise trombones; the recorders, very large
flutes up to four feet long, with sweet and solemn tone;
and the smaller flutes, the shawms and the hautboys. Besides these there are the instruments for real musicians—the
small *organs portatives*—actually a kind of portable accor-
dion slung on a strap over the shoulder and played by
the right hand while the left hand works the bellows, and
last but not least the great and truly powerful church
organs—although these as yet are of only one manual and
completely innocent of bellows.

There remains an instrument in which Mistress Anne
takes great satisfaction and which is constantly becoming
more elaborate. The tall harps of the professional minstrels
are still fairly common, but for ease in playing they are
now often being laid on their side over a sounding board.
If you smite the strings of these horizontal harps with
hammers held in your hand you have a dulcimer; if you
simply pluck the strings you have a psaltery. There are
other forms but the most important is when instead of
hammer or fingers the strings are played through an elaborate keyboard which works on wooden "jacks" that in
turn cause a great series of quills to pluck at the strings.
The commonest name for this expensive new-fangled instrument is now the virginal. With her virginal Mistress
Anne can produce delightful melodies far beyond the
power of any ordinary lute or harp player. It has a very
clear, bright tone and if it lacks the shade, light, and
power of what will some day be called the pianoforte, undoubtedly the virginal marks a real advance in the art and
must render great developments in music possible.

With all these instruments the household of Hollydean
and the good town of Boroughport cannot lack real bands

or even orchestras. Sir Walter can regale his guests any dinner time with a "consort" of lute, cittern, shawm, treble viol, and viola da gamba, played by servants off duty; while his Worship the Mayor never advances in a civic procession without an enormous braying of brass, wood, and stringed instruments not to mention an unconscionable number of cymbals and drums both great and small.

Sir Walter has also insisted that his son should pick up a polite something of another part of genteel learning— heraldry. Heraldic insignia have practically disappeared for military purposes, but in an age when the possession of "coat armor" is an essential part of any claim to respectability, it is a most desirable thing for every "armiger" to be able "to blazon his own proper coat."

Andrew was therefore taught by his father the rudiments of that science which could have no meaning to the menial and vulgar. The Hollydeans are enormously proud of their three griffins and try to make you believe that the founder of their house wore the selfsame emblem upon his shield at Hastings; although the patents affirming them are no older than a Garter king-of-arms under Edward III.

The three griffins have been carved by the owner not merely over the main portals and chimney pieces of his new mansion, but the "family animal" appears on all sorts of ornaments around the hall—newel posts, panels, friezes, and laced into almost every design requiring painting or carving. Lady Catherine and Mistress Anne work griffins incessantly into their embroidery; and when the gentleman ushers and all the liveried servants attend their master in state they are dutifully proud to display the three griffins embellished upon their sleeves or bosoms.

All the Hollydeans unavoidably deplore the horrid cheapening of coat armor which has lately manifested itself all over England. The new wealth which has made many a "butcher, shoemaker, tailor, cobbler, yea, tinker, pedlar, and swineherd" seek to be called by the vain name of "Master" impels them (and still more their pertly dressed dames) to seek for the glories of a coat of arms.

It is charged (alas! too truly) that her Majesty's heralds and pursuivants are corrupt men who ask an applicant more about his fee money than his ancestry. In the London comedies vulgar characters boast: "I thank God that I can write myself 'Gentleman' now; here's my patent! It cost me thirty pounds by this breath!" And the fellow flourishes about a document with "the crest of a boar without a head rampant" but done in beautiful colors. The usual way is to discover suddenly that the applicant had some ancestor of "singular virtue and discretion" who rendered the king remarkable service, but whose worth somehow missed proper recognition. Now his great-grandchildren are suddenly rewarded with a magnificent charter, with the new arms shining in gold and colors and the seal of the herald-king dangling from it.

These things make Sir Walter pluck his well-peaked beard with rage. What makes him swear blasphemously, however, is when a case is exposed as recently when a king-of-arms deliberately assigned to a vulgar embroiderer, named Parr, without any proof or right, the time-honored arms of a Sir William Parr, of a noble Northamptonshire family, but who died in 1571 "the last male of his house." The new Parr is unquestionably the son of a pedlar. Like honors have been purchased by a stocking-seller, a printer, and a haberdasher. But what is this save another sign that the times are evil and woefully on the change!

Captain Andrew can descant about roundels, gorges, and marks of cadency, about blazons, crests, supporters, augmentations, and tinctures, but a fluent knowledge of heraldry is only a small part of a polished gentleman's accomplishments. More justly he takes pride in having attended Cambridge University.

It is now extremely proper for scions of even the highest nobility to be sent to either Oxford or Cambridge. The day has come when a certain reputation for learning is a decided advantage at court and in diplomacy. When her Majesty visits one of the university towns it is the settled thing to greet her with an interminable Latin laudation, make her sit through a ponderous Latin sermon, regale her and, we trust, her courtiers with a play from Plautus or Terence and top off with a veritable Greek oration. Gloriana will interrupt from time to time with "impromptu" rejoinders in Latin and will answer the Greek orator in his own language. All this shows the trend of the age.

Young men of fashion—'tis to be feared—often go to St. Johns, Merton, or Corpus for somewhat other reasons. Near them are said to be the best fencing and dancing schools in all England. If you get a lax tutor, the next step is to be "initiated" by the older students at a tavern. Then you learn to excel in tennis. In dull weather you can find light literature somewhat amusing, and in the college library you will improve your knowledge of heraldry and train yourself to become "a gentleman-critic in pedigrees." Of grosser pleasures there is no need to say anything.

There lack not, however, young men of the greatest families who are students of great industry, imitating my Lord Treasurer Burghley who (in his Cambridge days) rose at four in the morning and studied until late into the night. Andrew Hollydean, after he matriculated at Pembroke, steered a middle course between the roistering and the grave extreme. He certainly never shone as a Latinist, but developed enough histrionic talent to be assigned a good part in the *Aularia* when it was produced one Sunday night in honor of some visiting noblemen. The discipline appeared to him (just escaped from Master Thwacker's tender mercies) a decided release, but actually —save for the sons of great personages who laughed at all regulations—could be counted severe. It was a serious offense for a student to be caught attending a drama in *English*—as sometimes given in the town by companies of strolling players. It was another gross misdemeanor to play the most unacademic game of football within university bounds, or (theoretically at least) to frequent taverns. Students were forbidden to keep firearms, ferrets, and hawks, and Master Andrew was roundly mulcted for keeping a small dog in his chambers without getting a special license. The university had its own jail into which even masters and fellows were sometimes locked for defying the statutes, and for the younger students there was tingling proof that the days of painful correction were not yet over—public floggings before the whole student body were still in order for serious offenders.

Concerning the studies and modes of instruction at those "most noble and equal sisters, Oxford and Cambridge," there is little call here to say anything. If Andrew had desired he could have frequented lectures on philosophy (based upon Aristotle, Plato, and Pliny), on medicine (based on Hippocrates and Galen), on mathematics (founded on Euclid), on astronomy (resting firmly on Ptolemy), and on cosmography (equally dependent upon Pomponius Mela and Strabo). He actually did condescend to take some interest in rhetoric—which made him open the pages of Quintillian and Cicero.

Andrew speedily learned his place just as in the great outside world, for theoretically Cambridge and Oxford are "republics of learning"; actually as in other republics class distinctions are drawn with amazing sharpness. First there are the idling sons of great nobles who are formally permitted, thanks to their fathers' ranks, to take their degrees in four years, though seven is the residence usually required to become a Master of Arts. Then there are the heirs of rich gentlemen, like Master Andrew, who are expected to live within the rules and show certain signs ot studying, but of whom little erudition is expected. Then there is the army of "younger sons" of poorer gentlemen, or the sons of ambitious merchants who rattle fewer dice boxes, study harder, and sometimes make a career out of their learning. Finally there are the veritable beasts of burden—the down-trodden "sizars" or "servitors" who are sons of yeomen, tenants, and tradesmen, and who are practically servants of their fellow students. They lodge in comfortless chambers without winter fire, and their lot is a degrading round in which "bed making, chamber sweeping, and water fetching are great preservatives against too much vain philosophy." [1]

The majority of Andrew's fellow students have drifted back into the world, where it is to be hoped their Latin, and their fencing, dancing, and tennis have made them accomplished if not learned gentlemen. The minority have pried their way into the Church (whereof more hereafter) to become "Dons" themselves at the various colleges, or join the unhappy army of poor schoolteachers.

The "Dons"—the fellows supposed to rule the colleges —too often are far from being men of erudition. It is much too common to give the fellowships to sons of rich men, lawyers, royal officials, and so on, who have, or who can, render large services to the colleges. Such magnates of course make up in social pretention all they lack in the stiffer learning. At the other end of the scale of university

---

[1] However, be it noted, Spenser was "sizar" at Pembroke, showing how a man of real ability could work his way successfully through the university.

men are the poor scholars, who fight their way to a degree
as servitors or even by getting licenses to beg during the
long vacations. They are turned loose by their Alma Mater
into a very cruel world. There is little before them but the
poorest kind of a curateship in some desolate country hamlet or still poorer schoolmastership in a starving parish. All
their lives they will struggle against poverty and demon-
strate the futility of mere learning, and inevitably they will
become embittered against a social system in which their
richer fellow students are suffered to "study little other
than histories,[1] tables, dice and trifles, and ruffle and roist
it out, excusing it all by saying, 'They be gentlemen.'" In
another generation such learned malcontents will supply
plenty of reënforcements to the Puritans.

Master Andrew was not expected to remain on through
the seven years admitting him to a degree. Like most of
his well-born companions he dropped out at the end of
three or four years because his parents felt he would profit
by breathing a certain legal atmosphere—as became the
son of a wealthy house and a destined justice of the peace.
He, therefore, was sent to London to frequent Inns of
Court, that ultra-genteel institution for training lawyers.
Doubtless many of the young gentlemen there will become
ornaments to the bench and bar, but Andrew learned
mainly "to be distinguished from a (university) scholar by
a pair of silk stockings and a beaver hat." He became inordinately critical about his clothes and "marked any man
whose bard sat not well." He learned enough law to pretend to quote Plowden and Littleton, but of more importance gained a real reputation as an amateur actor in
English plays by robust London playwrights.

[1] History was still much at a discount as a learned subject, although
in 1597 Francis Bacon was advanced enough to write, "Histories make
men wise."

By this time the heir of Hollydean's education was completed. If times had been peaceful he might have been sent on the "grand tour" of the Continent to France, Germany, and Italy. As it was, a commission in the English contingent assisting King Henry IV of France seemed entirely the proper climax to the training of a fine young gentleman. The grammar school, the college, and the Inns of Court saw nothing more of Captain Andrew for several years.

ILLUSTRATIONS TO "SHEPHERD'S CALENDAR," 1597. MAY.

S IR WALTER HOLLYDEAN, unlike his son, has never resided at the university, but that fact does not prevent him from being a well-read gentleman with a fair claim to some literary discernment. There are plenty like him. Wrote George Pettie in 1586—himself a gallant soldier—"Therefore, gentlemen, never deny yourselves to be scholars; seeing the only way to win immortality is either to do things worth the writing or to write things worth the reading."

Hollydean's good friends Philip Sidney and Walter Raleigh have shone alike as courtiers, soldiers, and authors, and it is not surprising that his own mansion contains a very tolerable library of well-selected books.

Not all country gentlemen, by any means, patronize the booksellers. A hard-drinking boor like Sir Walter's fellow-justice, Master Heavypate, never talks about anything but the price of corn and grumbles because his wife must needs buy a Bible, a prayer-book, and a Foxe's *Martyrs*.

Nevertheless, even in cottages and tradesmen's living rooms, there is often now a growing shelf of quartos and folios. The English tongue is finding itself as a literary language. It is no longer needful to learn Latin, not merely to read the Bible, but to feed the imagination with all sorts of tales, true or false, of that wonderful world the new inventions and discoveries are just disclosing. Such books as Lyly's *Euphues* and Spenser's *Shepherd's Calendar* command the praise of the most finical, but prentices and plain folk's lads—such as that William Shakespeare who is now prospering as a playwright in London—waste their candles and feed their imagination, for example, upon Painter's *The Palace of Pleasure*—a collection of wonderful tales and fables, including such stories as "The True and Constant Love of Romeo and Julietta"; or they dote upon the translation of *Gesta Romanorum,* a real treasure house of pseudo-history and ancient lore collected by the mediæval monks.

If you ask why many of the writings of this age seem charged with a wonderful imagination and bid fair to last across the centuries, the answer partly is that the world is still full of the mysteries and unknowable, and this sense of mystery unconsciously permeates innumerable books. When the laborer quits his darkening field it is promptly filled up with goblins and will o' the wisps. You can be sure the night woods are full of fairies; under the yew tree in the churchyard very likely the ghosts keep gibbering all night long. More than one old woman near Hollydean is suspected of being a witch; and Squire Rackrent's cattle have sickened undoubtedly because of the evil eye. When a criminal is caught it is manifestly God's direct revenge for murder, and during the great drought the parson was rather expected to draw down rain by his fervent prayers.

All this reflects itself in literature. The imagination has not been blunted by a daily stream of so-called "facts" and cheap explanation. The most vulgar form of composition, the street ballads, and the alehouse songs contain much that is coarse and brutal, yet at worst they are simple, earthy, natural, and devoid of the sophisticated smirk and leer. When really able men take pen in hand in such an atmosphere—what wonder some can write their names among the immortals. *Fortune My Foe* is ever a better touchstone for great literature than *The Reign of Law.*

We are not dogmatizing concerning the literary spirit of the Elizabethan age but reciting its matter-of-fact outward expressions. Around Boroughport there lack not various young gentlemen who think they have "slept on Parnassus and drunk of the font of Castaly." There is the exquisite Master Fripper; he thinks there is no modern author like the affected Lyly. Like his example he covers pages with classical allusions, forever dragging in Diogenes, Pythagoras, Plato, Lycurgus, and Milo. He wastes a whole inkpot discussing the nice question, "Did Gyges cut Candaules's coat by his own measure?" Then there is his friend and rival, Master Hotpassion. Sometimes he sings the praise of his mistress in stanzas in the accepted model of Gascoigne's

> Amid my Vale I bathe in bliss,
>   I swim in heaven, I sink in hell:
> I find amends for every miss.
>   And yet my moan no tongue may tell,
> I live and love, what would you more?
>   As never lover lived before. . . .

No doubt this is very fine, but equally fine are the pastorals of that other votary of the Muses, Master Sonnetmonger. He composes nothing but pastorals. The world, for him, is a glorified sheepwalk; its inhabitants, nymphs and shepherds who are devoted to the sway of love and are flitting their time away amid discussions of the divine passion in terms mixed with very conventional remarks about flowers, lambs, and pleasant weather.

Then, too, there is Master Knowitall, who is indeed a young prig and who, exactly as does another young prig, Francis Bacon, informs his familiars, "I have taken all knowledge to be my province." Just at present he is devoting his self-admitted talents to a history of Britain and is writing eruditely of how Brute, a hero escaped from Troy, while Æneas was founding Rome, voyaged on to

Britain with his sons Lucrine, Camber, and Albanact, drove out the giants who infested the land, and founded "Troya Nova," later better known as London.

Boroughport and Thorpshire thus are doing their share to add to the portentous list of volumes which every year

PRINTING PRESS, 1511.
Title-page of "Hegesippus," printed by Jodocus Badius Ascensius, Paris, 1511.

now are registered in Stationer's Hall; but Sir Andrew wisely does not confine his book buying to local authors. Whenever he visits London the good knight is sure to wander down into St. Paul's churchyard. The vaults of old St. Paul's are used as storage places for the booksellers' stocks, and the actual bookstalls are clustered closely around the big gray cathedral. Here is the literary center for England. Here you can meet Master Lyly the Euphuist, Master Spenser (if he is back from Ireland), that rising Master Shakespeare, dissolute Master Marlowe (if he has not just been stabbed in a brawl), or that returned soldier young Master Ben Jonson who may perhaps have some future as a playwright. They are always elbowing about, and talking with the booksellers (who are also their publishers) as to how their own printed works are vending. Outside of London there is no such focus for bookdom; although Oxford and Cambridge have many good "stationers" and a great many volumes can be purchased elsewhere. At the country fairs there is sure to be a booth selling romances and songbooks, and itinerant hawkers with popular ballads pester you everywhere.

Sir Walter trades much with Master Whitepaper who conducts in Boroughport a snug little business both as printer and stationer. In the latter capacity he maintains his shop at the sign of the Keys and Crowns. Like every retailer his stalls are quite open and customers are free to wander about and browse. All around the shop and on the pillars before it are posted up the title pages of recent books. This is a regular method of announcing new publications and explains why the title pages of a volume are so handsome, so elaborate, and contain so complete a description of the contents inside. Master Whitepaper has two or three smart clever prentices who begin their jargon the moment a gentleman in prosperous grave clothing or scholarly black and bards comes in sight: "What d'ye lack, sir? See a new book come forth, sir? Buy a fine new play, sir—*True Tragedy of Master Arden of Faversham?*—Or will your Worship like a Sir Thomas North's *Plutarch's Lives;* new printing all in white vellum and gilt."

Whitepaper prints certain books on his own presses but

the great majority of his wares come from London or from abroad. The book trade is now barely a hundred years old, and as will be wisely said, "All the books are new books." Considering the cost and trouble of bringing out a volume the appearance of a really new book is, for a select circle, a really exciting event. Master Whitepaper's shelves are always well lined with neat editions of the ancient classics —mostly printed in Venice; he has, too, a good many modern works in French and Italian, or more scantily in Spanish.[1]

There are heavy shelves loaded with all permissible brands of Divinity—very often in Latin even if the authors are English. Then there is a solid stack of translations—racy tales from France and Italy, and a great collection of versions from the Greek and Latin although the great poems of Homer are only available in a clumsy French translation; but Master George Chapman is likely to end that lack in a few years. As for modern English books there is a goodly collection alike of romances and plays, and a good many works of practical value like that of John Maplet's *A Green Forest or a Natural History*—a wonderful description of beasts, birds, and beetles that has fascinated all the young Hollydeans; or Turner's *New Herbal,* a really scientific attempt to explain British flora.

There is a good demand too for books dealing directly with the occult and marvelous. Volumes on sea voyages and adventures of the Spanish and Portuguese explorers in the newly discovered Indies are in great demand, as are the later stories of the valorous English seamen in the volumes of Master Richard Hakluyt which are just coming off the press. Marvels are marvels and the age abounds so in won-

---

[1] Only most exceptionally would a cultivated Englishman read German and then not for literary purposes. The frequent intercourse with Dutchmen would probably be in French or, failing that, in Latin.

ders that there is a good sale for such a book as *The History of Serpents,* in which it is solemnly stated that dragons are wont to hunt elephants in packs. At some narrow place dragons tie their tails together, trip up the elephant as he goes along, and then the whole pack falls upon him. Other dragons however are smaller, mild, and tamable; children enjoy riding about on their backs and then sleeping with them curled up in their beds.[1]

Even considering the value of money the prices of most books seem reasonable, especially if in the common limp vellum binding. A new London play or an ordinary pamphlet can be had unbound for four or six pence; in vellum you must pay eight- or nine-pence. A heavy folio in fine print can cost up to a pound. Many solid books are much cheaper, but there are no inexpensive reprints in "popular editions." Furthermore the age-long complaint about publishers abusing their authors has begun already. No writer ever bothers his head about accountings for royalties. It is exceptional for a printer to pay more than forty shillings cash down for a fair-sized pamphlet, although in good nature he may throw in "an odd pottle of wine"; also if the book is promising some copies may be given the author to sell on his own account. The learned Master John Stow is now finishing the manuscript of his *Survey of London,* destined to endure as a monumental work. He will probably get three pounds cash for his manuscript and forty free copies to sell off as he is able. Plenty of authors will echo Drayton's angry protest that booksellers "are a company of base knaves whom I scorn and kick at."

Master Whitepaper, of course, has his own troubles as a printer. Nearly a century and a half has fled since Gutenberg's press began its clangor at Mainz. The printer's

[1] This standard work on the subject, Topsell's *History of Serpents,* possibly did not appear until about 1600.

mystery is now common enough but there is still a little of the unusual about it. A good many manuscript books are still in circulation, beautiful products of the professional scrivener; and often an author can become well known before a line of his efforts has been set in type. Sir Philip Sidney wrote his "Arcadia" in 1580-1583. The poem was famous by 1587, but it was not printed until 1590. Then too the governments have discovered that the printing press can be a diabolical engine for spreading rebellion and heresy. Not to mention the Papal Index and the Spanish Inquisition, here in England printing presses are supposed to be permitted only in London, Oxford, and Cambridge—where they can be under the sharp eye of authority. It is by some special dispensation that Master Whitepaper lawfully keeps a press in Boroughport.

Usually as with Whitepaper a printer combines his business with that of a stationer (bookseller). The processes of printing have not been greatly changed since the art of type founding was discovered. There is still the slow clumsy hand press worked by a screw-lever and the equally slow inking-balls stuffed with feathers. Up to about 1553 every printer cast his type; then type-founding became a separate business. Most of the casters in England are visiting Frenchmen, but some of the faces they produce are certainly beautiful. There have been Greek fonts used in England since 1541, and lately in 1592 a font of Hebrew. With the leisurely processes involved a first edition of a book will seldom exceed five or six hundred copies,[1] and if the author lives in the same town as the printer he can visit the office as the work goes along and make his corrections before later sheets of the issue go to press. There is no such thing as electrotyping and if, by some great luck, an edi-

[1] This was probably the size of the First Folio of Shakespeare, which apparently sold for one pound.

tion of more than twelve hundred and fifty copies is needed all the type must be distributed and the book reset. The statutes of the Stationer's Company require that, to make a fair balance in business between the pressmen and the compositors.

English printing does not on the whole compare with the Continental, with the products of the presses of Antwerp, Paris, Geneva, and Venice; nevertheless much of the typography is beautiful. It is a real art to give a clear even impression with the old hand presses; into the making of a book can go the joys of personal craftsmanship. The title pages are elaborate and often elegant and handsome copper plate inscriptions are coming into vogue—for example, Master Harrington's recent translation of Ariosto boasts forty-six fine engraved plates.

Worthy Master Whitepaper will tell you of his troubles as a printer. The whole trade is under control of the royally incorporated Stationers' Company in London, and some of its regulations are severe and unreasonable. Many of the most profitable books are government monopolies— only a Master Jugge has the right to print Bibles and Testaments. Master Tottle alone can issue law books, Roberts and Watkins possess the extremely desirable publication of almanacs and "prognostications," and a Master John Day is growing rich with his monopoly for A B C books and the Catechism. Then there is the troublesome fact that all attempts to manufacture paper in England have thus far proved unprofitable; every sheet of it has to be imported. The foreign rag paper is excellent and very durable but equally expensive. Last but not least there is illicit printing. Presses are clumsy but so simple they can be hidden and worked in many an innocent-looking farmhouse. The Catholics are always bringing out uncensored tracts and books of devotion; the extreme Puritans are doing the like with "hedge presses"—especially the famous *Martin Marprelate* pamphlets in which her Majesty's bishops are held up to pitiless ridicule. In addition forbidden books are constantly being smuggled in from the Continent—and all reports are that the trade is extremely lucrative.

Law-abiding printers have to submit to a fairly stiff censorship. No manuscript can be issued without a license, usually by the Bishop of London. The Puritans complain bitterly that godly works of Divinity are thus delayed in publication three months to three years, even if finally passed, while many secular works "full of all filthiness, scurrility, baudry, dissoluteness, cosenage, and conycatching" are licensed immediately. As for unlicensed books every now and then the justices exert themselves, lay hands on sundry copies, and Tom Hemprope the Boroughport hangman, imitating his brother practitioner in London, burns the deadly volumes in a great fire before the Market Cross; after which ceremony Captain Andrew and his gossips, Masters Fripper, Sonnetmonger, Knowitall, and the rest, take pains privately to obtain copies for themselves—at the contraband price.

Being a printer Whitepaper also employs bookbinders, and volumes are not often sold without their covers. Limp vellum is the commonest binding for small cheap books, but worthier volumes demand solid plain brown sheep or calfskin reinforced by metal clasps. However very elaborate bindings are obtainable, and when a handsome gift is desired you can obtain a splendid volume done up in gold or silver, velvet, or even embroidery—but such pomposities are works of art not tools for a scholar.

Sir Walter, we have seen, is filling his "closet" with a very tolerable library—at least three hundred volumes. Of course his poorer neighbors are less fortunate, but collections of one to two hundred books by solid country gentlemen and the better type of curates and vicars are by no means rare. Some works you can be sure of seeing in even a very small and unlearned collection. Romances of chivalry often translated from the French are very popular —such as *The Four Sons of Aymon;* then there is that good old story *Sir Guy of Warwick,* and its counterparts *Bevis of Hampton* and *Arthur of the Round Table.* Less sophisticated still, and pored over by the young are *Robin Hood, Adam Bell, Friar Rush,* and *The Fool of Gotham.* You can hardly fail also to meet *The Court of Venus*—a collection of songs denounced by the clergy and therefore the more delectable; *The Hundred Merry Tales,* a very popular jest book, and (devoured by every literate teamster and milk-maid) *The Book of Riddles,* a treasury of very elementary word-puzzles with appropriate answers; *e.g.,* "How many calves' tails will reach to the moon?" Answer: *"One,* if it be long enough."

But the Hollydean library goes far beyond this; there are the more classical satires and fables, Æsop, Erasmus's *Praise of Folly, Raynolde the Fox, Piers Plowman,* and the invaluable *Palace of Pleasure.* There are such standard Latin classics as Vergil, Seneca's plays, and Apuleius; upon a separate shelf stand the solid "Books of Instruction"— treatises on all kinds of practical subjects, the perusal of which has been so urged upon Captain Andrew and especially Mistress Anne that they have come somewhat to hate them: *The Book of Courtesy, The Book of Chess, The Book of Cookery, The Book of Nurture for Men Servants,* and so on.

Lady Catherine could hardly have won her fame for piety unless Master Crabtree had been authorized to assemble a fair collection of works of piety. Naturally there are several huge and handsome Bibles, some velvet bound prayer-books and only a little less honored a great Foxe's *Martyrs.*

Then there is the extremely popular Latimer's Sermons, and the simpler theological books of Whitgift, Cartwright, John Knox, and (in translation) Luther. Lady Catherine constantly strengthens her faith by reading Craddock's *Ship of Assured Safety,* and her Protestantism by *The Hunter of the Romish Fox.* She has a French Bible and several other French and Italian books (which she can hardly read) but which are all of a very pious cast.

Sir Walter being a wealthy and liberal man with a reputed taste for letters has not escaped the fate of most gentlemen like him—he has been singled out for the honor of being "patron" by several needy ink-spillers. Since authors' royalties are unknown and printers' cash payments are insignificant, there is really no other way for an author, not blessed with an independence, to eke out a living, save by wheedling good money out of some rich patron who is rendered "immortal" by a dedication.

This is a recognized procedure, and Sir Walter was resigned and a little flattered when Master Quilldrive, a threadbare, over-clever gentleman of Boroughport, suddenly dedicated to him a ponderous *Calliope Reducta,* or *Veritable and Indubitable History of the Deliverance of England from the Assaults of Spain Told now in Epic Verses.* Master Quilldrive had begun by dedicating his not few hexameters to my Lord Fatacres, another landed magnate; but his Lordship scandalously failed to recognize the honor and give the poet anything, and the accommodating printer caused a new dedication leaf to be struck off and bound into all the later copies of the edition transferring all the honorifics to Sir Walter Hollydean.[1]

This dedication (ah! pity) will not go down to admiring

---

[1] A transfer of allegiance which happened fairly often. The first copies of Sanford's *Garden of Pleasure* were dedicated to the Earl of Leicester; the succeeding ones to Sir Christopher Hatton.

ages but its tenor can be guessed from that which Master Sir Philip Sidney says of the character of dedications in general—"(if you turn patron) you shall be (hailed) as the most fair, most rich, most wise, most (everything); thus doing, you shall dwell upon superlatives; thus doing your soul shall be placed with Dante's Beatrice." If Sir Walter is proclaimed merely "President of Noblesse and Chivalry" and "Hope of All Learned Men," he is getting rather less than seems his due. "Love" in current parlance is being constantly used as a term for "friendship," and the stout and ruddy knight is addressed in terms hot and sentimental enough for amorous sonnets.

What is the reward for this violent admiration? The patron's gift for the dedication of an ordinary London play is standardized at forty shillings. Master George Peele has received three pounds for a poem celebrating the installation of the Earl of Northumberland as Knight of the Garter. Master Spenser enjoys a pension of fifty pounds per annum from her Gracious Majesty for the glory shed upon her reign and person by the *Faerie Queene*. Before long Master William Shakespeare (it can be rumored) will receive an outright gift of one thousand pounds from the Earl of Southampton—but this is amazing generosity. The Earl of Leicester (so long as he lived) and my Lord Burghley have had any quantity of books dedicated to them; sometimes they rewarded the authors handsomely, sometimes proved absolute niggards.

Sir Walter, a lesser personage dealing with a somewhat minor poet, sends Master Quilldrive perhaps ten pounds. The recipient is reasonably content.

There is another kind of literature very current around Thorpshire, though it finds no honored place in a regular library—popular ballads. They are hawked everywhere at markets, fairs, and especially at such extraordinary concourses as public hangings. So much are they in request among the vulgar that very many "idle youths loathing honest labor" go about vending and singing them. Often a pair of fellows, "one with a squeaking treble and one with an ale-blown bass," will collect a crowd of nudging clowns and get them all gaping and admiring while they begin some such prologue as:

> Now listen all good people
> Unto a strange event,
> That did befall to two young men
> As they to market went.

There follows a blood-curdling recital about desperate highway robbers, their capture and execution—all just recently in the next county. "A goodly matter!" "Bravely wanton!" cry the yokels; and soon there are halfpennies in the hat and more pennies paid out for broadsides of the song itself to take home or roar over again in the ordinaries.

Some of the ballads are very pious with a pat moral, "The Lamentation of a Damned Soul," some are political as "Lady Jane Grey's Lament"; many are simply hearty popular jingles—"Ruffs, Sleeves and Hose," or "God Send Me a Wife that Will Do as I Say"; some are absolutely ribald and demoralizing as "Watkin's Ale" and "The Carman's Whistle." The best of them, however, are very genuine poetry that will last long after Master Quilldrive's productions are embalmed in dust; "The Ballad of Chevy Chase" is one of these, of which Sir Philip Sidney wrote, "I never heard the old song of Percy and Douglas that I found not my heart more than with a trumpet, and yet it is sung but by some blind crowder."

Good or bad all the ballads are intensely loyal, profess intense detestation of malcontents and traitors, and very often conclude with these lines testifying the popularity of her Majesty:

> Lord, save our gracious sovereign
> Elizabeth by name,
> That long unto our comfort,
> She may both rule and reign.

¶ *Chapter* XI: Concerning True Religion and Its Ministers

DEVOUT Master Crabtree (did we consult him) might surely be scandalized, if we proceeded thus far and gave no formal attention to the forms of Pure Christianity as practiced in Gloriana's England—another instance, he would certainly assure us, that our guides, like so many fair-weather believers, have, like Demas, forsaken the ministers of religion "having loved this present world."

If till now we have not examined strictly into the religious atmosphere of Hollydean Hall and Boroughport, it is not because the subject is unimportant. Compared with men of an another age our Elizabethans are the most pious if not *piosus* of folk. Men are constantly proclaiming their religious beliefs without the least affectation or hesitancy. "If God wills"; "So Heaven has ordered it"; "We bow to the behests of Providence"; "I beseech you as I hope for salvation"—these are the merest small coin of conversation or correspondence about extremely mundane matters. When Francis Drake first saw the Pacific he fell on his knees before his comrades and prayed aloud that God would suffer him to sail on that unknown sea. When the pickpocket last hanged at Boroughport was at the foot of the gallows, a kind of etiquette compelled him to utter a deeply moving speech thanking the Almighty for cutting him short in his sins to be a saving example to young men who might imitate his doings. Every one takes religion seriously, whether he is a Church of England man, like the great majority, a Catholic Recusant, or a student Puritan. There may be a very few atheists, but they are openly diabolical skeptics, not smiling cynics who mask their disbelief under a smug indifference.

Religion owes much of its importance to the fact that it is almost the sole intellectual and moral influence of the age. Men interested in intellectual matters cannot find their outlet in pure science, or the study of human relationships divorced from any supra-mundane theories. The fact that it is so important is one of the reasons why men wrangle so vehemently about it, make laws about it, and imprison and even put to death the wrong thinking mortals who defy proper authority. Sixteenth-century religion unfortunately, however, although it says a great deal about one's duty toward God, says far less about one's duty toward man. Here is room for the critics—but not in the reign of the dread Virginia.

Since universal scientific laws hardly exist, a belief in "direct providences" is decidedly keen. Perhaps angels no longer visit a man's house as they did Abraham's but if a rascal is thrown from his horse it probably is a "judgment." God may no longer divide the Waters of the Red Sea before Israel but He certainly aided the English fleet with favoring winds on those fateful days when it fought the Armada. Also there is very vivid fear of hell fire. Not one of the jangling persuasions has any doubt about its reality. Churchman, Recusant, and Puritan unite in commending that declaration in the well-known *Repentance of Robert Greene,* where the author declares that by his pious reading "he discovered the miserable state of the reprobate, what Hell was, what the worm of Conscience was, what torments there were appointed for the damned souls, what unspeakable miseries, what unquenchable flames . . . weeping and gnashing of teeth and all these horrors world without end."

When we pass from these generalities to certain particulars we are on much less certain ground. England has passed through the great shock and roar of the Protestant Reformation; and the process of adjustment within the Established Church is not ended—and will not be for nearly a hundred years, when it will be determined by 1700 that the English Church will not return to Catholicism, while the Puritans will have to secede and set up churches of their own.[1]

There are plenty of old people around Boroughport who remember the general astonishment when Henry VIII, "Defender of the Faith," broke with the Papacy in order to marry Anne Boleyn; the bewildering change on change —the monasteries abolished, Protestantism slightly favored then savagely repressed; men going to the stake because they denied Transubstantiation and on almost the same day other men going to the block because they denied the King could replace the Pope as head of the Church. Then the swing to violent Protestantism under Edward VI; then the swing back to equally violent and even more sanguinary Catholicism under Mary; and then the restoration of Protestantism (a little subdued and modified) under Elizabeth again. Let the theologians say what they please, it is enough to perplex honest, simple-hearted men. The only safe thing to do is to obey the laws as the King or Queen for the moment command—if these enjoin heresy the punishment falls on those who ordain them.

Up to 1588 Protestantism was weak because it seemed so provisional. Until 1587 the lawful heir to the throne had been Mary Stuart, a devout Catholic. What if she became

---

[1] In discussing the popular attitude toward religion the case is made more difficult by the fact that playwrights were strictly forbidden to touch on religious matters. This great source of information is sealed to us.

monarch of England? Then came the tragedy at Fotheringay, followed during the next year by the utter defeat of the vast project of Philip II for restoring Catholicism by means of a Spanish conquest. Protestantism has seemed triumphant, assured, and its profession intensely patriotic and national. Catholicism is subject not merely to theological criticism; its professors seem disloyal to the Queen and probably flirting with the public enemy. The question is no longer "Shall England be Protestant?"—but "What form will English Protestantism take?"

Of course there are certain regrets still for the old religion; for the gray Franciscans, the black Dominicans, the white Carmelites; for the hospitality of the richer abbeys; for the stately liturgies, the treasures of plate, the cloth of gold and velvet around the altars. Old persons still grieve sadly for these without becoming really disloyal. But by the 1590's England has been officially Protestant for well over thirty years. A new generation has grown up, most of it taught to shun Catholicism. Besides that the old Church has never lived down the bitterness and horror caused by the Marian persecutions. The martyrdoms of Smithfield, the "candle" which Latimer and Ridley lighted when they were burned at Oxford, seem a warning to every moderate man of what might be repeated on a more horrid scale if Catholicism gained the upper hand.

Following on this after Elizabeth was Queen came the bull of Pius V in 1570 excommunicating the Queen and releasing her subjects from obedience to her government. Every zealous Protestant could now argue that no man could be a sincere Catholic and not be a latent traitor. The position of the Catholics presently became intolerable. The more desperate of them conspired vainly; the less convinced

of them fell away—and Protestantism was again strength-
ened.[1]

Excluding the Catholics and Puritans (elements more
conspicuous than numerous) the great run of Englishmen
are loyal adherents to the church of England lawfully
established. "Sir" Charles Surplice, the parish priest at
Hollydean and Master Tony Chanter his clerk are as much
members (very humble) of her Majesty's official body as
her captains or civil justices. A clergyman you can know
instantly from his everyday uniform—a black gown with
small ruffs and his "Corner Cap." "Sir" (or *Dominus*)
Charles Surplice owes his position—like all of his fellows—
not to his piety, nor his learning, still less to the desires of
the majority of the flock to which he ministers. He was a
poor "servitor" at an Oxford college, but at last scraped
through to his degree. Ahead of him seemed only a hungry
chaplaincy in a shabby-genteel country gentleman's family
or an even hungrier career as a petty schoolmaster. Fortunately just as he was quitting Oxford a relative left him a
very small legacy. The old vicar of Hollydean parish had
just died and Sir Walter as hereditary patron held the
advowson—the right of naming the new incumbent. Surplice was a Thorpshire lad and negotiated discreetly
through a Boroughport solicitor. The legacy just met Sir
Walter's minimum price, the pious knight knocking off
ten pounds because Lady Catherine said she liked the way
young Surplice sang the psalter, and Captain Andrew said
he played a good hand at primero.

Surplice therefore became "Sir" Charles. He had to be
licensed and ordained by the bishop—no great difficulty
when the fees are paid and the candidate's orthodoxy proves

---

[1] Of course such events as the massacre of St. Bartholomew (1572)
and the cruelties of the Duke of Alva in the Low Countries greatly
intensified English Protestant feeling.

unimpeachable. Henceforth he is set over the Hollydean villagers—to read prayers, bury, christen, and marry for the rest of his days unless he should commit some great crime or cause some outrageous scandal.

"Sir" Charles is counted a fairly lucky man. The parish pays him tithes of full forty pounds per year. Thus, with the parsonage and a garden worked largely by his active thrifty wife, he is infinitely better off than very many coun-try vicars and lower still the country curate. He is tolerably learned, and is no "blind Sir John" like so many men of the cloth who are unable to preach and can barely stumble through the service. Sir Charles sometimes actually preaches himself—his discourses contain plenty of long "comfortable words," and Sir Walter finds them pleasantly soporific. More often he drones off homilies approved by the bishop —this is always safer and wiser, you do not unwittingly slip into dangerous expressions. He is not a sporting clergy-man, like his associate Sir Jack Hardrider set over Squire Heavypate's parish, a holy gentleman who always tries to be first with the hounds. As stated he plays well at primero, and he can tuck down a second bottle without doing any-thing foolish. Among the villagers and tenants he is reason-ably popular. He is naturally kindly and tolerant, and has won a considerable reputation as an unofficial peacemaker and arbitrator in matters that might well have gone to the lawyers.

Under Sir Charles is Master Tony Chanter, his clerk who sings the responses in the service, keeps the parish records, and acts also as sexton and verger. Master Chanter counts himself a man of large importance and enjoys making official visits to the sick—if these are not of enough standing to warrant a pastoral call by his superior. The secular affairs of the parish are supervised by two church-wardens, elected by most of the substantial parishioners.

One of them keeps the tavern, the other is a prosperous yeoman. They also are proud of their office which involves the onerous task of assigning the seats in church, and thereby proclaiming the social rank of every regular attendant.

Greatly do we fear that the reputation of the cloth has not increased during the reign of Gloriana. No new churches have been built. The men who think more earnestly or acutely upon religious subjects are very often either Catholics or Puritans—alike under disfavor as parish clergymen. Most country priests have to struggle along on ten to thirty pounds per year—they are lucky if they do not lose one third of this through many deductions and charges. Stories are direfully current that very many clergymen are not merely semi-literate and slothful, but are "riotous, drunken, and licentious." Few of them can marry to advantage. Sir Charles's spouse was only the daughter of a middling yeoman; many a parsonage has a former milk-maid or even barmaid for a mistress. As for Mistress Anne the bare suggestion that she wed a clergyman will seem almost an insult—unless he can command such patronage as to be sure of a deanship or bishopric before long, and a canonry or very fat prebend as soon as he quits the university.

Sir Charles's one great task is to read the service at seven o'clock every Sunday morning and administer communion to those who remain to receive it, then read afternoon prayer at two. He is expected to cause various young people to remain in the afternoon and learn their catechism. Going through the prayers is the great thing—sermons, homilies, and psalm singing are not strictly necessary. The services are attended fairly regularly, for law compels every one without proper excuse to be present under a shilling fine, and householders are responsible for their families and servants. Needless to say such compulsory attendance does not always promote a reverential attitude. There is much coming late, walking and talking in the Church, and slipping over from the ale house just as the last bell is sounded. Abuses are so common that ministers are required publicly to remind the churchwardens and other sworn officials of their proper duties, and flagrant offenders can find themselves summoned to stand trial (with a jury) before the arbitrary ecclesiastical courts.

Sir Charles is also expected to do what he can to enforce the law about the numerous fast and fish days. Especially must he enjoin his flock not to eat flesh on Fridays and Saturdays. Unfortunately he collides alike with human inclination and the direct desire of so many to have a fling at Rome. At Hollydean and many another wealthy house *both* fish and meat are served on these days. The guest can take what he chooses—but if he leaves meat entirely alone his companions will wag their beards: "He is no sound Protestant."

The vicar has, as may be surmised, a formidable professional rival in the godly Master Crabtree. Private chaplains are common enough in the families of country gentlemen, although the government tries to confine their employment to the households of the nobility. Their lot is sometimes simply degraded. Many a fox-hunting rural justice takes in a "trencher chaplain" as tutor for his sons. He is usually a poor scholar just turned out of the university and grudgingly admitted to "holy orders." He is supposed to read prayers to the family and exhort on Sundays, but his real task is to be a cheap schoolmaster. For sixty shillings and a "winter living" per year he must sleep in a truckle bed in the same room as the young master, never presume to sit above the salt, never "charge his trencher twice"; be very subservient to all the family, and never beat his charge without asking the boy's mother: "How many jerks shall I give him?" Such a life surely permits a chaplain to cultivate the Christian grace of humility.

Master Crabtree is of a superior sort. His employers are genuinely pious and take their religion in steady doses. Master Crabtree is not expected to follow the hounds though he sometimes helps out at cards and can stand a decent amount of Canary. He dresses in severest black, quotes the Scriptures in every third sentence, and wears an official frown on May Day and Twelfth Night. But he is neither a knave nor a fool, and lacks not in worldly sagacity nor real kindness of heart. Morning and night he reads prayers to the household. On Sunday afternoons he supplements the homilies of Sir Charles at the parish church, with less formal sermons drawn from his own eloquence. Lady Catherine insists that he explain every dark passage in the Bible while he reads it—and this leads to endless expositions and observations full of quotations not merely of the Prophets and Apostles, but of St. Basil, Chrysostom, and Augustine, not to name Luther, Calvin, and Cranmer. The Hollydeans do not always understand him, but they are intensely proud of him—"*Our* chaplain is no Sir John-lack-Latin" like so many of them in squires' families. As for Lady Catherine she is never happier than when Master Crabtree is admonishing her (and Mistress Anne) in her ladyship's closet, upon grace, election, and the foreordained damnation of the wicked.

Master Crabtree is unmarried: "Far be it from him to commend the Papist's practice of celibacy—but the Lord hasn't yet called him." Captain Andrew profanely hints to his familiars that when the chief parish church in Borough-port falls vacant Master Crabtree will not treat it wholly as a "chastening Providence" if Sir Walter and the others who control the endowment think well of his learning and piety. There is a certain widow—relict of a rich maltster—but the rector although old and doddering delays in passing to his long rest and Lady Catherine will not lose her ghostly counselor yet awhile.

As doubtless is fairly plain the Hollydean family(especially the female end of it) is somewhat of a Puritanical cast. Puritanism does not at all imply desire to sever from the church. On the contrary the great hope of the Master Crabtrees is to bring the Established Church to their way of thinking, and it is a great pity that her Majesty and her ministers have not consented to a more thorough "cleansing of the Temple," that is, clearance from the Church of the remnants of "Romish superstition."

Puritans neither condemn good sack nor good velvet. They believe they understand the just use of physical blessings, "Let your moderation be known of all men" is frequently enough in their mouths. Just at present their movement is only in its fair beginning. A few simplifications in the liturgy, a change in church government, making it more like a Geneva presbytery, probably will content them. But let opposition and repression increase, let the contest intensify and extremists become fanatical, there is no telling how Puritanism will really end. In the 1590's, however, it simply represents an austere, earnest party within the Established Church.

Certain Englishmen are not within the Established Church. Protestantism is somewhat unevenly distributed. It is very strong in London and nearly all the coastwise towns, where constant warfare with Catholic Spain has convinced the great trading and seafaring population that Rome and the "Scarlet Woman" are the selfsame thing. It is accepted almost everywhere by the small traders, the weavers, the industrial workers. It has been tolerated, if not joyously adopted, by the run of the yeomanry and the rural

tenants. However, a large proportion of the country gentlemen keep their loyalty or at least their hankering for the
old Church; and in this they are joined by certain of the
very proudest of the nobility. Generally speaking the number of Catholics increases as you go north and inland, away
from the towns. In moments of Catholic boasting or Protestant despondency, people tell you "half of all Englishmen" still lean to the old Church, although the probability
is there are nowhere near so many.

Thorpshire, being in Southern England and containing
the brisk trading town of Boroughport, is overwhelmingly
Protestant. Still Master Crabtree grows solemn descanting
about "the devilish boldness of the Recusants." Be it confessed that among the country clowns "religion" consists
still of pattering off a Creed or a Hail Mary and tumbling
into bed. A leader like Sir Charles Surplice is no kind of
man to make his flock cease mumbling such jargon verses
as the following, and thinking that Heaven is somehow
more favorable:

> White Paternoster, St. Peter's brother;
> What has't i' th' t' one hand? White book leaves.
> What has't i' th' t' other hand? Heaven gate keys.

Such yokels are too loutish to be any real danger. The
peril to Protestantism comes from the great scattering of
respectable country families who go to parish church as
little as possible, or not at all; who avoid receiving the
sacrament from any Established clergyman, and who are
strongly suspected of harboring "massing priests."

The first anti-Catholic laws date from 1559, but only after
1570 and the great conspiracies have the Recusants felt their
increasing severity. Good Protestants in any case sincerely
believe that their Catholic neighbors cannot, in view of the
Pope's Bulls, be anything but latent rebels; that Jesuit

emissaries are constantly entering England not only to stir up rebellion but to compass the murder of the Queen, and that any assertion of loyalty merely to the old religion without any intention of subverting Elizabeth's government is simply so much hypocrisy. This makes the public acquiesce in the pitiless arrest and execution of Jesuits and seminary priests, not as being misbelievers but as traitors.

The position of peaceable and sincere Catholics is deplorable. They can hold no kind of public office, nor enter a grammar school, take learned degrees, become lawyers, nor serve in the army or navy.[1]

If they do not attend the parish church and come at intervals to communion they are subject to ruinous fines, enforced intermittently indeed, and with a certain eye to the question whether the offender's estate can pay them. If they are caught harboring Jesuits or other churchly emissaries from abroad their plight is still more miserable.

Not five miles from Boroughport there has been lately a "blessed deliverance" from the "plottings of the Beast," as Master Crabtree energetically put it. A certain well-to-do squire, Master Manyoaks, was suspected of being a "Church Papist." He and his family at long intervals attended the parish church barely enough to avoid the fines. But for years he avoided the Sacrament alleging "he had a quarrel on his conscience" and so could not communicate "being out of charity"—a technical excuse for avoiding the Lord's table. Nevertheless everybody was confident that the smooth, quiet "tutor" he kept at his house was no tutor at all but a disguised priest from the English seminary at Douai, who said mass privately before the Manyoaks family and a few sympathetic neighbors.

---

[1] During the Armada crisis this barrier against military employment was less rigidly drawn, and many persons who were at least Catholic sympathizers rendered gallant patriotic service.

In any case, her Majesty's council at length heard something which caused the sheriff of Thorpshire himself with a strong band of constables to descend suddenly on Manyoaks Hall and search the mansion from cellar to garret. Everything seemed harmless and lawful but with the sheriff was a shrewd Sir Edward Prywell, especially come from London. He heeded none of Master Manyoak's protests that he was a "true Englishman," and went over the house as a cat noses for mouse cracks. He tested for hidden vaults in the foundations, sounded and examined all chimney corners, put gimlets into the thicker partitions, and hunted for any hidden lofts. At last (just as the search seemed to have failed) he discovered a certain upper chamber was a little broader than the room below it. A panel was torn out, and there—behold! from a narrow stifling closet were dragged forth two gasping, hungry men—the tutor and a strange fellow disguised somewhat as a shipwrecked sailor who had been begging his way on land. Sir Edmond instantly pounced on this victim as Father Anthony Softspeech, a Jesuit envoy of the worst type, and on his person were found a quantity of tracts denouncing the Queen as an immoral usurper and alleging that the Pope released her subjects from "all fealty and service that is due her."

Master Manyoaks, the tutor, and Father Softspeech are now in Boroughport jail awaiting the next assize. The squire may escape with long imprisonment and the loss of half his property, but the tutor and the Jesuit had better prepare themselves for the gallows. So one "priests' hole" and "nest of iniquity" is broken up, but Master Crabtree is mournfully confident that Thorpshire contains several others.

Right in this same jail, however, is another victim of religion who may well dread Tom Hemprope. It is hardly safer to be an ultra-Protestant than to be an avowed Catholic. The more pronounced Puritans are usually unpopular and often run foul of the law as the Justices can stretch it. In Boroughport are several small tradesmen and master craftsmen who seem to reproach their fellow citizens by their abhorring of starched collars, by clipping their hair extraordinarily short, by forcing their wives to wear only "sad colors and little ruffs," and by keeping a Bible ostentatiously open upon their counters and flatly telling neighbors who keep a jolly Christmas or May Day that they are "men of sin." Such pious folk with their "Yea, verilies," and constant quotings of Scripture usually keep out of jail, but almost everybody jibes at them as "Precisians."

Many, however, carry their convictions beyond this. The breakdown of the old religious barriers has opened the way for many fantastic notions. Only a little while ago London was astonished by one William Hackett, who gave out that he was "Christ come to judge the world." He was soon joined by two "prophets" as unbalanced as himself, and roundly and openly they denounced the Queen and her ministers. All three of course perished on the gallows. Then even in Thorpshire there will sometimes appear "Anabaptists." They are counted the most dangerous of fanatics, and are said to take after the old Anabaptists of Munzer in Germany who called infant baptism sinful and practiced not merely community of goods but plurality of wives. The English Anabaptists certainly condemn the taking of oaths and teach that no true believer can refer any dispute to the law courts or hold any office under existing civil governments. They are mostly vulgar, mechanic people deserving little consideration; and their anarchic ideas are punished not merely with death but with the good old remedy for heresy—burning.

But in Boroughport jail there is now a solid peaceable yeoman, Master Myles Readbible. He is not as violent as the Anabaptists but has become infected with "Separatism." He is probably a follower of that defiant pair, Greenwood and Barrow, who were executed in London in 1593 for the "Brownist" heresy—that the Church of England is hopelessly bad, that the rule by bishops is unscriptural, and that true believers had better set up a new church for themselves under a very democratic type of government. Such amazing opinions can well bring Master Readbible to the same gallows as awaits Father Softspeech (whom he abominates most heartily). If he escapes hanging, perhaps he will presently find England so uncomfortable that he will flee with his family to Holland where greater toleration prevails, and possibly if he wearies of Holland, consider further emigration to the new lands in America.

One last comment upon the books upon which Elizabethan religion seems to be founded. Barring the Bible and the Prayer Book, by far the most important volume for English Protestants is the oft-mentioned *The Acts and Monuments of These Latter and Perilous Days*—in simpler title Foxe's *Book of Martyrs*. First published in 1563 it has run through a vast number of editions. It is adorned with vivid wood cuts. Its vehement intolerance of Catholicism and its glorifications of Cranmer, Rogers, and all the other "Marian Martyrs" is reinforced by an extraordinarily picturesque and forcefully simple style. No boy or girl brought up on it can easily escape becoming a violent Protestant.

As for the Bible the world is still awaiting that Authorized Version which will become the eternal possession of the English-speaking race. Bibles however are now very common; and it is no longer so needful to keep them (as earlier in the Reformation) set out, fastened by a chain, for general reading in churches. There is still much use of the *Great Bible,* the old version of 1539, which supplies the Scripture selections and Psalter retained in the Book of

Common Prayer; but in 1560 there followed the *Geneva Bible,* the version favored by the Puritans, and often printed with pictures, maps, and pithy notes flavored with a strong Calvinism. In the churches all Scripture reading (not from the Prayer Book) must be from the official *Bishop's Bible* of 1563-1572. The Bishop's Bible is pretty manifestly an inferior piece of work, the complaints against it are many, but her Majesty's government has not yet got around to providing a satisfactory substitute.[1]

[1] Apparently Shakespeare gained his Bible knowledge from the old *Great Bible.* The Catholic translation of 1582 (completed in 1609), the *Douai Bible,* apart from criticisms concerning its theological bias, was alleged to have been the work of persons who were not perfect masters of vigorous, idiomatic English.

ILLUSTRATIONS TO "SHEPHERD'S CALENDAR," 1597. JUNE.

¶ *Chapter* XII: CONCERNING PLAGUES, PHYSICIANS, AND FUNERALS

"ALL flesh is grass," Master Crabtree continually warns us. "Today we are here, tomorrow we are— where?" Today we are gay, lusty, and wanton. Tomorrow we are brought low with mortal ills. The next we are cut off in our sins, our bodies the prey of the worm; it is an unspeakable mercy if the undying worm does not prey upon our souls eternally!

Undeniably the span of life is shorter in the sixteenth century than it will be in subsequent ages. How many fine young fellows, how many blooming young matrons are suddenly laid away in the churchyard! Dame Motherwell the midwife boasts her skill and her luck that three out of four of the infants she brings into this evil world somehow survive the initial process, and that only four of their mothers during the last year died in childbirth. Every birth is of course a sheer dice-throwing between Life and Death alike for mother and for child; and after that there is perhaps only an even chance that the babe safely christened will live long enough to be confirmed in the church. Catherine of Aragon bore Henry VIII six children; all but one were stillborn or died in infancy, although they received the most skillful care possible. Conditions have hardly improved since her time, and plenty of English mothers have been no more fortunate than poor Catherine.

Hints have been dropped already about the sanitary conditions at Boroughport and Hollydean Hall. Many little villages and farmsteads are styes of filth.

Gallant courtiers "compound with cleanliness" by a free

use of oils and scents, and seldom waste money on soap which is mainly used for laundering. Almost everybody commits acts every day which in another age would shock all public decency. The water used at Hollydean comes from springs decidedly near to vast manure heaps; no one ever troubles his head about it. Fresh air indoors is more or less dangerous, and the great curtains around the beds cut it off absolutely. Vermin are unpleasant but are never associated with disease. Truly Thorpshire, we may say, breeds up a sturdy race; so many persons, despite everything, manage to live to respectable years.[1]

Besides all other agents whereby a wise Providence keeps England from the evils of overpopulation there is the plague. It will be a mistake to imagine later that the Great Plague of 1665 in London was more than the climax and the worst of the visitations which never were completely absent from the metropolis, and which break out incessantly in Boroughport and many smaller places. Just now in 1593 London has been hideously scourged; some 15,000 persons have been taken off with it in the city and suburbs, including the Lord Mayor and four aldermen. Conditions in Paris are frequently almost as bad. After the horror had descended, wiseacres said they always knew the plague was coming for all the signs foretold it; the harvest season was stormy and tempestuous, there were fiery comets in the sky; and there suddenly appeared great numbers of small frogs, toads with long tails, and an abundance of gnats, spiders, and moths—proving that the air had become corrupt. Certain learned doctors admitted that the air had become corrupt but assigned possibly a different cause; they

---

[1] It has been conjectured that Shakespeare died when he did, because a very noisome resort for straying pigs, Chapel Lane, ran beside his house in Stratford-upon-Avon. Such an atmosphere could well have undermined his health.

said that the summer had been hot and rainless, and that the enormous garbage heaps had bred a fearsome quantity of flies which conceivably had infected the air.

Whatever the cause, the plague is a hideous visitation. It can be fought against by special forms of prayer, enjoined by the bishop, to be said by the master of a house with all his family kneeling and responding "Amen" in a room perfumed with frankincense, or at least with juniper, rosemary, rosewater, and vinegar. Then various mundane precautions seem to help. There is a sudden zeal by the city magistrates to abate all "stinking dunghills," to wash down the streets with plenty of cold water, to make innholders clean up their stables, to stop the free emptying of filth into the streets, and stop nondescript cats, dogs, and swine from running about as usual.

No doubt these things avail, but who can search the purposes of God? The plague breaks out suddenly in the most unexpected places. Only last year in Boroughport Goodman Shuttlethrow, a respected weaver, after a brief indisposition discovered to his horror a huge carbuncle appearing upon him. Instantly he was shut up with his household, the formula "Lord have mercy upon us" inscribed upon his door, and a stout watchman stationed to prevent egress or entrance. The carbuncle is called "The Lord's token" and is supposed to be a sure sign of death. Actually this is not so. A certain number of afflicted recover and then as "safe men" or "safe women" are in profitable demand as nurses for those later afflicted.

Panic of course reigned in Boroughport. All Shuttlethrow's neighbors drank every morning a concoction made of boiled ale mixed with aristolochiaceous, angelia, celandine, mithridate, and ivory "dragon-water"—whatever these terms mean to the apothecaries. The moment several of them felt the headache, inward burning, and weakness of the stomach which were the first signs of infection, they took large doses of mithridate and dragon-water. They also used hot cloths and bricks to make them sweat freely. If "the sore" actually arose they applied a fowl cut in halves, or a plaster made of egg yolk and certain chopped herbs.

By an astonishing mercy only four or five persons actually died in this visitation at Boroughport, and Goodman Throwshuttle was back singing psalms at his loom as heartily as ever. But this "pestilence that walketh in darkness" is always a fearful scourge that can descend any moment on any English community. Even more deadly though fortunately less common is the sweating sickness which has also ravaged London—although not lately. This fell disease begins with "a burning sweat which invades the body and vexes the blood, and with a most grievous heat infests the stomach and the head grievously." If you survive the attack twenty-four hours probably you are safe—but very few are those who can endure so long.

In the villages and country districts smallpox probably carries off more victims than any other scourge. Nobody understands it; even those who survive are probably pitted for life. The only approved thing to do with a sufferer is to place him in a meat-pickling vat and fumigate him with cinnabar, after which he must be given a drastic sweating treatment and kept on a low diet. There is then perhaps a chance left that he may recover.

To fight these and more ordinary diseases what progress has been made since the feudal ages! Much less we fear than in many other fields of human knowledge; however conditions, in say the time of the Crusades, were so primitive they could hardly have been worse, and most changes in the healing arts have been on the whole improvements. In 1518 the royal College of Physicians was chartered at London, and since 1582 it has provided learned lectureships; but its main duty is to license candidates to practice the mystery of medicine, and this means at least a slight examination into their competence and character.

Beyond a doubt the ablest physician in all Thorpshire is the celebrated Doctor Bleeder. He has studied first at Montpellier and then at Padua (that seat of wondrous medical learning). His rivals complain that long residence in France and particularly in Italy has relaxed his opinions and corrupted his morals; but it has never been charged that he ever gave a rich patient a "mortal mineral"—the alleged practice of corrupt physicians and wicked heirs. It is also hinted that he does not practice in London, because the doctors of the metropolis hate competition and enforce examinations of extreme severity upon would-be London practitioners—although affably lax if the candidate will migrate to the shires.

Doctor Bleeder beyond a doubt is a responsible and intelligent man with a high professional honor. True, he firmly believes that many diseases can be warded off by wearing an Eastern "hyacinth" (or jewel), and promptly advises applying the fowl plucked of its tail feathers to the carbuncle of his plague patients. This is only the best orthodox practice. He makes all his patients close their windows at night, but causes fires to be lighted in sick chambers "to consume the evil vapors." He always talks of "the influence of the stars" upon sickness and healing, and assures sufferers that Jupiter, Saturn, or Venus have much to do with their gout and ague—but we suspect he is not quite confident about the matter himself. Unlike less successful rivals he is known to wash carefully his instruments used in treating "plague, pox, measles, ulcers, and boils"; alleging (a very hard thing to believe) that if he failed to do this the disease somehow might be transferred to the next patient touched by the instrument.

Most of his herbs and medicines he prepares himself, and in the rear of his chambers there is really a considerable pharmacy. Of course he fails not with such recognized remedies as mixtures of chopped mice, lynx claws, and elks' hoofs for baffling cases of rheumatism, and he will order oil of stags' blood for wealthy sufferers with the gout; but in his arsenal are pills, powders, and tinctures of a slightly different variety: rhubarb, senna, bitter apple, turpentine, camphor, mercury, mastic, and the like. He has doses brewed from poppy and other "drowsy syrups"; but no real opium or laudanum. Also he possesses a good many dangerous drugs such as henbane and poisonous yew, which he uses with reasonable caution. He makes all kinds of plasters and has handy a hot iron for cauterizing any wounds. His bag is full of "tents"—rolls of lint with which wounds are searched and cleansed. Lately too he has invested in a watch;[1] this is much better for timing a patient's pulse than the old way of counting the heart beats through the interval taken for reciting the Lord's Prayer. Every day, naturally, he passes out pastils of mastic, wax and strong pepper for "head rheum" (head colds), and flasks of gargle for sore throats, made of barley water, vinegar and syrup of mulberries.

But his infallible recourse in nearly all cases is phlebotomy—otherwise blood letting. Dr. Bleeder, like all his brethren, draws out his lancet and opens a vein almost before he examines a patient's tongue or feels his pulse. Countless lives, say the medical books, have been saved by timely blood letting. Most people have too much blood; the mere act of reducing it relieves them. Then, too, by a careful scrutiny of the blood as it flows, by noting its excess, deficiency, etc., invaluable assistance is given to diagnosis.

[1] Physicians without a watch or clock often carried with them "timing glasses"—sand glasses especially made for taking a patient's pulse.

Dr. Bleeder is firm in the opinion that perfectly healthy persons ought to be bled several times per year merely to remain healthy, and he goes regularly out to Hollydean with his assistant and his basin to bleed Sir Walter, Lady Catherine, and all their relatives and upper servants. The thing is cheerfully submitted to, as a somewhat unpleasant operation which prevents troubles much worse.

Dr. Bleeder is a really intelligent man at the top of his profession; quite often because of (or in spite of) his professional training he has cured really difficult cases. Empirical knowledge can sometimes circumvent much remarkable theorizing. Less praise can be given certain of his rivals; for example Master Veinknife, the surgeon. The surgeons [1] are counted inferior to the physicians, although they have their own Royal College. They never quite escape association with the barber-surgeons who are permitted to bleed tradesmen and rustics when they are not clipping and frizzing. Master Veinknife can perform various simple operations with fair success. At the College at London he has dissected dead felons, the charter allowing the society four malefactors per year. He extracts teeth—hardly painlessly—and can "stop" or repair decaying teeth to a modest extent. When, however, Master Veinknife is confronted with a really difficult operation the patient had better make his will and send for the parson. He will probably not survive the shock of the scalpel used ruthlessly without anesthetics, and if he does a few days of lingering will very likely produce mortification and his heirs can soon divide his property.

Lower still are the apothecaries of which Master Strongphysic is a fair representative. He has no official status and maintains his small shop nominally for the sale of herbs,

[1] In 1587 while the learned fraternity was dissecting a criminal, the corpse suddenly came to life!

essences, and drugs for the use of the physicians or any laymen who will take their chance. Actually he prescribes and passes out purges and cordials to those people who grudge the noble (six shillings eightpence) which is Doctor Bleeder's regular fee. Master Strongphysic's shop smells of stale herbs, and many of his drugs are direfully adulterated. He has not the slightest theoretical knowledge of medicine, but has learned its jargon and a certain native acuteness helps him to pick up enough practical information sometimes to cure instead of promote the simpler diseases.

All three of these good men have a fair standing in the community, but Boroughport lacks not its sprinkling of downright quacks. For a while there was a Doctor Slaughter. He pretended to have studied at Heidelberg, but probably had never quitted England. He was full of merry tales and stale jests to make the old folks laugh, and his pockets were laden with comfits for the children. But his practice consisted invariably in bleeding his patients thrice as much as Master Veinknife and then administering a desperate purge. He boasted much of his remarkable cures, but before too many of his victims died the jealous Doctor Bleeder discovered that he was a horseleech out of Staffordshire who had run away from his debts. His creditors suddenly pounced upon him; he vanished into debtors' prison and Boroughport was saved from further devastation.

Of other quack practices what need to speak? Many "wise women" will tell you that the best way to cure toothache is for the patient—while he sits by the fireside—to hold his mouth open over a basin of water. Then the woman casts into the fire a handful of henbane seed likely to be full of worms. The seeds break in the fire with a kind of cracking sound. Often some of the worms snap out and

[169]

fall in the water. "These," the beldame affirms, "have dropped out from the teeth that are diseased." By this time the toothache is perhaps letting up. Such a "cure" can well demand a shilling.

This is no place to discuss the "royal touch" for epilepsy. The hand of a God-anointed monarch can well work miracles. Henry VIII and now Queen Elizabeth have often touched long lines of sufferers presenting themselves in a formal ceremony at court. Certainly many cures are reported; but possibly the fervent belief of the patient has something to do with it.

As Doctor Bleeder is wont to observe piously, all too often "his skill is futile before the decrees of Heaven"; and all that remains for his patients is a befitting burial. Very recently Sir James Broadheath, an old neighbor of the Hollydeans, breathed his last. Immediately after he died came Master Coffin, the best Boroughport undertaker, who took possession of the mansion and caused all the chief rooms and the great staircase to be draped in black. More particularly he set in place a perfectly black mourning bed; and Master William Broadheath, as heir and now the new head of the family, lay down for some hours upon the sable black bedclothes and there received set visits of condolence from all his father's friends.

These "mourning beds" are kept in a household sometimes for generations and are loaned around among the relatives along with the black velvet window curtains and black carpets which go with them. Furthermore since Sir James was the honored member of one of the Boroughport trading companies, his worshipful brethren brought over an extremely handsome pall of purple velvet and cloth of gold which was kept especially to honor the mortal exit of the members.

After proper delay Sir John was laid out in his very elaborate coffin resting in the family hall.[1] A clergyman made a short oration dwelling on the virtues and piety of the deceased. Upon the coffin stood a large pot of wine which was next passed around as a loving cup among all the assembled friends and relatives; after which every person present laid sprigs of evergreen (tokens of immortality) upon the coffin lid. To the children present were next passed out direct gifts of small coins; their elders received bolts of ribbons, scarves, and gloves. Next rosemary was produced; some of it was also laid on the coffin and bits of it tied to the mourners' hats. After that the time was come for the regular procession to the parish church.

A funeral procession tells all the world just how important is the family of the deceased, and every effort therefore is put forth to make it just as imposing as possible. The worshipful trading company marched first, then followed a platoon of their clerks and other employees who were able to chant psalms; after these advanced all the friends and relatives, male and female, black-clad, melancholy, and important. The well-born mourners all carried small branches of bay, rosemary, and evergreen, as did a much greater throng of mourners who were simply all sorts of poor folk, paid a trifle to look sorrowful and march in the procession. Sir James's coffin, under its magnificent pall, was carried along in a horse litter, over which was borne the *hearse*—which was not a conveyance at all, but a fine black canopy, carried over the coffin by four cousins of the deceased.

The burial service was read and then the coffin lowered down not into a grave dug in the churchyard, but, in honor

[1] For people of poorer condition it was usual to keep up a *wake* or riotous feasting all night before the funeral, as well, of course, as a second and more regular feast after it.

of Sir James's rank and his ownership of a good part of the parish tithes, directly into an opening made in the pavement of the chancel itself. The vicar was wholly agreeable to this for custom permitted him to exact a very round fee. After the coffin was in place most of the evergreen branches were decorously cast down upon it. After that nothing remained except for all to go back to Broadheath Manor for an enormous feast. Sir James, like many another prudent man, had set aside a sum in his will for this feast and even specified the exact bill of fare. The gorging and guzzling was enormous—"to do the departed knight honor." Even more exciting to the meaner folk, however, was the generous distribution of black gowns to many poor men and women who had come flocking from miles around expecting just such liberality.

After all else was over a handsome effigy of Sir James Broadheath was presently set upon his tomb in the church. It was in the good old style—a full-length figure of the knight clad in brass armor (which he never wore), his hands elevated in prayer and all the heraldic bearings of his house blazoned conspicuously about him. A person of slightly meaner rank would have had to content himself with a casque, sword, and coat of arms hung up over his tomb. Being an undoubted magnate, perhaps it is needless for the family to put up the somewhat customary tablet warning against "disturbing these bones." Had Sir James been a common mortal buried in the open churchyard, such a request however would probably have gone absolutely unheeded. The average churchyard is small and all the parishioners are mortal. Next to the north wall of the chancel of many parish houses there is the charnel house or "bone-house," into which the bones dug from the neighboring graves are flung with no more ceremony than with so many clods. Twenty or thirty years at most (long enough for many of your friends who grieved for you to die off themselves) is the average time you can hope to sleep in most churchyards unless you come of a fine family that can provide a fine tomb. By that time good Christians trust that all ghosts are laid, and the grave diggers are always asking, "Whom can we dig up next?" [1]

[1] Hamlet's Yorick was dug up after only twenty-three years to make room for Ophelia's body. There was grim necessity behind the plea on Shakespeare's own grave:

> "Blessed be the man that spares these stones
> And cursed be he who moves my bones."

And this, too, although the poet as a part owner of the tithes of Stratford church and a man of local consequence was entitled to burial in a grave directly before the altar.

¶ *Chapter* XIII: Concerning the Cottages and Farms

ENGLAND is overwhelmingly an agricultural country; successful as have been many trading ventures, marked as has been the multiplication of looms, nine Englishmen out of ten still live as toiling farmers or as those farmers' employers or lords of the manor.

Heaven forefend that simple persons like ourselves should have to understand, much more to explain all the details of rural land tenure, a subject fit only for the most learned of the Queen's sergeants at law and high judges. In general we may say that the later years of Elizabeth have brought welcome respite in the distressing changes in land holding and farming which began with the Black Death in the fourteenth century and continued with increasing severity until the passing of the unfortunate Mary Tudor.

Under the old manorial system most of the parishes of England were divided into three sections—the lord's demesne land, worked by the personal services of the peasantry; the village farm, divided up into temporary holdings assigned among the villagers; and the "commons," wastes and woodlands shared in use alike by the lord of the manor and the village folk. This was an utterly inefficient system. It meant that the lord was always trying to get as much unpaid labor from the peasants as possible, and that the latter were always evading their customary duties.[1]

Also no peasant had more than the temporary occupation

---

[1] Often this labor upon the demesne land would be compounded for by a customary money payment. This probably made the situation a little more comfortable.

of the fields he cultivated for himself. From seedtime to harvest merely he had possession of it, with human and four-footed trespassers kept out by the proverbially ineffective "hayward," and crows and pigeons by the equally futile "crow-keeper." Then on every Lammas day (August 12) the crops were supposed to be cleared away, the fences removed, and the arable land suddenly became "common" —to be grazed over by the villagers' herds attended by the general neatherd, shepherd, and swineherd; and so until the next seedtime when the cattle had to maintain themselves on the heath and waste land, unfit for cultivation. Finally at varying intervals (local custom would largely settle it) there might be a redistribution of the peasants' small holdings; certain families would be assigned more fields, others must be content with less. In any event almost no one could assert confidently "this is mine" and improve his lands with the assurance of firm ownership.

Since about 1480 this grievously imperfect arrangement has for the most part broken down. As usual the first gainers have been the great landlords. It was discovered that there was excellent money in sheep grazing, with Flanders providing an insatiable market for English wool. "The foot of the sheep has turned the land to gold," became the saying. But to develop great sheep runs the landlords used every unscrupulous means to force the "customary tenants," the peasants, to abandon their rights to the common village farms, and content themselves with a mere cottage and garden plot—if they were lucky enough to keep that. The lawyers cheerfully aided the "gentle" owners. There was the breaking up of the great monasteries —very easy landlords assisting the process; Henry VIII closed his eyes while the magnates who clutched at the abbey lands proceeded next to put the screws on their helpless rural population. By 1560 an enormous number of small farmers, cotters, and rural handicraftsmen lost their hold on the land by this ruthless process of "enclosures"— conversion to strictly private ownership.

Furthermore the demand for sheep runs has implied the deliberate turning back of plowland into grazing land. One shepherd can tend the flocks where once the arable lands gave honest work for twenty men. Whole villages have been pulled down. Not ten miles from Hollydean there rises a handsome parish church. The tithes still levied on the grazing lands about pay the vicar, but he often reads the prayers to an empty church with only a doddering old clerk to quaver the responses. Around the building are simply the manse and a series of moss-crusted cellars. A hundred years ago here was the good village of Merryfields. Today Squire Merryfields in the great house is only interested in the price of wool.

Ballad mongers, of course, are forever lamenting the situation:

> Sheep have eat upon meadows and our downs,
>   Our corn, our woods, whole villages and towns;
> Yea, they have eat up many wealthy men,
>   Besides widows and orphan childer-en!

Nevertheless this "enclosing" (a process now pretty complete in Thorpshire, but by no means over in certain other parts of England) has brought good as well as loss. The worst distress of a change to a new system is over. And there are some direct gains. For example, on the old "common field farm" it is impossible to keep the common stock pure, the scab is rarely absent from the common fold, the rot from the ill-drained land. No one owner can improve his live stock; mating is utterly haphazard of "everybody's son with nobody's daughter." Cows are pitifully small in size, and sheep are so lean that they are raised more for fleece

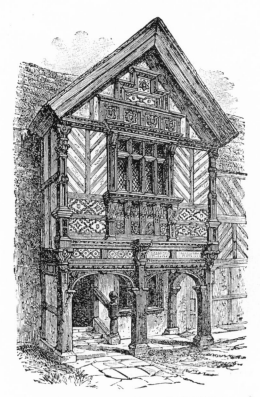

FRONT OF TOWN HALL, NANTWICH.
Built 1611.
Richardson, "Old English Mansions."

CARVING ON WALL BY CHARLES BAILLY, PRISONER IN THE TOWER, 1571.

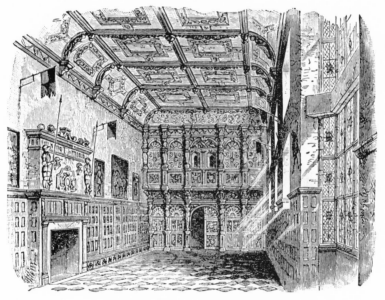

HATFIELD HOUSE: THE GREAT HALL.

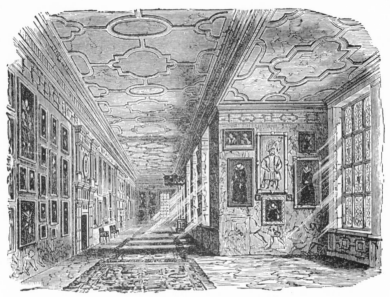

HARDWICKE HALL: THE GALLERY.

Me that giueth meafure,
God bleſſeth with treaſure.

It makes a poore man,
To ſell flower for bran.

Wake well to thy ſeaſon,
With cunninge and reaſon.

Be iuſt with thy weightes,
God plague falſe ſleightes.

Who ſo followethe theiſ preceptes well

BAKERS OF YORK, A.D. 1595—1596.
Ordinances of their Gild.
Collection of Miss Toulmin Smith.

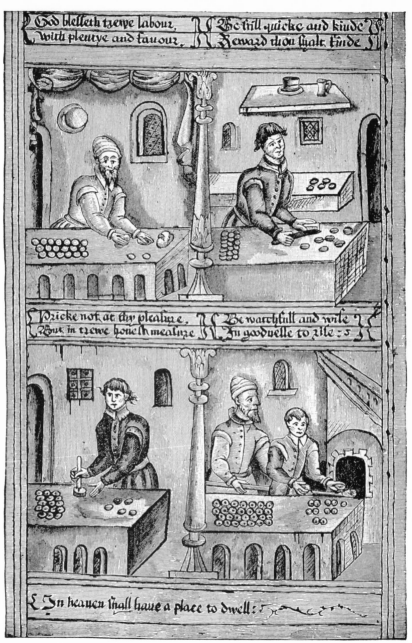

BAKERS OF YORK, A.D. 1595—1596.
Ordinances of their Gild
Collection of Miss Toulmin Smith.

OLD TOWN HALL, LEICESTER.

Drawing by Miss Edith Gittins.

CHAINED LIBRARY, FOUNDED 1598, IN ROOM OVER PORCH OF GRANTHAM
PARISH CHURCH.

Blades, "Bibliographical Miscellanies."

THE FULLER'S PANEL.

Carved end of a bench in Spaxton Church, Somerset ; late Fourteenth or early Fifteenth Century
Proceedings of Somerset Archæological Society.

WESTGATE STREET, GLOUCESTER.
Showing the house where Hooper was imprisoned.

FRIARS' STREET, WORCESTER.
Britton, "English Cities."

THE NEW INN, GLOUCESTER.

and leather than for mutton, although ewes are kept often just for their milk—for six ewes give as much as one cow. You can tell "common land" cattle when you see them; the animals are extremely lean and with very long legs, because they are seldom in the stalls and often have to wander miles in search of food.

Hollydean Manor has passed through the pains of transition and the villagers are sufficiently contented. They are direct tenants now of Sir Walter who like many another landlord finds it to his personal interest to be reasonably humane. While the new direct rent system was coming in there were fearful abuses. In Edward VI's liturgies there were direct petitions begging God to incline landlords "not to stretch out their rents but to be contented with sufficient." Now local custom has hardened and rents cannot as a rule be arbitrarily increased without making the landlord dangerously unpopular—not to mention certain legal protections for the tenant.

"Farming in several" has thus become hereabouts the order of the day. The first result has been marking off the lands between the various estates and leaseholders by the very picturesque hedgerows which are becoming a feature of the English countryside. Sir Walter is developing a fairly intelligent system of agriculture upon the lands which he works direct by hired laborers. He encourages his tenants to imitate his methods although of course they are stupid and unprogressive. Wheat is rising again in price, and a good part of the quondam sheep-lands are going back to the plow. Outside the arable fields there are still the huge stretches of woodland under which the pigs run for their beechnut mast or acorns, and the villagers seek their fence and firewood, hop poles, and farming tools; there are, in any case, other wide stretches on which vast herds of sheep are grazing. Most of these sheep are Sir Walter's, but the tenants and the neighboring yeomen have certain grazing and woodland privileges also.

If the day is fine and the crops have been good there is no need to condole over the lot of the rustics around Hollydean. Go out into the meadows and count the wild flowers waiting to be made into garlands—"blue-veined violets," "daisies pied," "pansies that are thoughts," "ladies' smocks all silver-white"—these in season are only a few.

Just before the hay harvest look for the orchises, the blue and white wort, the yellow rattlegrass, and the tall "moon daisies." Plunge into the greenwood behind the pasturelands—what perfect delight in its tangles, its glades, its dingles! Hear the milkmaid singing at her tasks! We are told that her chief desire is "that she may dig in the springtime in order to have a store of flowers stuck upon her winding sheet." Hard toil, long hours, most certainly. But there are no sweat-shops and factory systems near Hollydean, and blessed very possibly are those simple souls who are never vexed with that little knowledge which is a dangerous thing.

The testimony to the lusty happiness of much of rural life is far too cumulative to be whistled away as merely poetic imagination. We hear of hale, middle-aged farmers who tell their gossips "what with hay in the barn, horses in the stable, oxen in the stall, sheep in the pen, hogs in the sty, corn in the garner, milk in the dairy, ale in the tub, bacon in the roof, herbs in the garden, whole clothes on our backs and some money in our purses—if we serve God at all, what in God's name can we deserve to have more?" On bright days why pity the shepherd? "Give him fat lambs and fair weather and he knows no happiness beyond. The sweet fountain is his fairest ale house, the sunny bank his best chamber." Or round the barns of Hollydean Hall go the healthy strapping farm maids. "Their lips are a little chapped though pleasantly red, they have good complexions a bit peeled by exposure to wind and sun. They trip about with a mincing walk; they rise with the merry lark, tie handkerchiefs over their black hair, work cheerfully from morn until dark—and are content with one holiday per year in town—generally at Easter."

Creatures of fancy, doubtless, but fancy can only exist when founded upon reality. So then it is not the least of the blessings of Gloriana's England that the country folk of England are on the whole better off than in very many earlier and succeeding ages, however circumscribed and benighted their lives may seem.

How are these "ungentle" rural folk divided? At their head no doubt are the substantial yeomen. These worthy people in the grand shuffle of the agricultural changes kept their ownership of the land and now possess it absolutely. They have their twenty to forty acres which they work with their own hands, so putting themselves automatically below the gentlemen. But Goodman Steady, near by Holly-dean, though he dutifully uncaps to Sir Walter, knows that the knight amply respects his position. Steady can read enough to con the Prayer Book, to learn how to treat the murrain among his oxen. He has a few good hawks and dogs, pays his reckonings promptly, and never is caught in ale-house brawlings. He hates Spaniards as a good Protestant should, and makes a reliable man to draw for juries.[1]

He wears solid russet clothes, though his daughters can go to church almost as bravely clad as proud Mistress Anne. Such a yeomanry you will not find in France or in Italy. They are spread from Northumberland to Sussex, a solid barrier between the top-lofty rich and the toiling poor. It is

[1] Technically to be a yeoman it was needful to be the freeholder of land worth forty shillings per year—implying modest competence.

[179]

the yeomen that are the surest stay and promise for the future of England.

The yeomen like Steady seldom have a bigger income than the tenants, but of course they have a much more self-respecting position. The number of the two classes is probably about equal,[1] with possibly the yeomanry more numerous.

However, the tenants and the hireling laborers have much the same social status, and are always rising or falling to one condition or the other. In any case the lot of a tenant depends much upon the character of his landlord. Sir Walter lives on his estate, administers it directly or with close scrutiny of the steward, and understands well that a kindly interest in the tenant's affairs is by far the best policy. Hodge Littlefarm never hesitates to tell his Worship whether it is because his cattle are sick or his wife down in childbed for the eleventh time that the rent will be a little delayed. Less fortunate are the tenants of Sir Francis Spendpenny, a Thorpshire magnate who haunts her Majesty's court seeking preferment. Only rarely does he reopen great gloomy Spendpenny House; and perpetually he writes down from London bidding his agents to press the tenantry for every possible fee, to renew leases as illiberally as possible, and to evict for the slightest delinquency. These absentee landlords can be the curse of the countryside, and around Hollydean plenty of honest gossips will shake their heads every time Captain Andrew rides off to the metropolis: "Will he too live away from us when he gets the manor?"

Part of the Thorpshire tenants are leaseholders: they have hired the land for a term of years or for so many lives and until the period expires when they must bargain afresh,

---

[1] In 1696—a very late date for any generalizations about the reign of Elizabeth—it was computed that there were in the realm 180,000 "yeoman" families and 150,000 "farmer" or "tenant" families.

are firmly protected. The majority of them are "customary tenants"; their families have probably held their lands for very many years and consider the acres their own morally if not legally. Their rents are established by very ancient custom, but whenever a son or other heirs take over the lands they have to pay an additional fee or "fine" to the lord of the manor. These people are called "copyholders" for having the payment of these fines—confirming their lands, entered in the manorial court rolls.

Eighteen acres of arable land, two acres of good meadow land, and grazing rights on the uncultivated "common land" of the old manor not yet enclosed, make up a satisfactory tenant holding. Such a property ought to suffice for a large family except in very bad years, although on many estates there is complaining because the rents are paid off in grain, and the landlord's agents use "iniquitous bushels" and so cheat the tenants of one quarter of the entire amount, or else deduct for the alleged bad quality of the grain—unless they are quietly bribed.

Under the tenants are the great armies of the rural hirelings. The yeomen employ many, of course the thriftier tenants also employ many, but the landlords with the big estates, which they work directly, employ the most.

Sir Walter keeps busy permanently about a score of these hard-working folk. They are under the direction of upper servants and overseers, but the excellent knight like the wise "husband" that he is never fails to cast an eye on their general doings and know who is laggard and who is skillful. Many of them are married and live in little cottages in Hollydean village; the remainder find quarters, decidedly primitive, among the barns and outbuildings. Besides there is seasonal work for a small company of harvesters, hedgers, ditchers, thatchers and the like who may often have quarters in the village, but often are rolling stones, drifting around from manor to manor as employment presents.

The wages paid all these toilers may seem amazing when seen from another age. The Hollydeans have the name of good masters, but they only pay at the rate laid down by local custom reinforced by the direct terms of the law. If they paid more they would make themselves hopelessly unpopular with every other landowner, besides being subject to prosecution. Their laborers nevertheless enjoy their service, because they are paid promptly in ready money, not in kind, and enjoy various unstipulated gifts and extra holidays. Jack Mattock is a typical superior farm worker. He is employed for the entire year, although not on precisely the same tasks. He can sow, mow, thresh, thatch ricks, and kill and dress pigs. He is perfectly content with his forty shillings per year plus eight shillings every Christmas season for a new livery. Helping him is a tow-headed lumpish fellow, Ned Wantwit. Ned will never be anything but a most ordinary inexpert laborer. He gets sixteen shillings per year, and four more for livery. Jack tells him to thank God that he gets that much. His general clownishness should make him "content with his lot"—if he has the least Christian virtue.

In the dairies and kitchens Lady Catherine has a superior woman, Joan Griddle; she can cook, bake, make butter and malt, and direct the girls. She has risen to the proud scale of getting twenty whole shillings per year plus six shillings eightpence for clothes. Such a young assistant as Meg Muncher, a little more hopeful mentally than the doltish Ned, is getting twelve shillings annually, with four more for garments. Of this income she is trying to save half to fill her hope-chest against stepping off with Archie Tinker.

The day laborers of course are paid not by the year but by the day. Wages vary slightly from county to county and of course are highest in thriftless extravagant London. Here in Thorpshire you can get a master-mason or expert carpenter or thatcher for fourpence per day "with meat and drink," but must give him eightpence if he must find his own food. However, the journeymen who accompany him will probably only demand half as much. Common field workers during sowing and harvest will be satisfied with twopence or at most threepence per day—including board. In the springtime there turned up a fairly capable plowman; the Hollydeans gave him a shilling per week "and found" during the season. He had not the slightest right to complain.

How on such wages can it be possible for Jack Mattock and Tibbet Talkapace his consort to appear fed and clothed decently enough for the back pew in the parish church Sunday—especially as there is a whole brood of little Mattocks, increasing in annual succession? In the first place Jack has the use at a very low rental of a small cottage and four acres of tolerable land. Up at the great house Jack gets his own dinner with a big bowl of porridge for breakfast and a hearty mess of scraps for supper. His family have a kind of prescriptive right to appear for so many meals at the manor, and if at times their father and head tucks a loaf or the remnants of a flitch under his jerkin before going home, "Sir Walter is far too liberal a gentleman to let the steward say anything about it." If you are a gentleman you must submit to petty plunderings. The fare for the hinds at Hollydean may lack in puddings and sweetmeats, but there will always be plenty of beef, salt fish, and carrots.

Then Tibbet and her brood work the four acres carefully if unintelligently; the boys know how to pick up scraps and live on next to nothing. There are absolutely no luxuries except an occasional pot at the ale house; and as for school fees—"what use is schooling to simple folk like us?" The only intellectual pleasure is listening to Sir Charles droning through the prayers and the homily every Sunday, "not that such as we should make bold to understand them." Three or four times per year, Jack, like every other honest farm worker, gets gloriously drunk. That is as inevitable as short nights in summer. Every other month, more or less, he comes home in a foul temper and gives Tibbet a smart beating; but she has never lost any teeth or had a collarbone broken or a wrist dislocated. She is furthermore no delicate dame herself, and can usually keep her spouse at a respectful distance.

To add to the family income Tibbet has a loom, and at odd intervals through the year she turns off a good many yards of good stuff for the wool merchant. The oldest boy now can tend the pigs and weed the garden; the oldest girl is learning to spell her mother at the loom; the next oldest girl can tend their own and their neighbors' flocks of geese. With such resources the Mattock family are in nowise miserable if the crops are good; if the year is a poor one they face actual want, except as charitable Lady Catherine makes it a point of honor to see that none of the regular helpers on the estate suffer too much privation.

The Hollydean estates are far better tilled than many of those around, but even then farmers of other days can rub their eyes at some of the methods. There is no understanding of the proper rotation of crops. The old style "three field" method, whereby one "common" field was sown annually with autumn wheat, the second with spring barley or oats, and the third lay fallow, has largely broken down with the coming of enclosures and private ownership. Every occupant wants to force his land to yield as much as possible—often by very unintelligent methods. The Bible tells of the enemy who sows tares among the good wheat

and causes a disastrous harvest, but such farmers as Myles
Littlefield sow themselves plenty of weeds along with their
grain, then lament at what their acres bring them. The
June weeding is likely to be careless and imperfect. As for
manure, Sir Walter amazes his neighbors by insisting that
ferns be gathered up and spread out over the land in the
autumn. He also does another amazing thing: he forbids
the gathering up of the sheep manure, deposited through
the autumn and winter among the stubble fields. Since
England was, such manure has been carefully gathered up,
dried, and used as a common fuel—so much less trouble
than going into woods for sticks! Can this possibly be the
reason why the Hollydean fields yield considerably more
than Squire Hardpate's acres? But Sir Walter never
bothers his head by putting to use the great dung and
garbage heaps which gather around his barn doors and
around the front doors of most of the cottagers. The only
thing to do with those is to let them dry out until late
in the summer. When they are ripely offensive they can
be burned in great bonfires to the joy of all the lads and
girls.

Still Thorpshire fields are counted fertile and their
owners thanked God last year for a good harvest. The
standard crop, of course, is grain—red or white "rivet"
wheat on light soils, red or white "pollard" if the ground is
heavier. Plows are not very efficient; better go over each
field three times. At the end of September the sowers go
out with their seed-corn, and expect to finish broadcasting
the new crop by Hallowmas (November 1). But rye rather
than wheat is the bread corn of the country, and makes
that bread "brown as a nut," which is the common diet
for the poorer folk of England and is counted more sustaining than wheat bread whether crunched by mean folk
or by gentle.

Rye ripens slower than wheat. It is sowed earlier, is more hardy, easier to work, and its tough straw can be plaited up in the winter into many things—especially hats. Barley is very common but is raised mostly for the sake of the ale. Hops used to be imported, but now are largely home grown and counted a needful reinforcement for the barley. Oats are very exhausting for the land but some have to be raised for the sake of the horses. However, it is oxen not horses that pull the plows and the big wains. They cost less to feed, they require less care, and when they have tugged and bellowed to a venerable age can be beefed and eaten. There are ten oxen to one horse all around Thorpshire.

Hollydean Parish and Manor is so near Boroughport that there is a fairly constant coming and going, and many things are bought in the town market which the villagers might well make for themselves. Go ten miles inland; the roads are so poor that any communication is at best difficult. At Hazelthorpe, for example, the "drift lanes" which lead from the village to the cultivated fields cease at the bounds of the parish. Very little coin circulates in the tiny community because it buys next to nothing from the outside world. The fields and live stock provide almost all the necessary food and clothing even for the landlord.

Hazelthorpe has its mill,[1] its village institution, and every house has its oven and brewing kettle.

The women spin and weave up the wool into coarse cloth, and the hemp into linen. The men tan their own leather and make their own rough tools and household utensils. In the long winter evenings the farmers carve up their wooden spoons, platters, and bowls, rivet on the bot-

---

[1] A water mill if a good stream were available; but in some parts of England a stately, solemnly revolving windmill—in any case a picturesque object that contributed much to the landscape.

toms to the big horn mugs, and close the leaks in the leathern drinking jacks. The abundant osiers are plaited up into baskets, handles are fixed on the scythes, flails are cut from holly and thorn and fitted to staves, and the teeth of the ashen rakes and harrows are sharpened.

Many villages are too small and poor to maintain a regular smithy, but there are traveling smiths who trudge about with a forge and anvil on an oxcart, and almost every good farmer can do some light work for himself.

Meantime during the long winter slumber of the fields there is incessant bustle among the women. Their spinning wheels, distaffs, and needles rest not from sunrise to sunset. If not busy preparing cloth there are the neck collars to plait, the sheepskin bags to stitch, the rushes to peel for wicks to make into candles. Take the good old names "spinster, webster, malster, brewster, and baxter," and you know at once how the Hazelthorpe, and almost equally the Hollydean women spend their time—spinning,[1] weaving, malting, brewing, and baking.

Winter is then anything but a time of busy idleness for honest rustics, but oh! the joy when the frost begins to relax and the buds to swell, and the birds begin calling in the hedgerows. The ditches have to be opened, the meadows searched through to catch the moles, the sheepfolds insured against prowling dogs; then all the hop poles (carefully stacked through the winter) have to be set out—and the field work is near its beginning. The toil is very hard but by its very character allows long intervals when tired nature can relax and animal spirits release themselves. May Day is likely to be one amazingly prolonged drinking bout, and so is Whitsuntide. If the day of

---

[1] Spinning was likely to be more common among the cottage industries than weaving, because one weaver could use up yarn faster than several good spinners could produce it.

the patron saint of the Parish falls anywhere in summer all work will stand still. In any case there is the mirth and merriment of the hay harvest. Sir Walter, like every honest friendly landlord, provides unlimited food and drink to all his regular toilers, hires in others, and lets the girls romp through their share.

The hay ought to be gathered in July; the more serious work of the grain harvest comes late in August. Then all the rest of the countryside stands still for this one thing. A good landlord drives his assistants to the limits of their strength, but keeps the black bowl ready in the hall the moment work knocks off for the evening. He swishes his stick toward loiterers but makes all his helpers wear rough gloves to protect their hands, and poor widows and their children are always encouraged to glean after the regular harvesters. After the grain harvest in September comes the gathering from the orchards—more merry noise, frantic energy, and free providing. Then the winter is drawing on; the wool from the summer shearing must be bagged and sold off; the logs stacked for the winter and the supply of salt fish for Lent is bought in the town and laid out to dry. Given fair crops Hollydean is in a mood to look forward to a roaring Christmas.

Look again at Jack Mattock, for after all it is the Jack Mattocks, about half a million of them, that provide the human foundations for such assorted things as the *Faerie Queene,* Master Shakespeare's comedies, Master Bacon's sage philosophizing, Gloriana's glittering court, Sir Walter Raleigh's Virginia voyages, and Vice-admiral Drake's shrewd blows which are establishing the sea power of England.

Jack Mattock has seldom a crown in his pouch but all Hollydean esteems him as a charitable, hard working fellow. He is short, thick, with nose and cheeks as red as a brick, and has perhaps picked up enough learning barely to make out the figures on the marketing lists. His cottage is very humble with a hard earthen floor, whitewashed walls, and thatched roof, but many children are in it and none but the baby idle. There is bacon hanging from the rafters, and on the little green are pigs, hens, and "gaggling geese." He loves being out in all weathers and so "keeps gout at bay." It has never crossed his mind that there is anything wrong in Sir Walter Hollydean being a wealthy squire and he and his lady enjoying infinite luxuries, thanks to the toil of Jack, of Tib his wife, and all the other Jacks around Hollydean; and a very few simple things can make Jack Mattock very happy.

Sometimes there comes a dead point in the working of certain human problems which perplexes the nations world without end. The 1590's apparently witness one of these dead points. Her Majesty's Council is troubled with many things—but the wider issues of "Capital and Labor" are hardly among them.[1]

[1] Of course the good fortune and contentment of the English lower classes in say 1590-1600 can be overstated. Earlier in Tudor times matters had been infinitely worse. On the other hand, rural conditions continued apparently very tolerable until well after 1700.

¶ *Chapter* XIV: Concerning Rogues, Vaga-
bonds, and the Queen's Justice

THERE is a very heavy deduction to be made if we praise the condition of the farming classes; never in England have there been so many vagabonds and downright felonious rascals roaming about betwixt Berwick and Dover. At best they are a nuisance; at worst they are a menace to the Queen's peace and betray a rotten spot in society.

What causes their multitude? Many things all working toward one bad end. In the first place the dissolution of the old monasteries turned loose a great quantity of formerly harmless parasites; the process of enclosures forced out as desperate wanderers very many poor, dispossessed farmers; the rich merchants who have bought up many ancient estates are less careful of their dependents than the old hereditary landlords and do nothing to help their feebler retainers. Then too have come the incessant wars in Flanders and France; groups of disbanded English are always drifting home. These Sons of Wars were probably vagrants or real jailbirds when they enlisted. After the roistering life of the camps they have gained an even greater distaste for honest work. They are strong of arm and despise the constables, and can make horrid disturbance of peaceful life—especially in the inland villages.

Then too, although rural labor conditions have improved, the generally adventurous restless spirit of the age keeps the next generation of vagrants from rapidly dwindling. Behind the packs of disbanded soldiers drift other strollers; "ballad mongers" and "minstrels" (with crazy lutes as an excuse for sheer vagabondage); "bear wards," dragging on mangy bears and using their antics as means of levying tribute; "common players" who profess to give comedies and tragedies in barns or inn-courts but who have no license and who probably are more interested in thieving; "scholars" who claim to be begging for their fees at Oxford or Cambridge, but whose begging licenses are probably forgeries; and finally a constant mob of jugglers, tinkers, and petty chapmen of very debatable honesty. All these take their toll from rich and poor; and beyond these regiments who perhaps think it safer to beg than to steal, there are plain rogues who get their living from the world by unabashed felony.

At the best the number of vagabonds is a matter for grave public counsels. In London it is estimated that there are twelve thousand "begging poor," almost one tenth of the population, although many of these are doubtless honest unfortunates.

But it is also reckoned that there are at least ten thousand genuine outlaws spread over the kingdom, and every year three or four hundred are "eaten up by the gallows," with the fair surmise that the number of felons still at large is something dangerous. Learned gentlemen write that if all the able men among these elements were organized into an army, they could give the Queen's most powerful enemy "a strong battle," yet as the case stands they are merely so much strength to the adversary.

The roads swarm with these creatures. For a traveler to set forth on a lengthy journey without making sure of honest, well-armed companions is an act tending to emptied pockets if not a bloody grave. The letter of the law of course ought to terrorize the vagrants and rascals, but (more the pity!) there is a vast difference between passing an Act of Parliament and seeing it enforced by the constables. So many rogues go scatheless all the year long that it is a mere turn of fortune if one of them is entrapped. As he sits in the stocks or even as he mounts the gallows, probably he will curse his ill luck rather than reflect that honesty is the best policy.

Every parish rejoices in the constable. At Hollydean Will Proud marches about with his truncheon and makes all the little boys peep around the hedges in awe of him. It is a reasonably important thing to be constable. Proud was a middle-aged carpenter when the last constable died; he finds his red coat, his baton of office, and some very tolerable fees a fair equivalent for his former wages, not to mention a seat of vantage at the ale house. In gloomier moments he complains of his fate as a hard working servant of the Queen—he has to duck scolds, stock and whip rogues, see that no flesh is eaten on fast days, make every idler go to church on Sundays, and drag before the Justice all cursers, swearers, and drunkards. Besides that he has to start and lead the "hue and cry" whenever there is a serious crime. Will Proud is a just, efficient constable. He is not corrupted by a small bribe, he is fairly alert to the ordinary tricks of the lawless, he shows a passable courage if he has to clap his hands on a hulking villain. By general admission he is a much better limb of the law than sottish cowardly Frank Weakly, his colleague in the next parish beyond.

In Boroughport the local constables are eked out by the night watch. These powers of justice would be more formidable if they were not elderly ex-craftsmen who have outlived their usefulness as wage earners and are given their posts largely because his Worship the Mayor fears that otherwise they might make demands upon charity. They go clattering about the streets with their staves and lanterns, making plenty of noise so they will not have the bad luck to run on lurking evildoers. One night lately certain watchmen did indeed pluck up courage and proceed with a certain care to nip a suspected housebreaker, but they found him not; for they had all eaten onions that evening to keep themselves awake, and the approaching scent gave the shrewd warning that it was time to slip away. However the city watch have at least a "drowsy charm" about them as they make their rounds. It is pleasant for honest folk to hear the singsong under their windows:

> Give ear to the clock, beware your lock,
> Your fire and your light, and God give you good night—
> One o'clock.

And turn over in the feather bed and drift off to sleep again.

On the day of our first visit to Hollydean we have seen that Will Proud by a certain exertion has gathered around him several fellow champions of the law, and pounced down on sundry evildoers who had been infesting the neighborhood. He caught the rascals at a kind of camp on the edge of the woods, and since they were chicken-hearted wretches the constables were quite brave and strong enough to nip six of them and drag them securely roped before her Majesty's Justice of the Peace, Sir Walter himself.

The worshipful Justice sits enthroned in his great armchair at the head of the table in the Hall. Beside him upon a stool sits lean, sharpnosed Master Nibquill his clerk, who can help out with knowledge of the law if his superior hesitates. When the prisoners are brought in it soon develops that Constable Proud has made no common haul. He has caught a whole graded fraternity of hardened rogues, who by the testimony of a score of farmers or their wives have been preying upon the countryside by sham appeals to charity and probably by deeds much worse. "Plain caterpillars of the Commonwealth," Sir Walter promptly calls them, and then proceeds to closer interrogation.

The first prisoner, it soon comes out, is a "Counterfeit Crank." He has excited charity by pretending to fits of epilepsy. He is naked from his waist upward save for an old patched jerkin of leather, and his face is smeared with blood as though he had just fallen down and "been tormented by his painful pangs." A bladder of sheep's blood has actually been found about him from which to daub his cheeks from time to time, and in his wallet are thirteen good shillings levied only yesterday among the soft-hearted housewives in Boroughport.

His next companion is a "Palliard." He also works on the charitable, but by displaying hideous artificial sores and sham wounds made by tying arsenic or ratsbane to spots on his legs and ankles.

The third affirmed he was a "begging proctor," presenting a justice's license to beg for an impotent person over in Southampton. A very scanty examination showed that the license was a forgery and that probably the helpless cripple was a myth.

The fourth claimed to be a wandering minstrel. He had indeed a kind of bagpipe on which he could produce most lamentable noises. It was manifestly a mere excuse for tramping the roads and watching any opportunity for plunder.

The fifth fellow refused to give any account of himself but he had been seen going about the villages carrying a long stick with a hook. Many women were lamenting the loss of linen hung out on the bushes to dry. He was beyond

question an *angler* angling for unprotected garments, some
of which were found in his bag.

The sixth rascal had terrorized any number of housewives into giving him messes of victuals to take himself
off. He was an "Abraham Man" or "Poor Tom o' Bedlam,"
who shammed violent insanity and could get anything he
wanted lest if angered he proved a raging maniac. He
seemed the adroitest and most composed of all the gang.

These six types are familiar enough, only it is unusual
to catch such an assortment together. The law is plain and
Sir Walter is just putting on his best "justice frown" and
making rumblings in his throat preliminary to ordering
stocks and whipping post, when Master Nibquill, who had
been gazing very hard especially at the Abraham Man,
suddenly whispers something to his superior. Instantly Sir
Walter's countenance betrays a great light. He turns
roundly upon the ex-maniac:

"Hark you, sirrah—were you not that 'Upright Man' last
winter in Winchester?"

The Abraham Man, who had seemed to be awaiting,
with considerable composure, a long morning in the stocks
and a sound flogging, suddenly is seen turning white under
his ears. "Upright Men" are the very aristocrats among not
merely vagabonds but thieves, chieftains of the whole fraternity, with the choice of all *doxies* (female companions),
and authority to extort contributions from all pilfering fra-
ternities.

The fellow quickly recovers himself, "How could his
Worship imagine such a thing of a poor unfortunate trying to scrape a living by a few harmless tricks!"

But Sir Walter's suspicions are amazingly aroused; other
questions follow answered with increasing awkwardness.
Also more questions are flung at his companions. Soon
it appears that the Counterfeit Crank and the Palliard, who

are after all mere spiritless beggars, are willing to convey favor by telling on their companions. The angler also is browbeaten into one admission after another. The end of the whole matter is (to the swelling glory of Constable Proud) that the sham maniac appears to be none other than Hal Liftpurse, a notorious highway practitioner, and the minstrel and the angler are really his boon lieutenants, more professionally known as "Priggers of Prancers" because they shine most as horse thieves. The trio, finding pursuit in the next county becoming a trifle hot, had slipped over into Thorpshire and joined themselves with three rather harmless vagabonds with whom they planned to sojourn until the constables who had started the first hue and cry should become tired, the pursuit from parish to parish cool, and Hal Liftpurse and his friends could return to their old haunts and business.

The uncovering of such felons of course left Sir Walter nothing but to order the trio off to jail to be held against the next assize. The Counterfeit Crank, the Palliard, and the begging proctor would ordinarily now have been given a good broiling morning in the parish stocks, with half the Hollydean villagers throwing rotten turnips, following a thorough flogging by Will Proud, after which they would have been bidden "never to be seen again in the neighborhood if they'd shun the gallows."

But since these three vagabonds have promised to turn Queen's witnesses, the only possible thing is to clap them all with the guiltier comrades in jail for safe-keeping lest Liftpurse's comrades, still at large, cut their throats for their blabbing.

So to the unspeakable glory of Will Proud he is ordered to take them over to Boroughport jail. Plenty of daring scoundrels like the three chief prisoners have escaped from the constables while being taken to prison, but Captain

Andrew now valorously offers to provide the escort. He and five stout serving men will ride over. There is no need to provide horses for the prisoners. Each one of them is firmly strapped by his wrists to the saddle of a rider. If the six to be sure are nearly dead by the need of running at full speed for over two miles, when the captain playfully orders a canter, that is only what such wretches deserve, and they can recover their breath while Master Locktight the jailer sends over to the blacksmith's shop for a proper man to rivet the leg irons.

After Hal Liftpurse has been duly shackled, a good part of Boroughport pays its two pence to the under turnkey for a chance to see him. In fact he is exhibited somewhat as was the great ape at the last town fair. Former victims on the highway identify him, and he boasts complacently of how he plundered them. Several fine ladies seek excuses for peering in through the barred door at him; all the clergymen visit and pray with him, and Master Brush the local portrait painter craves the honor of taking his picture.

Soon stories multiply of his adventures. Before he took to the road he was a pickpocket in London, not a common *nip* who slips up behind persons in crowds and cuts off their dangling pouches with a knife, but a daring adroit *gentleman foist* (a being of a far higher order) who slips his fingers into his victims' pockets and draws thence their valuables by sheer sleight of hand. Such a good foist must have "an eagle eye, a lady's hand, and a lion's heart." Liftpurse was such an expert, being especially successful in churches where he excelled in lifting his eyes piously toward the preacher while exploring his fellow worshipers' pockets.

But something made him leave London and take to the road. He became soon a king of his profession: all the "Roaring Boys," "Bravados," and their kin as well as the

"Priggers of Prancers" took his orders and made him their hero. With one female companion he went through the form of a wedding. A Vagabond *patrico* or hedge priest, a kind of clerical gipsy, performed a marriage valid "until death us do part." But after six months they tired of each other and divorce was charmingly simple: the man stood on one side of a dead dog (or other animal), the woman on the other. Then they shook hands above the carcass, and "death" parted them forever, and Hal took another consort.

Such a leader of course was Master of "Pedlar's French" or the "Canting Tongue," the special language of rascals. He taught some of his disciples "Vincent's Law," otherwise the art of fraudulent betting, "Coney-catching Law" or how to cheat at cards, and "Cheating Law," less technically the use of false dice. If a younger reprobate proved proficient there was a regular initiation at a friendly ale house; much liquor was tossed off at the candidate's expense and the Upright Man solemnly pronounced the formula of admission after "a gage of a bowse" (otherwise a quart of liquor) had been poured over the neophyte's bare head: "I, Hal Liftpurse do *stall* thee to a rogue, and henceforth it shall be lawful for thee to *cant* for thy living in all places."

Liftpurse thus had a long career. His fast horse, his pistols, the daring with which he stopped and terrified small bands of peaceable country traders out of their wallets made admirable stories. His fame might have grown like that of the famous Ratsey up in Northamptonshire who is still at large,[1] and he become a sort of Robin Hood, if now, in a most inglorious manner, the devil having saved him so long had not decided to abandon him.

Stripped of his halo Hal Liftpurse appears a most cow-

[1] He was at last betrayed and hanged in 1605.

ardly commonplace scoundrel who has perpetuated his exploits through the sheer inefficiency of the peace officers. In any case all Boroughport talks of him: the women vow he is handsome; the lads almost envy his gyves and handcuffs—they decorate his notoriety, and there is infinite curiosity when the assize comes on and the prisoner's case is disposed of.

The very fame of Liftpurse provides him in prison with plenty to eat and drink and a certain grinning deference from his keepers. The plight of the obscurer prisoners however is sufficiently miserable. Master Locktight presides over the public jail in Boroughport, vulgarly known as the Clink. He is a sufficiently honest man so that Hal's companions still at large are unable to raise a sufficient sum to compass their leader's escape. The moment a prisoner is conducted inside he hears the dread word "Garnish." He then must pay his keepers liberal fees, based partly on his alleged crime and probable social condition. If he is liberal he can then command a tolerable room, luxurious food and drink, and the free access of friends. If he is poverty-stricken probably the turnkeys will strip him of any valuables the constables have left about him or, failing that, of his coat or doublet, and fling him into a black dungeon where it is only the mercy of God if he does not starve. He must also pay another fee (or part with more garments) to provide a sousing round of drink to all the earlier prisoners who welcome him into their brotherhood. Should he fail in this there are a thousand ways for making his life one torment.

The Boroughport Clink is neither better nor worse than its more famous London contemporaries, such as the Fleet, the Cage, the Marshalsea, the Compter (especially for debtors), the King's bench, and the rest, where, as a writer pungently puts it, "prisoners are lodged like hogs and fed like dogs." Of course every prison is a perfect pesthouse; "prison sickness" often clears an entire jail without waiting for the assize, and a few years ago at Boroughport the contagion spread so during the trials that it swept off the high justice, the sheriff, half the jurymen, and a whole pack of lawyers, as well as a dozen rogues who thus cheated the hangman.

The abuses of the prisons are the same all over England. Master Locktight has been appointed by the town magistrates. So far from receiving a stipend he has bought his office by a round sum paid to the corporation and is allowed to recoup himself by his extortions. Thus he not merely charges fees for food, bedding, and fire, but actually collects a sixpence "fee for irons" every time a fellow's fetters have to be put on or struck off. Let the jury declare a prisoner innocent, let even the high judge say "discharged"; the blameless unfortunate cannot quit Master Locktight's hospitality until all arrears of jail fees have been discharged. Perfectly innocent men thus can lie in durance long months or even years until their friends raise the sum wanted or the jailer thinks his guests may die on his hands.

Such a fellow as Liftpurse is snugly lodged (when not on exhibition) in a well-barred strong room, but the run of alleged felons are allowed to rattle about in their gyves in the filthy central hall of the prison. Here men and women (not the most prudish) swig, gamble, riot, and curse all the day long. The sexes are allowed to be together constantly and the moral condition of the Clink is indescribable. Since, however, Boroughport is a much smaller place than London the company of the actual prisoners is seldom joined from time to time by rascals who have been at large but who know that a good jail is the last place constables and watchmen will think of searching, when the magistrates compel them to scour the streets and seize suspicious characters. In London the regular fee for an over night's lodging in a prison is four pence; also knowing felons can often get the privilege of going out for an entire day with a keeper who will not watch queer practices too closely. The regular price for this favor is twentypence for a whole day and tenpence for half a day. "But" (sighs Master Locktight) "we do not dwell in London and peevish people might cavil at such practices." Nevertheless every now and then a prisoner mysteriously disappears from the Clink in the nighttime. The Mayor and Aldermen may grumble but the jailer is undisturbed unless the runaway is a notorious fellow like Liftpurse.

The Clink is sharply divided into two wards, although the inmates of the two sections often are allowed to mingle. The second ward is the debtor's prison. Imprisonment for debt is as common as rainy weather. Most of the victims are young spendthrifts who are fair prey for usurers, or slippery "cozeners" who have slid close to fraud and embezzlement, but every now and then an honest but unfortunate tradesman or farmer is seized under a writ, and he then enjoys Master Locktight's company until he can discharge his debt, or until his creditors are tired of paying the fees for keeping him. Debtors are usually kept in shackles but they are allowed to see their friends frequently and often can pursue their handicrafts in the prison. If they have any means they can order in good food and furniture. But the run of debtors are of course almost penniless. Such "poor debtors" are beyond words miserable. The jailer gives them just enough food to keep them from escaping by way of the undertaker. As you go along the street by the Clink you see a little window, heavily barred, and behind it a woebegone emaciated face.

"Alms for the poor debtors for the love of God!" groans a voice. This form of begging is a recognized institution. The voice is probably that of luckless Cuthbert Wantpenny. Years ago he was a self-respecting grocer, but in an evil hour went surety for a friend. The friend disappeared; Wantpenny's little property was seized, and for lack of twenty pounds after its sale his body was taken. That may have been six years ago. He is helpless, hopeless, in rags, and starved till his ribs stick out. His stony-hearted creditor believes that he has a brother who is a prosperous yeoman up in Wiltshire. Can he not be driven into paying Cuthbert's debt? In hopes thereof the Master Criper will let his victim stay a year longer—but in the meantime "death will doubtless bail him out."

But now it is assize time and Hal Liftpurse and his companions begin to lose part of their swagger. The details of royal justice we gladly omit, merely saying that one of the Queen's high judges has come down on circuit to Boroughport, that all the justices of the peace have come down to sit with him; a perfect swarm of lawyers has assembled, dandies parade about in their bravery, and sober yeomen appear alike to answer their jury summons and do much trading. Some of Hal's professional friends are in evidence in the crowds, for Justice Solemn has his purse taken while he goes to hear prayers at St. Michael's just before the opening of the session.

The court sits in the great hall of the gild house. There is the usual procession of the red-robed judge, the parti-colored gowns, blue and green, of the serjeants at law, the sad-colored gowns of the ordinary barristers and solicitors, the coifs and the caps, the white wands of the gold-laced sheriff, the tipstaves and bailiffs and all the other paraphernalia for making justice awesome to the multitude. This is most necessary, for so inefficient are what could be called the police, it is reckoned that only one person in five who ought to be laid by the heels for felony is ever indicted and plenty more escape by hook or by crook betwixt arrest and trial. There is ordinarily no regular public prosecutor, but that advantage to the defendant is offset by the fact that alleged felons are allowed counsel only on matters of law, not of evidence, and that the judge takes a most vigorous part in examining all the witnesses and is continually expressing his mind.

Most of the cases at the session are civil—contracts, torts, and the like. This is what fattens the great buzz of lawyers. The pleadings are indescribably technical. Much of the verbiage in the documents is in a jargon which to the outrage of Cicero is called Latin. The least slip in the formulas probably makes his Lordship throw out the whole suit. From any discussion of this common law of England we pray humbly to be excused, but at last the final case of wrangling heirs is settled until their solicitors can draft new papers, and the judge can give attention to offenses against the Queen's peace.

The letter of the criminal law is terrific, the list of felonies is startling, and the penalty almost invariably death —death for conspiracy against the Queen and death too for carrying horses into Scotland, stealing hawks' eggs, or taking goods from a dead man. On the other hand the law has some curious loopholes. It is hanging to steal a horse outright by violence; but to get one by fraudulence means only to pay a fine of forty shillings and stand all day in the pillory. "Cozenage" (swindling and cheating) is in general only lightly dealt with—putting a great premium on using your wits instead of your fingers to get rich. One of the first cases before his Lordship is of the son of a good yeoman charged with deer stealing in Squire Oldcastle's deer park. There is a certain jocularity when the case is called. Plenty of brisk young gentlemen take their chances with rabbits and venison and nobody shuns their company. The defendant promptly pleads guilty and is sentenced as per statute to three months' imprisonment and payment of triple damages. The court orders Master Locktight to "use him well" and the deer stealer will probably spend his three months in prison ruining himself with strong ale.[1]

Petty offenses of course are dealt with directly by the lesser magistrates. Boroughport has a whole series of sumptuary laws such as those against giving false measure, which was punished by the mayor only the other day by making the offending green grocer sit in the stocks for three hours with his false scales hung over his head and a paper pinned on his breast "For bad measure." Of course he can never vend again in Boroughport. Almost any day there is the sight of a sturdy beggar who has defied ordinary stockings, floggings, and warnings being burned through the gristle of his ear with a red-hot iron. If he then will not turn to honest toil his next reward will be the gallows. Then too there are the female backsliders. About twice per month the mayor has to order the ducking stool. Beldame Martha lately drove her neighbors frantic by her incessant quarreling and vituperations. She was cooled and quieted by being set in the ducking stool and held fast with iron staples and locks until this open seesaw could be dragged by ropes and wheels down to the river where (to the admiration of all youths and maidens) she was dipped thrice in the water—then released to drag herself home again, almost drowned.

Last year an extremely profligate "bona roba" (of the tribe of Rahab) was stripped to her waist, dragged about

---

[1] According to familiar tradition young Shakespeare was taken on the lands of Sir Thomas Lucy thus offending, and after the usual penalty had to leave Stratford for London "to his great advancement."

the streets at the tail of a cart, ducked soundly, then forced
to stand "doing penance" in only a sheet all through Sunday morning prayers at St. Michael's—many of the congregation regarding her more than they did the rector.
All these nice matters the Queen's judge scorns to concern
himself with; he does however confirm the sentence of
the magistrates that Arthur Backbite, who has openly railed
against the Corporation of Boroughport, the Laws of England, and (fearful to recite!) the mysteries of "the Queen's
justice" itself, should lose his ears. They are presently
cropped off with clumsy snippers in a grand ceremony at
the market place. By a special leniency of the court Backbite's wounds are seared with a red-hot iron lest he bleed
too much.

All this is small coin for the good people of Boroughport—"no hangings yet." Furthermore, the court being in a
lenient mood and influential cousins suddenly coming forward, the two priggers of prancers taken with Hal Liftpurse are given another lease of life. It appears that although they have undoubtedly stolen horses this has been
done without violence, burglary, or putting anybody in
bodily fear. They are therefore advised to "plead their
clergy."

Under the old church priests were given special privileges before the law. This has been extended to all "clerks"
—*i.e.*, people who can read and write. Only the less serious
felonies come under the privilege, and in theory common
clowns must go to the gallows for sheer illiteracy. But any
prisoner charged with a "clergyable felony" promptly learns
by rote—be he ever so unschooled—the famous "Neck
Verse" which he is always asked to read, and no other.
It is Psalm 51:1: *"Have mercy upon me, O God, according
to thy loving kindness: according to the multitude of thy
tender mercies blot out my transgressions."* The two horse

[205]

thieves mumble through the verse, and are forthwith branded on the right hand with a red-hot iron. The scar will tell any justice, if they are taken again, that they are old offenders. A second conviction inevitably means the gallows; but with their permanent warning they are immediately turned loose, free after paying their jail fees, to join the curious multitude that follows the mortal exit of their hero Hal Liftpurse.

No benefit of clergy for highway robbery. His Lordship, after a brief conference with Sir Walter, satisfies himself that the fellow is undoubtedly guilty; the session is becoming tedious, and not one terrorizing sentence has been passed. The court therefore acts promptly and takes unusual pains that no relative or boon companion of Liftpurse is among the stolid yeomen drawn for the jury— such things frequently happen. Liftpurse has to conduct his own case, although a barrister has been feed to make a few vain quibbles about the form of the indictment. The defendant cannot subpoena witnesses nor even take the stand in his own behalf, although he is very free to interject remarks calculated to excite compassion with the jury. He has plucked up a certain courage however, puts on a brag countenance, and pleads "Not guilty, my Lord" with a loud voice.[1]

Lawyers assert with pride, "There is no torture in the courts of England." This is not strictly true. Aside from the fearful coercion used to make a prisoner answer to his indictment, when the safety of the state seems involved as in the murderous plots against Elizabeth, the suspect is hurried to the Tower of London. There, upon a warrant from the Privy Council, he can be made to groan out all he knows. Sometimes he is coerced by the "Scavenger's

---

[1] If he had refused to plead one way or the other iron weights could be laid upon him until either he answered or was pressed to death.

Daughter," an iron hoop wherein his body is compressed and held doubled up in a fearfully small compass sometimes for well over an hour. More often he is confronted with the *rack,* a large open frame of wood under which the prisoner is laid with his back to the floor. His ankles and wrists are attached by cords to two rollers set in the ends of the frame. "Do you still refuse to confess?" Instantly by levers worked in the opposite direction the wretch is lifted to the level of the frame. Hanging there he is again questioned: "Still obdurate? Another stretch." And so until the truth is shrieked out or the prisoner's bones veritably start from their sockets.

Liftpurse being merely a felon and not a traitor has no such torments to fear—something quite different from like unfortunates in France, Spain, or Germany. There are shrewd methods however of getting the truth out of stubborn suspects, such as keeping them without sleep for three or four successive nights, more expeditiously, by making them stand close against a wall with their hands pressed upon the wall as high as they can reach. Few villains after some hours of this are not in a mood to "tell all." But Liftpurse has not been tortured. The court even allows him a certain cat-and-mouse "fair play"; but the judge himself examines the witnesses, and although the prisoner is permitted to crossexamine them, the constant interposition of the court makes his efforts mostly vain. One or two of Liftpurse's old comrades who have been summoned are browbeaten by the judge into giving reluctant testimony against him. Repeatedly there are undignified wrangles between court and prisoner: "You are hanging an innocent man, your Lordship." "Mark well, you of the jury, how this scoundrel would cozen you!"

Finally the case is complete: the defendant is suffered to deliver an ingenious harangue full of Christian piety and vows of innocence—"As I hope for Salvation before my Maker." The judge sums up dryly and concisely, practically telling the jury, "as they are good subjects and good Christians," to bring in a verdict of guilty. The jury retires. These twelve sworn *legali homines* know that they will be kept without food, drink, or fire until they agree. They also know that juries that persist in acquitting after such plain directions from the court, are sometimes clapped themselves in prison and fined stiffly. Fortunately no honest man has doubts of Liftpurse's guilt, and his Lordship has graciously saved the jury any need of wasting time over the evidence. Half an hour: "Guilty, my Lord." Then the black cap, the sententious remarks as to how "The way of the transgressor is hard," ending with the fearfully solemn death sentence.

Hal Liftpurse recognizes his doom and promptly sends for Master Crabtree as the most effective person in Thorpshire to smooth his way into the next world. The case is sent up to London, and there is just delay enough to allow a reprieve to come down, if any great folk wished to bestir themselves in the matter. But poor Hal has neither any money left nor influence. Master Crabtree wisely tells him to dismiss vain hopes and prepare himself to appear for yet a more terrible tribunal. The ten days are over, the dread timbers on Gallows Hill are ready, and there are no ratholes or twinks in the law that can be invoked to win any further delay.[1]

Hal ought to comfort himself that his is only to be very ordinary and humane hanging. He is not, as in great cases of treason, to be cut down from the gallows while still alive, disembowelled immediately, and his body cut

---

[1] When the case was near London the disposition could be fearfully speedy. A certain Crosby was convicted of murder on January 25, 1591. Two days later he was ceremoniously hanged.

into four quarters and thrown into a fire. He will not be burned alive—as was the woman over in Somersetshire convicted of murdering her husband. He will not be boiled alive in a cauldron as was that cook Rose, up in Rochester, who poisoned to death two persons. Not being a pirate nor a foul murderer he will not even be tarred and hung in chains on the gallows until his body slowly rots away.

The day has come. We hasten over it more lightly than does half of Boroughport which throngs the street. The cart sets out from Master Locktight's under the guard of the sheriff and many constables, for there is plenty of loose talk of "rescue." Liftpurse has found means to dress himself in tawny taffeta like a court gallant. In his buttonhole is a great posy. Nevertheless Master Crabtree assures us he is making a most edifying end, has repented heartily of his sins, and proffered thanks to God that he is cut off now before he can add to the list of his crimes. The chaplain rides in the cart reading and rereading the assigned prayers. The men and boys sympathetically shout; the girls gasp, "He's so handsome!" As the procession passes the hospital of St. Giles one of the male nurses as per custom presents the prisoner with a great bowl of ale—his last refreshment in this world. Liftpurse is observed to smack his lips.

Gallows Hill at last. In the coigns of vantage crowd numerous gentle folk, including Captain Andrew, Mistress Anne, and various young squires and ladies of friendly acquaintance. The cart halts; the prisoner in a quavering but fairly continuous voice assures Master Crabtree that he dies in charity with all men and beseeches all the lads of Thorpshire to take heed by his example and mend their ways. The chaplain utters a torturing lengthy prayer, then Tom Hemprope skillfully performs his office. The cart is withdrawn. The victim does not suffer more than ten minutes by the town clock. Soon all the multitude is drifting chattering homeward—all save Dr. Bleeder and Surgeon Veinknife; they are already chaffering with the hangman about the disposition of the highwayman's corpse.

Time fails us to speak of many everyday matters touching the treatment of the poor and the beggars and vagabonds. Very dimly it is being understood that many unhappy mortals need neither thoughtless charity nor brutal punishment. A body of laws is being built up providing for the systematic levy of funds in each parish for poor relief, for the opening of workhouses where the parish provides flax, thread, wool, and iron for making up into coarse articles and commodities. There is a gradual tightening up in the absurd "licenses to beg" issued by the justices. Besides the jails for criminals there are developing workhouses where not merely male vagabonds can be put to steady labor, but their female companions placed in women's wards under some "strong woman" as matron. All this means a gradual relief of the worthy poor. It also means something which the average vagabond hates far more than the chance of an occasional stocking and whipping, or even the remotest chance of a ride in the gallows cart—hard, continuous work.

During the seventeenth century England will still witness plenty of highwaymen and other picturesque criminals, but the golden days of tramp life, sturdy beggars, and vagabondage are over. The workhouses plus the increasing contentment of the rural classes will clear the roads of the great army of the idle and the unfortunate.[1]

---

[1] The great and effective Poor Law of Elizabeth, which for over a century brought remarkable benefit to England, was enacted in 1601. In the earlier 1590's the handling of poor relief, vagabondage, etc., was entirely in a state of transition.

¶ *Chapter* XV: Concerning Fairies, The Devil, and Witchcraft

SO far we have considered matters which Boroughport and Hollydean count tangible and the plain knowledge of Christians; but there is a vast unseen world around us, and about its nature even wise men differ. Sir Walter is counted a very solid-headed gentleman but he never thinks of questioning the existence of a personal Devil any more than he does of a personal God. He readily believes that certain alchemists and astrologers have decent fact behind them, though granting that most of the gentry he has met are cozening rascals. He firmly believes in the reality of witchcraft, although he keeps his right to declare that old Mother Herbsell is falsely accused.

Sir Walter however is branded "almost atheistical" by his neighbor Squire Heavypate. That gentleman is really guilty of superstition "of a godless religion and a devout impiety." If a hare suddenly crosses his path very likely he will turn back from a journey. If he meets a snake he imagines mischief. If at table the saltcellar falls over toward him he turns white and red, and demands that the waiter fillip some drops of wine upon his legs. When he sneezes he expects all his companions to take off their hats. Finally in his pocket he always carries an *Erra Pater,* an almanac marked with the lucky and unlucky days.

Passing to meaner folk we find small tradesmen, craftsmen, and still more all manner of rustics (not to mention their daughters and wives) live in a world that takes ghosts, fairies, goblins, and fiends entirely for granted.

Young Andrew and Anne, being much cast with the servants while they were growing up, have been filled with ideas that never in their most skeptical adult moments will they quite dismiss. Captain Andrew has been to the university and fought in great battles; for all that his hand goes instinctively toward his sword hilt when he goes by the churchyard on a dark night.

In 1584 an Oxford student, Master Reginald Scot, put forth a book which savors of sheer impiety if not rank atheism. In his *Discovery of Witchcraft,* by much astute carnal reasoning, he casts grave doubts upon the existence of witchcraft at all, and in so doing flings his stones at innumerable fond beliefs among the unlearned commonalty. Master Scot's book is so dangerous that if King James of Scotland ever comes to the English throne he will doubtless have the volume burned by the common hangman; still it contains matters worth quoting. For example, he tells how children are regularly made to fear their own shadows by "old wives' tales" of "bullbeggars, witches, urchins, elves, hags, fairies, satyrs, kit-with-the-candle-stick, dwarfs, giants, imps, changelings, the Incubus, Robin Goodfellow, Hob Goblin, Tom Tumbler, and other 'bugs.'" Anybody around Hollydean will tell you stories of "fairy rings" on the turf, and of how the sheep will not crop them because the "good people" dance there by night. Also in the region there are several miserable children looked upon as changelings: they are puny, wizened, half-witted infants, and very probably the fairies stole the beautiful human children right out of their cradles and put these ailing, puking brats in their stead.

Most farm hands dwell in constant terror of being "overlooked," and many a child has assuredly been ruined by being "overseen" at the time of its birth by some devilish practitioner. As for dreams few people are stolid enough not to give considerable heed to them. Only a little while ago Sir Walter dreamed that one of his eyeteeth was loose and that he thrust it out with his tongue. On consulting a dream book he learned that this surely meant the loss of a friend. He is now half expecting some such calamity. The dairymaids on their part are all agog against the warnings from Midsummer's Eve (June 24: the Vigil of St. John the Baptist). The bravest of them are trying to screw up courage to sit up all that night fasting on the church porch. If they do that (and don't hide their heads under their shawls) they will see all the persons destined to die in the parish in the next twelve months come and knock at the church door in the exact order in which they will take their mortal exit. Much pleasanter is such a practice as a pea's-pod wooing, which Toby Cowherd has just tried on Joan Milker. He took a pod from the pea vine, plucked it and presented it to the blushing lady. Perhaps she took pains not to shake it but certainly none of the peas spilled out—a sure omen that he will prosper if he grows bold with a tender question.

These are the barest samples of varied beliefs and usages which show that around us is a strange, unseen world whereof we poor mortals can know very little. Even such a learned personage as Master Crabtree, although always thundering against vain superstitions, will tell you "that often the future can be forecast by reverently opening the Bible at random, and taking the sense of the first verse on which your eye lights"—a sort of Christian *Sortes Virgilianæ*.

Pass now to such commonplace things as ghosts and goblins. Fortunate the Christian who after death can "sleep well," and never be obliged to wake save in Heaven or at the call of Judgment. Providence allows the dead to be constantly reappearing on earth, either because the conditions of their death do not permit them to have peace in their graves or because they have something to impart to their survivors. There are two kinds of ghosts, good and bad, but it is easy to tell the difference: the good ghosts have "a cheerful and merry countenance," and the damned "a heavy and sour look and are coal black." In any case they always appear between midnight and cockcrow, and usually "walk" in order to disclose some vile murder, to warn some kinsman or descendant or to watch over a hidden treasure. Of course they can glide through walls and doors, not to mention keyholes. They can speak only to the persons for whom they have a direct message, and then in a squeaking, gibbering voice, but other persons frequently can see them and be most certainly affrighted. Then too there are the specter dogs; these can be very dangerous to meet. Sometimes they are the foulest kind of original fiends who go around in the form of dogs seeking sheer mischief; but others are merely the spirits of wicked persons who have been given the forms of dogs as part of their punishment.

About ten miles from Hollydean there is an ancient mansion that has its "houseghost." This is an old woman who at rare intervals appears to members of the family just after midnight. Her appearance is an infallible sign that some near relative is about to perish. There are houseghosts in at least ten other old mansions up and down Thorpshire.

Most certainly it is inconvenient to be infested with a ghost, disturbing honest people by night walking, and very often "bewailing his torments" in the world. Fortunately God provides means of exorcising them. Sir Arthur has heard of a manor house near Dorchester that was direfully infested. The owner's chaplain, however, was a brave as well as godly man. The ghost was suspected to be that of a particularly wicked uncle of the present squire, who was now snugly buried in the churchyard. The chaplain went boldly up to his tomb, recited the Lord's prayer, then spurned the stone with his foot, and said in a loud voice, *"Vade ad gehennam!"* "Pack off to Hell!"—A great peace settled over the mansion; it was never troubled by a ghost again.

Much commoner and on the whole less dreadful than ghosts are fairies. There are undoubtedly great quantities of humanlike creatures round about us who are neither men, specters nor devils. Fairies are no more disbelieved in by most of the goodfolk of Thorpshire than is the existence of such countries as Turkey and Muscovy, which certainly they have never seen. Before she could talk herself Mistress Anne listened to her nurse's veracious chatter of fairies with wings of gossamer who peeped into her windows or goblins who quarreled in the thatch or tiles just over the gables. Not a child can sit in the ingle nook and listen to the incessant story-telling without hearing the "little people" made essential parts of every other tale. Is the milk sour this morning? The "little people" surely have done it. Kate Fearing was sure she saw them dancing in the moonlighted meadow just before her courage fled and she hid her head under the blanket.

The lore about the fairies is fairly systematic. We can construct quite a knowledge of them. They are genuinely "little people," shadows of humanity in miniature, full of whims, caprices, tempers, often rewarding or punishing humans, but in their own artless way. Men can only see them in "fairy time," which begins at midnight and commonly closes with the morning star though by great boldness sometimes they linger until sunrise. You can only meet them in the summer in England, for in winter they all flit off to the balmy Indies. They are immortal themselves, and if they carry off mortal children they can make them immortal by dipping them in a "virtuous well."

Such airy, graceful little beings are naturally gladsome and extremely fond of dancing, but are offended easily and can play humans most remarkable tricks. They possess some wonderful powers; for example, they can raise and disperse fogs. Sometimes they take a great fancy to a young man or woman, and to have a fairy lover is by no means impossible for mortals. Also it is quite natural for babies to have fairy godmothers, who do not steal them but assist marvelously after they have grown up.

The more regular and honest fairies are organized into a monarchy whereof the undoubted queen is Titania, a sheeny fay of the woodland, although Queen Mab, a tricky mischief-maker who robs dairies and pinches silly wenches, also claims wide allegiance. The regular king is Oberon, who holds his courts wearing a cobweb shirt, a waistcoat made of a Trent-fly's golden wing, a doublet of four-leaved "true love grass," and breeches also woven by the spiders. There are however various irregular fairies not wholly subject to Oberon's and Titania's authority; especially you may meet with Puck, Robin Goodfellow, and that most unruly Jack-o'-Lantern.

Over precise people may tell you that these are only three names for one and the same fairy, although this is vigorously denied by all the Hollydean wiseacres. It is certain the trio act very much alike. They all take delight in playing not very destructive tricks on mortals. Robin Goodfellow enjoys luring night wanderers by his cries and mutterings into brambly woods and founderous mires. He can change himself instantly into an ox, a dog, or especially a horse. Woe to the fellow who mounts him! Not twenty miles from Hollydean there has just died a yokel who swore that once in his youth he mounted a fine horse seemingly astray by the road at evening. No sooner was the beast stridden than away he went frisking and leaping over stock and stone, through woodland after woodland and at last through pools and ponds till he tossed his rider off into the freezing water.

It was Robin Goodfellow again or his double Puck who last year right in Graystone Hall, in the very next parish, when all the sewing maids were met after supper, suddenly blew out the candle and kissed the two prettiest. Also he undoubtedly pinches snoring house wenches to rouse them in the morning, and creeps into mousetraps, then leaps out with a "ho! ho!" and vanishes when you look to see if a mouse has been taken.

As for Jack-o'-Lantern he is the worst of all of them. He frequents the fens and pools, scurries along the marshes, skips over the hedgerows, and then disappears, leaving anybody who is befooled into following him floundering to his neck in slimy ditch-water. Another name for him of course is Will-o'-the-Wisp.

A really destructive fairy is called Gull. It is he that especially steals the milk and cream (though the poor cats are often blamed for it). At night he creeps into a man's bed, lies heavy on his stomach, and gives him the cramps and nightmare. He has a whole string of relatives: his brothers Patch, Pinch, and Grim, and his sisters Sib, Tib, Lick, and Lull, as noxious as he. Nevertheless Pinch is fairly popular with strict housewives for he takes special joy in visiting sluttish maids who sleep in the chimney corner, leaving the house "like a nasty dog's kennel," when they should be washing dishes or cleaning the kitchen. Such girls he nips "until their bodies are as many colors as a mackerel's back"; although servants slumbering after faithful toil he always befriends:

[217]

For to the good I do no harm,
But cover them and keep them warm.

This gives you some idea of the invisible world, but the chief potentate therein is beyond question the Devil. Good Christians have no more right to doubt the existence of the Devil than they have to question the existence of God. Andrew and Anne again have gained their lifelong notion of the Father of Lies from the talk around the servants' quarters. Says the almost satirical Master Reginald Scot, we are taught "by our mother's maids" to live in terror of "an ugly Devil, having horns on his head, fire in his mouth, a tail in his breech, eyes like a basin, fangs like a dog, claws like a bear, a skin like a nigger, and a voice roaring like a lion—whereby we start and are afraid when we hear one cry, 'Bow!'" Many authentic stories confirm this untoward aspect, though sometimes the Fiend can appear a little less dreadful; for example, in a reliable version of the fate of the famous Dr. Faustus we read that "Lucifer himself sat there after the manner of a man, but of a brown color, like a squirrel curled, and his tail turning upward on his back as the squirrels' do."

But the Scripture plainly tells us that sometimes Satan "himself is transformed into an angel of light." More frequently, especially when he has to deal with silly women, he appears as a spruce and plausible young man. Very many learned persons, overanxious for worldly knowledge, have had dealings with him, and his appearance was not overdreadful; among others such doctors as Cornelius Agrippa and the great Paracelsus are under such heavy suspicion, and probably have lost their souls. But the Adversary more often appears in horrid guise to work instant evil. Only the other day Captain Andrew brought home a pamphlet about the direful happenings at the parish church at Bungay near Norwich. One Sunday there was a terrible storm while all the good people were at prayers, and amid the noise and lightnings the Devil as a black dog deliberately entered the building and "wrung the necks" of two worshipers even as they knelt, so that they dropped dead; then he clawed up a third man's back so that his skin shriveled up "like leather scorched in a hot fire." [1] "A lightning bolt crashing down on frightened people," so vows the Captain to his fellows, but the most skeptical of them in his heart of hearts is not quite sure about it.

To fight off the Fiend good Protestants cannot be quite so free as are Catholics to exorcise him with holy water and frankincense, "to scald, broil and sizzle the devil"; nor have they the same confidence that the power of the Cross and the Sacrament can "torment the Devil and make him roar." Still he can usually be kept at a distance by loudly pronouncing the name of "God." Ringing church bells also can be effective. There is nothing like a good clangor from the steeple for scattering the collection of evil spirits who assist with if they do not create the greater storms. When old Goodman Wainwright lay dying, the parish bell was kept ringing all night by zealous friends to scare off the ministers of Hell who might be lurking right at his bedside to catch his soul as it popped out of his body. There are irrefutable stories of how on such occasions church bells refused to ring. Brave fellows investigated. There was the Devil sitting right on the clapper to keep it from tolling.

To deal with ordinary, capricious fairies and insure good luck in common matters much less drastic charms are sufficient. Sir Walter recently burst his spur leathers and had to put on a new pair. His serving man first threw three beans over the threshold to insure against a second mis-

[1] An actual pamphlet.

hap. His master laughed but did not prevent him. Lady Catherine herself and Mistress Anne let their maids give them a bay leaf, or better still a small garland of bays if they have to ride over to Boroughport when there is real chance of being caught in a thunderstorm. Down in the cottages no plowman ever thinks of paring his nails on Fridays or Sundays, but Mondays and Tuesdays are extra lucky days for the operation, and if a lover cuts his on Saturday he (or she) is very likely to meet the other party delightfully on Sunday. After the execution at Boroughport Tom Hemprope chipped up part of the gallows beam and sold the bits to pretty solid citizens. They would hang their purchases around their necks in little bags to fend off ague. As for the milkmaids, in every dairy if the butter making goes slowly, you can hear the singsong of the girls:

> Come butter, come!
> Come butter, come!
> Peter stands at the gate,
> Waiting for a buttered cake,
> Come butter, come!

All this goes to show how even honest, simple folk can assist themselves by the right charms invoked upon the invisible Powers. But what shall we say of those people who claim special ability in dealing with the mysterious? Among these, perchance, it is right to number the astrologers and alchemists, although many of them appear to be men of deep science, patronized by the mighty and vehemently disclaiming un-Christian compacts with the Devil.

Astrology is in considerable favor at London, and Boroughport is large enough to entertain intermittently a professor of the art of star reading. A few years ago there appeared a venerable gentleman with an inordinately long beard. He called himself Master Sidereus and claimed to be a pupil of the school of the famous Cornelius Agrippa of Pavia. Soon he was making good money casting the nativities of children born to wealthy couples, always making the stars predict great fortune for them. He picked out lucky days for important business transactions, resolved difficult family questions, and claimed to be able to recover stolen property. He was always talking about his friend the mighty Doctor John Dee, the Queen's personal astrologer; of the Pythagorean music of the spheres caused by the revolution of one heavenly surface upon another, and of how a comet had predicted the death of King Henry III of France.

All this was making him fairly wealthy and important, despite the fact that Master Crabtree and other Puritan divines cried out against astrology—"the bastard science," the foolish daughter of a wise mother (astronomy), and warned their hearers that "it is the wickedness of our own hearts which draweth us to evil, not the stars and planets." But in an unlucky day Master Sidereus was caught being hired by a Recusant gentleman to cast the Queen's horoscope—presumably to learn when her Majesty would die. The law instantly clamped upon his employer, who barely escaped the gallows; while the astrologer suddenly vanished from Boroughport—probably fleeing to Germany where his kind were in great acceptance at the courts of petty princes.

With Sidereus had been a smooth companion, Master Dulcify, an alchemist. This personage wheedled several local gentlemen into giving him many broad goldpieces on the promise that they should soon have them back again a hundred times multiplied. Alchemy differs from the very young science of chemistry in that the latter is based on the principle of the indestructibility of matter, and simply studies its real varieties and nature; alchemy rests on the theory that all matter is really of a single substance (a pure assumption in the schools), and you can change one apparent substance into another more fundamental by a few occult processes. Dulcify claimed to be the friend of that Cornelius de Alneto who engaged in 1565 for a very modest pension to provide the Queen with "50,000 marks of pure gold per annum" steadily—but by some slight mishap the promising business slipped through. He talked glibly of "subliming, dulcifying and calcining," of "ablution, ceration, and fixation." He claimed to be far on the way to discovering the Philosopher's Stone and the *Aurum Potabile* (about the same thing) that conferred long life and riches; but of course his great attraction was his alleged power of turning copper or even lead into gold.

Metals, he assured his clients, are composed of earth, water, and air in varying proportions. Only use the right process and you can vary the proportion and change them all into "the perfect metal," compounded in a state of absolute perfection—namely, gold itself. Apparently he was making rapid progress on the road to riches. He showed several curious gentlemen a piece of copper whereof half it seemed had been changed to gold already; but Sir Walter, who inspected it, shook his head: "He had heard how a piece of gold copper alloy had had part of its surface copper removed by heating in charcoal apparently leaving solid gold behind." Some of his friends were less skeptical. They gave Master Dulcify large sums, and he talked of soon making his patrons "richer than the Grand Turk or the Emperor of India." Then just as they were becoming a trifle anxious and importunate—lo! he vanished from Boroughport along with Master Sidereus whose fate has been noted.

Both of these pretentious personages passed as "gentlemen" and their clients were men of wealth and respectability. Doubtless it is unfair to suggest they ever had dealings with the Devil, but as much cannot be said of certain meaner folk who practice around Thorpshire. Very near Hollydean are several old women who seem unquestionably to be witches. "Cunning women" or "wise women" are about as common as graveyards or ale houses. They are not necessarily powers of evil. Take Beldame Agnes Simple who has a very small cottage on the edge of the village. Even Master Crabtree has a friendly word for her though scolding at her practices. She is a "good witch" who has a taking manner, considerable powers of healing, is a capital nurse, and can provide many effective drugs much cheaper than the apothecary. She is lucky as a midwife, but when not otherwise employed will (if you cross her palm with silver) provide you with a few primitive charms for making the deaf hear, for keeping the scab away from the cattle, and making a girl's lover return to her. Nobody thinks of molesting Beldame Simple. At worst she is harmless, at best a parish benefactor.

But even she shudders at times lest something suddenly be caught up against her. So many "white witches" are discovered to be "black witches." Perhaps the discovery begins with a quarrel over an unsuccessful cure, or a squabble between two lovelorn girls over one swain. No matter: old women are every day found to be practicing with the Devil. For reasons best known to the Author of Evil, although wizards undoubtedly exist, his best assistants usually are found among elderly females. His most trusted lieutenant is frequently a "beldame trot" with "wrinkled face, furred brow, hairy lip, a gobber tooth, a squint eye, a squeaking voice, a scolding tongue, having a ragged coat on her back, a skullcap on her head, a spindle in her hand, and a dog

[223]

and a cat by her side." Such a woman is sure to be suspected and often enough to be seized as a black witch.

The evidence seems convincing that in foreign lands black witches (not always as ugly as just described) have perpetrated most astonishing enormities. Hardly to be questioned is the story of the young English sailor who, landing in the island of Cyprus, strayed into the house of a woman who was a witch. He bought of her some eggs. The instant he ate one he was changed into an ass and of course was left on the island by his vainly searching shipmates. For three years he had to serve the woman as her miserable beast of burden. Finally in desperation he knelt down in a churchyard (not being allowed in the church) and bowed himself so devoutly as to attract attention. A sagely suspicious magistrate examined the woman and soon racked her into confessing her crime. She was forced to restore the youth to his human shape, then was promptly burned at the stake, while her victim "returned to his country with a joyful and merry heart."

Here in England there have been no such remarkable cases, but every now and then some person dies under horribly suspicious circumstances. Carnal wisdom might say "a disease that baffles the doctors," but eminent divines know better. Bishop Jewel as far back as 1560 besought the Queen in a sermon to enforce the law against witchcraft. "Your Grace's subjects pine away even unto death, their color fadeth, their flesh rotteth, their speech is benumbed, their senses are bereft." No part of Britain is clear of witches, but they seem to be more common as you go north, and are especially numerous in Scotland where his Majesty King James is learnedly zealous against them.

To take a random case, up at Chelmsford in Essex in 1579, sixteen women, mostly very poor and of sordid morality, were caught in the law on charges of witchcraft. They were easily scared and certainly their foul Patron did not teach them clever denials. Several confessed to most amazing charges of keeping house devils for the ruin of their neighbors. One Ursley Kemp kept "a white lamb, a little gray cat, a black cat, and a black toad." All these were at her constant bidding and she had a whole retinue of other demons disguised as blackbirds. The case finally ended with three of the witches being hanged, the others barely escaped. People still argue about "mistaken mercy."

Only two years ago all Thorpshire was excited by a very typical case of witchcraft at the Boroughport assizes. First there was a boy named Darling who kept falling into fits. "Epilepsy," at first said the gossips, but very soon he began saying that in these fits he saw green angels and a green cat, and then he named a certain old woman, Alse Gooderidge, as being responsible.

Poor old Goody Alse certainly could pass for a black witch. She was an old weather-beaten crone—"hollow-eyed, untoothed, furrowed on her face, lips trembling with palsy"—who went about, it was alleged, saying *"pax, max, fax"* as some kind of spell. The charges against her were at once snapped up by Justice Zealous, the landlord of Darling's parents, a veritable terror to evildoers. Goody Alse being at last hailed to prison by constables who were half afraid to touch her, all sorts of stories were soon brought out at her examinations and the final trial. There was no doubt that in her youth she had been a "mort" (female beggar). As she grew older she had been something of an herb healer and something of a fortune teller. Plenty of rustics swore to the fact that she had cured sick people against a fee of one penny and a loaf of bread, muttering a charm over them. This she did not in the least deny but vowed that her only charm was this:

[225]

Thy loaf in my hand,
And thy penny in my purse:—
Thou art never the better,
And I am never the worse.

All this was very sinful but possibly not felonious. However soon a whole volley of charges were flung against the prisoner. In her direct neighborhood there had been a run of cases of sheep with the "giddies," hogs with the "mumps," and horses with the "staggers." Alse had certainly demanded alms of the owners of the creatures, had scowled and muttered so maliciously that one sagacious farmer nailed four horseshoes and bunches of pine and rue over his stable door—undoubtedly the reason *his* cattle were not afflicted. But what undid the defendant was the testimony of many small and very excited children, who had heard Goody Alse talking most confidentially to the black cat she kept around her cottage.

After all this Justice Zealous took round measures. The statute against torture can be winked at if the cause is good. Alse had tight new boots placed on her feet and then was set so close to a fire that the extreme heat caused extreme pain. Still she held out while Squire Zealous began consulting with his assisting clergymen as to other tests. No real witch can say the Lord's Prayer without stumbling. She can only weep three tears and these only from the left eye. If you tie her right thumb to her left toe, and her left thumb to her right toe and fling her into water—if guilty she will not sink. Fortunately just as they were considering this last test she gave way. Amid much screaming she confessed that her black cat was named "Satan," and was really an emissary of the Devil. She had also three other imps—dun-chickens called Pluck, Catch, and White—whom she called by smacking her lips. She had blasted corn by spells, had sent snakes into a meadow to suck dry the udders of the cows, had "overlooked" an unbaptized child so that it grew up an idiot, and as for Goody Long-tongue (who owed her six shillings and was a chief accuser) she would have killed her cow except that the owner prudently had tied a piece of mountain ashwood to its tail.

Amid her screams and moans the one offense she would not confess to was that of stealing away babies, and seething up their fat and bowels for making an ointment which would enable her to ride through the air along with other witches to meet the Devil himself. However, if this last charge was not quite proved, all the others were ten times over. The final trial was a most perfunctory affair. The Court complimented Squire Zealous, the jury never left the box, but Alse Gooderidge, by a great stretch of mercy, was hanged and not burned. At the gallows, to the general scandal, she repudiated the confession as "forced out of her" and died gasping out something about innocence. Thorpshire generally agrees it was saved from a terrible public menace, though Captain Andrew (to his pious mother's regret) sometimes hints: "Perhaps the old hag was harshly dealt with."

Such an ordinary case is nothing to what in 1591 they unearthed up in Scotland. Here King James personally had a superior witch, Geillis Duncane, and her assistant, Agnes Sampson, tried, "the pilliwinks" put on their fingers, and soon the fearful truth came out, although not until their bodies had been searched for "devil's marks" and one token found on Geillis's "fore crag," or the front of her throat.[1] Agnes however was the most communicative. She

[1] Torture was legal in Scotland. The unhappy women also had their heads "bound and wrenched with a rope." This Scotch case of 1591 is famous historically.

[227]

confessed that on the night of All-hallows' E'en, she with two hundred other witches all went to sea in sieves and while drinking merrily flagons of wine came to the church in North Berwick. Then they landed, took hands, and danced a reel, singing with one voice:

> Commer, go ye, commer, go ye!
> If ye will not go before, let me!

While they danced thus Geillis played for them on a jew's-harp. Next they went into the church and here was the Devil himself in the likeness of a swarthy man. He stood upon the pulpit, and (shame for Christians to recite it!) made every witch do homage to him in his well-known hellish way—by kissing him directly under the tail. After this all the witches returned to the sea and rode home again in their sieves.

Agnes Sampson went on to confess how she had hung up a black toad by the heels for three days and gathered its venom as it dropped into an oyster shell. If she could only have smeared this on some bit of dirty linen belonging to King James he must have died. In this she failed, but she did manage to christen a cat with the King's name and carried it out to sea in a sieve and drowned it just as his Majesty was on a ship from Denmark. This caused a terrible storm but God mercifully brought the King to land.

Needless to say all these Scottish witches were packed off to damnation by the executioner according to best North Country methods. No such case has there been near Hollydean, but this shows what the Devil can inspire his votaries to do. The whole problem is full of wonders. Can witches whiz through the air on broomsticks? King James after careful investigation has just affirmed that they can, but not for a great distance. They can only fly "so

far as they can retain their breath." "Good lungs, therefore, appear to be needful for Satan's service."

Around Hollydean the truth of all the foregoing is taken
for granted by everybody but perhaps the overdoubting
Captain Andrew. He has read Master Scot's almost atheistical book and says he would like to come on a plain case
of witchcraft, where the defendant was not a feeble old
woman, where she was not put in bodily fear, and where
the witnesses were not credulous rustics and imaginative
children.

ILLUSTRATIONS TO "SHEPHERD'S CALENDAR," 1597. JULY.

"MERRY ENGLAND!" Yet what is so "merry" in all this toiling, and schooling, and grave piety, and punishing the wicked? We have come to Hollydean on days of honest work; may not our license carry to the days of honest mirth and pleasure?

Her Majesty's subjects have long hours of labor, but then in mitigation there are many holidays. England is so far north that in midsummer there is plenty of light late into the evening. In winter it gets dark so soon that work has to stop early—then there are plenty of sports that can while away the time in dim candle light. The English are a lusty, hearty race, as already remarked, with plenty of the animal still about them. They enjoy very simple and decidedly violent and primitive amusements, nor is there much delicacy and humanity in certain popular pleasures. It is a common enough sport to hang a cat in a leather bottle and shoot at it with crossbows. The length of time poor Tabby can survive this brutal archery probably gives the basis for her proverbial "nine lives."

Other outlets for animal spirits are less cruel though even less sophisticated. Almost any day Hollydean's parish church bell begins to ring like something possessed. Fire? Are the Spaniards raiding the coast? Nobody in the least stops his business. Simply a few idlers at the ale house have suddenly caught the notion of "a turn at the ropes" and rush over to the churchyard. They take passionate delight in hearing the clamor in the steeple, and one fellow will relieve another, perhaps keeping up the din for hours.

until arms are weary and possibly some rascal falls fainting.[1]

When the schoolboys escape from their prison, very likely they will fall to "filliping the toad"—putting a toad on one end of a short board placed across a small log, and striking the other end with a cudgel—thus flinging the luckless creature high in the air. An equally desirable pastime is plucking live geese—but geese are more valuable than toads and boys caught at this are likely to rub themselves after a hard whipping. As the lads grow older they will invariably take infinite pleasure in wrestling, pitching the bar and fighting with singlestick, and that extremely violent free fight called football. As spectators they will be equally keen for cockfighting and bear- or bull-baiting, and of course every fellow (and lass) who is not wrong in the head is decidedly fond of dancing.

If you would move as a gentleman, physical accomplishments are even more needful. It is part of your regular education "to run comely," "to vault lustily," "to play at all weapons," "to shoot well with bow or gun," and to be able to leap, wrestle, and swim. In addition you must be a passable dancer, sing tolerably, play the lute, and hold your own at hawking, hunting, and tennis. It was not the least of the glory of Sir Philip Sidney that, besides being a poet and a wit, an accomplished courtier, and an equally accomplished soldier, he was versed in "all the sports." Thousands of young gentlemen try to follow his example.

In the long evenings and during the harsh winter, however, one cannot bowl on the green or follow the dogs. Lutes, viols, and virginals can become tiresome, and there are various quiet diversions at which, however, Precisians

---

[1] Well known is the delight John Bunyan took, years later than this narrative, in bell-ringing during what he considered a very wanton youth.

sometimes raise their eyebrows. Least do they cavil at the ancient and royal game of chess, at draughts (in another land and age checkers), and at tables (otherwise backgammon). The Queen loved to play at draughts and chess with her old tutor Roger Ascham as long as that famous worthy lived; and chess has always something aristocratic about it. We fear nevertheless these games call for too much noble knowledge to be popular with the run of Englishmen. They like other and less thoughtful amusements. The standard indoor diversions will thus be listed not long after the age of Gloriana: "cards, tables, dice, shovelboard, chess play, shuttlecock, billiards, music, masks, singing, dancing, Yuletide games, frolics, jests, riddles, 'questions and commands,' and merry tales."[1] Here surely is variety enough for learned and simple; but beyond doubt the princes among these diversions—if not the ones most in pious favor—are cards and dice.

Cards began their sway in England about 1450.[2] Henry VIII, always careful of his subjects' morals, vainly tried by law to restrict their use to the lax season around Christmas. Now it is a regular thing at a dinner party after the table is cleared for a waiter to bring in a "fair silver bowl full of dice and cards," and for the host to enjoin, "Now, Masters, who is disposed—fall to!" In many circles he may add, to start the excitement, "Here is my twenty pounds—win it and wear it!"

There are many card games, of which we will only name —primero, trump, gleek, new cut, knave out of doors, nuff, noddy, pace; but by far the most fashionable and popular is primero. Originally it was a Spanish game brought to England when Philip of Spain came to wed Queen Mary.

[1] Listed in Burton's *Anatomy of Melancholy,* first published in 1621.
[2] It is curious to note that until after 1600, a pack of cards was technically known as a pair of cards—whatever their number.

Now it is in vast favor at her Majesty's Court. It is played incessantly right in the august Presence Chamber, Sir Walter Raleigh in particular being devoted to it. The preachers are scandalized at the amount of gold that can pass of an afternoon between noble if not royal hands. Among very rich hosts who wish to put their guests at ease, it is customary to distribute sums of money among the players, to be gamed for after dinner. Sir Christopher Hatton, the royal favorite, has been known thus to put £1000 at the disposal of his "gambling guests," and then to order that the stakes should be reckoned at only twelve pence to the pound—to make the wagers even greater.

There are other card games of the highest acceptance. Maw, played by two to six persons with a pack of only thirty-six cards, is gaining at court upon primero. Gleek, played by three persons with forty-four cards, has its votaries, and then there is trump which somebody will develop into whist. But primero still holds its own. It is with this game that the Hollydeans kill time for twopenny stakes during the long evenings, and Sir Walter frequently loses or gains a few shillings to or from his friends the mayor and aldermen after they have finished any business at the Gild Hall.

Cards undoubtedly ruin many fortunes and demoralize the young, but they cannot compare with the mischief wrought by dice. To throw dice requires the brains of a sheep, and the magic cubes are capable of infinite practicing at the hands of cunning scoundrels; although the "card cozener" is certainly in the land, giving his pasteboards private pinches with his nails, marking the backs with fine spots of ink, and sometimes getting a "friend" to sit behind the victim and signal his hand and plays.

But where a shilling is lost through marked cards a pound goes off through cogged dice. The falseness of dice and

[233]

dicers' oaths is proverbial. To succeed with bad dice calls for a certain sleight of hand. Young Master Innocent, a cousin of Captain Andrew, was lately induced to "adventure a few throws" with a smooth fellow, Master Anybody, he met at a Boroughport ordinary. At first Master Innocent seemed fairly successful. Then luck turned amazingly against him. He had lost all his purse, his fine ring, and was just risking his silver shoe buckles when Captain Andrew entered the tavern. "Let me see these dice, sirrah!" Instantly the stranger started for the door, but the suspicious landlord stopped him. The dice proved to have been cogged with quicksilver. The gamester had dexterously substituted them for the honest ones which he had slipped up his sleeve. Anybody was held and forced to confess that he made a living by false gaming; that the dice had been made for him by the notorious "Bird of Holton," who, although confined in the King's Bench prison in London, was allowed to make false dice and sell them to any applicant.

The cheat brazenly boasted that he had sworn to Master Innocent to play honestly with him, "by Saint Martin" and "by salt," the victim not understanding that such oaths were to be taken as meaning the precise opposite of what they seemed to affirm. The dice used were arranged to throw "the main chance" (some number between five and nine inclusive, always in a combination favoring the manipulator).

By that time the ordinary was full of angry people and Master Anybody was fain to plead for his life. When all Master Innocent's money had been given back and the rest of the fellow's purse had been confiscated for the poor, he was allowed to go—after Captain Andrew's and Master Innocent's serving men had tied him to a post and flogged him till their arms were tired. Probably he has slunk off to renew his work at Portsmouth, but it is too much trouble to prosecute at law.

When the weather gets better few honest Englishmen prefer indoor gaming to outdoor pleasures. Already we have noted the delight taken in merely ringing the bells. Feasts and festivals, funerals, marriages, election of town officers, royal birthdays, all are reason enough for the prodigious clangor! For miles out of Boroughport along with the singing of the larks you can often hear the silvery pealing of the distant bells. Then on the fine evenings there is a constant lighting of bonfires. Old country folk tell you this is to drive off the dragons and other evil spirits constantly hovering in the air, and plenty of uneasy mortals will use this notion as the apology for setting off a great blaze now on this hill and now on that. Besides the bonfire and the bell ringing, there are the frequent and uproarious "wakes." Nominally these are to celebrate the dedication of a church. All night long people are supposed to "watch" piously in the building, and in the morning they certainly give themselves over to the crudest forms of rural merriment. The church wardens vend "bread, wine, and ale" (presumably for the profiting of the parish), and the hinds certainly empty their pockets while guzzling; hawkers and pedlars set up their stalls in the very churchyard, and half-drunken youths are soon breaking their heads at cudgel play—all somehow in the name of religion!

But most sports are of a more orderly character. The usual day for them is Sunday. If it is a fine day after Hollydean Parish has heard Sir Charles go through his prayers and homily, out they stream into the golden weather. The viols are sawing on the green, the local ale house has just broached a tun; all the youths and girls begin dancing, and plenty of the married men too, barring those unfortunates condemned by jealous wives "to sigh away Sunday." The great folk of the Hall would be a little unpopular if Captain Andrew and Mistress Anne did not let themselves take a few measures with this good yeoman's daughter and that good yeoman's son; Sir Andrew and Lady Catherine for a few minutes beam exalted approval. Master Crabtree sighs because of the world's evil, but thanks God nevertheless that the whole company breaks off well before curfew, and does not keep up strange practices well into the night (as in some villages) and also that the revels are all under the control of "discreet and substantial men"—as by Royal Proclamation of 1569 provided.

Over at Boroughport on certain Sundays a juggler takes his post by the market cross. Ned Nimble can make balls multiply, vanish, or combine into one large one. He can pass a coin through a table, work numerous card tricks, and alter grain in a box from rye into barley by uttering some "magic words." If he sees plenty of silver ready when the hat goes around he can actually swallow knives, push a piece of lead into one eye and out the other, and really "plunge a dagger in his guts" and recover immediately. How can he do it? Doubtless by having a false breast and belly of pasteboard hidden under his jerkin, plus a bladder full of sheep's blood which will squirt out in a most life-like (or deathlike!) manner. Under all he has slipped a metal plate to protect his body. They tell a story of a juggler who made bright shillings by this trick until the day he became so drunk he forgot to put on the plate. He got some one to stab him, fell down with no pretended groan, and soon miserably died.

Ned Nimble's great feat, however, is the "Decolation of John the Baptist." This he will only do before a worshipful patron and a round fee in advance. But right before unbelieving eyes he will exhibit a bowing victim and an executioner. A shawl is held before the scaffold momentarily, "a fearful swishing of steel and groan is heard," and lo! right before all doubters there on the scaffold lies the headless body and at some distance away a dissevered head upon a platter. Mistress Anne explains with superiority to her younger sister that it is understood that the head belongs to one of Nimble's assistants and the body to another, and that clever means are used to conceal the remainder of their anatomies. But how all the prentices and maids are shouting and shrieking!

Nimble does not exhibit his tricks on Sundays when there are too many counter attractions. These are likely to be cockfighting and bear- and bull-baiting, and Sunday is a very proper day for such diversions. Cockfighting, to be sure, is frowned on by many non-Puritanical people, but the schoolboys and not a few of their betters delight in it. In London there are three very famous public cockpits, seldom vacant long. There is another in St. James Park near Whitehall, especially for royalty. The Queen herself looks in pretty frequently. Good fighting cocks must be of a stout large breed, with very long collops hanging down on either side of their beaks; these, however, before a cock is sent into actual battles must be cut away close to the head, or the adversary will take hold and gain an easy victory. Aside from Sundays the great day for sportive schoolboys is Shrove Tuesday (just before Lent). As per custom Master Nicholas Thwacker graciously unbends and lets the boys exhibit their fighting cocks to him for his august approval. After that the whole school enjoys a holiday while pair after pair of birds are set out to fight.

Cockpits for adults are undeniably noisy, roaring places, notorious for their blasphemies and clamor, although the clergymen who frequent them (not Master Crabtree's best companions) say that there can be no great cruelties to cocks; for they are the Devil's messengers because one crowed for joy after Peter denied our Blessed Lord.

Much more respectable is bear- and bull-baiting. The Queen often deigns to honor the London exhibitions with her presence, and in 1591 issued a royal edict forbidding stage plays on certain days lest they interfere with the audiences at these sports "maintained for her Majesty's pleasure." The chief London resort is the "Queen's Paris Garden." It is actually on the Surrey side of the Thames, convenient for the vulgar, but the bears are often brought over to Whitehall, so the monarch can watch the sport from the gallery of the palace. There are a master and two keepers of the bears, who rank somewhat as royal officials, and every now and then they can exhibit their charges and the "royal mastiffs" not merely before the Queen but before any ambassador or visiting prince their sovereign condescends to honor.

Boroughport is not London, but all but the smallest community must have its bears. Up in Cheshire a certain petty borough has suffered a sad loss—its "town bear" is dead. The corporation has at once voted to sell the church Bible in order to buy another bear! Nobody thinks this astounding, probably least of all the vicar.

The Boroughport bear is a local institution kept very possibly in a den near to the Gild Hall. In honor of a distinguished London bear he is named Tom o' Lincoln, although the most famous bruins that perform before her Majesty are Harry Hunks and above all the great Sackerson. Tom (when not professionally employed) is the pampered darling of all the youth of Boroughport, and somewhat overfed with sweetmeats. His coat is terribly mutilated and his muzzle is covered with scars but these are merely honorable wounds. We shall pass lightly some details of his exhibitions; enough that on certain Sundays and Thursdays Tom o' Lincoln is led out to a field beyond the gates where a ring has been surrounded by a barrier of solid stakes, outside of which are rude benches for the people of worship and green turf for the multitude. The bear is fastened in the center of the ring by a collar and a thick rope some five yards long, tied to a stake in such a manner he can circulate freely. When all is set the dogs are turned in—mastiffs with short noses "that their teeth may get a better hold." The dogs, four or five at a time, creep up upon the bear while he writhes and tugs this way and that, more and more furious, and his eyes changing to balls of pinkish fire, while the betting among the onlookers grows reckless. Then a brave mastiff shoots in to seize Tom's muzzle. At once the creature is caught in a mortal hug that squeezes the life out of him, but while thus occupied the whole pack flies at the bear. Instantly there is nothing visible but a swirling mass of animals "biting, clawing, roaring, tossing, and tumbling." The bear suddenly emerges "all blood and saliva," and drives back the surviving dogs with great bats of his paws. A second mastiff lies motionless, the others retreat to bark at safe distance; but attendants rush in, drag away the fallen, and lead forward fresh dogs. The contest thus continues until Tom is so exhausted that another attack may kill him (an expensive business for the town) or so many fine dogs have been slain or maimed that further bloody work is again too costly.

Bull-baiting is very similar though not quite so popular. The chained bull catches the dogs as they try to creep under his belly and "stamps their guts out," or more often he will toss his tormentors on his horns and fling them sometimes thirty feet in the air. For the sake of the dogs, therefore, a bull ring is always on soft sand to break the fall.

The Puritans rail against bear-baiting with **more than**

wonted violence. "What Christian heart," cries Master Stubbes, "can take pleasure to see one poor beast rend and kill another? To be plain, I think the Devil is the master of the game, bear ward and all."[1] But most fine gentlemen, and certainly the multitude, agree in praising the sport as "a sweet and comfortable recreation, fitted for the solace and comfort of a peaceable people."—Who are right? This is no place wherein to pass judgment.

The more extreme Puritans also denounce "the horrible vice of pestiferous dancing," but their anathemas are much less fervent than those against bear-baiting, and those of the type of Master Crabtree admit that dancing done innocently and moderately is "a wholesome recreation of the mind and also an exercise of the body." Outside of the violent Precisians nobody frowns on decorous dancing. The Queen is passionately fond of it, and decidedly proud of her own grace in the exercise. It is written of her, in 1589, "that she is so well that six or seven galliards (rounds of vehement exercise) in the morning is her ordinary exercise." Though her years are increasing she dances now more vigorously than ever to give the lie to the rumor that she is turning lame. Very lately, they say, she danced a galliard with a visiting French duke who was so delighted with her performance that he artfully made shift to kiss not her hand but also her foot.

Of course dancing at court and dancing on the village green are very different things. The country folk do not care for complicated and stately measures; what they like are jigs, hornpipes, rounds, the famous "Morris Dance," and the ever popular *"Hay"*—something very like a reel. Up at Hollydean when Sir Walter kept open house to all

---

[1] It is unjust to assert that the Puritans condemned bear-baiting simply because it gave pleasure to the spectators. The brutality and inhumanity of the sport appealed to them keenly.

the gentles of Thorpshire against Captain Andrew's return from the wars, the rich squires and dames marched through the solemn Pavane, the Cassamezzo, the Lavolta, the Coranto, and especially the Galliard, and other dances with imposing foreign names.

"Treading a measure" in these stately dances fits in well with the stiff and cumbrous costumes and fashions of the day, "but some of the performances really call for much agility and real gymnastics. Court customs are forever changing. Mistress Anne complains that she has barely learned the dances in favor at Greenwich or Hampton when she hears that the noble lords and ladies have dropped them for others. But it will be some time ere the various types of galliards are discontinued. These are of an ex-tremely nimble type:

> A gallant dance that lively doth betray
> A spirit and a virtue masculine.

Sometimes a galliard involves regular capers. Usually if properly conducted it begins with the slow pavane, which is not much more than a dignified processional march "suitable to the gala mantles of princes and the robes of magistrates." But the music gradually quickens and the actual galliard begins, whereof the essential feature is always five skillful steps forward then five taken back. The climax is likely to come with *la volta,* a series of veritable springs in the air, in which her Majesty takes pleasure, often displaying her personal agility to her admiring cour-tiers.

When the galliard grows tiresome gentle folk often turn it into the "Cushion Dance." A man or a woman dances vigorously around the room then suddenly stops before one of the opposite sex, bows, and sings lustily:

> This dance it can go no farther.

Which is the signal not for the dance to end, but for the other party to bow, step out, and begin revolving with a partner; and so they continue until the whole company is whirling around the great hall or gallery in a kind of reel.

Very proficient persons like to exhibit their skill in single dancing; Captain Andrew prides himself a trifle on his accomplishment with the Capriole, literally "goat's leap," which consists in great leaps upward so that the feet are beaten together in the air. But any public festival (be the audience gentle or vulgar) is not likely to be complete without some morris dances—executed often by paid performers.

Morris dances are supposed to come from Moorish Spain—the land of the "Moriscos." They are violent ballets, not unlike the pantomimes of another day, in many features. Certain stock characters always appear—a Moor, Robin Hood and Little John in their forest green, Friar Tuck, a wonderful hobbyhorse, and an equally nimble dragon. The dancers have sewn to their arms and legs many bells, which tinkle musically as the wearers leap about. The hobbyhorse cavorts in a most lifelike manner, with "careers, prankers, false trots, and Canterbury paces," and the female part is always taken by Maid Marian, sometimes a boy prinked out in stomacher and farthingale and chosen because of his extreme agility. The morris dance is usually the climax of the great Maypole festivities, and to provide one on any other gala occasion is a sure road to local popularity.

ALL these things rejoice in their season but they hardly meet the need of vigorous men blessed with decent leisure, especially when the weather is just right. For then there must be the constant outlet of field sports. A man of family thinks himself a little disgraced if he is not tolerably proficient in tennis and bowling, cannot pull a fair bow in archery, cannot keep near the dogs in hunting, cannot carry a good falcon on his fist, and if still fairly young, cannot make a good figure at running, swimming, shooting, and even wrestling.

Bowling and tennis of course are games that do not take one far from home and can be indulged in when a dash with the hounds is quite impossible. Every gentleman's house has its convenient bowling green, and for less prosperous folk there are several public bowling alleys near Boroughport. The latter are not favored by the better people; they are often the scenes of much gambling and worse things despite regulation acts of Parliament. Sir Walter is by no means too old to take his turn with the balls in friendly contests with friendly squires, upper tenants, and even with his more favored servants. Around Hollydean they are incessantly talking about the "bias" of the green, about the "rub" which is anything that disturbs a ball on its course, and about the "Jack" which is a small ball used as a mark for the player to aim at.

Captain Andrew being younger prefers tennis, whenever he can get a good opponent. This is an extremely respectable game. Henry VII and Henry VIII alike were expert players and there are tennis courts at all the royal residences over Christian Europe. At London there are four-teen public courts, certain of them however restricted to men of rank, or those who can show goods or land to the value of at least one hundred pounds. Such courts vary from eighty-four down to only fifty-five feet in length and usually are covered. You can play in them either with a racket or with only your hand; if with only the latter and your opponent keeps his racket you are allowed fifteen points. A special form of tennis is "balloon" played with a "great ball" of leather filled with wind. You drive it about with the strength of your arm aided by a stout wooden bracer. The proper name for a racket is singularly enough a "net," and the small hair-stuffed balls that are used in the ordinary game are not driven over an actual net at all but only over a rope stretched tautly across the center of the court. The method of scoring however, by "15," "30," "advantage," etc., will seem remarkably like that in vogue at another day.

Tennis matches between two high-born gentlemen are ordinary enough. Everybody remembers how in 1565 Lord Leicester and the Duke of Norfolk played a lusty set, with the Queen as their very close witness. A moment for rest, and Leicester "very hot and sweating" plucked the Queen's "napkin" (handkerchief) from her royal hand and wiped his face. Norfolk furiously rated his opponent for his im-pertinence, but the Queen laughed and took Leicester's side. That was the beginning of the estrangement between the Queen and the Duke which brought the latter to the scaffold. Often however large groups of persons play in a single tennis game; for example, in 1591 ten of the Earl of Hartford's servants went into the court all together and played a long contest before the Queen five against five, "to the great liking of her Highness."

Common folk find tennis a little too aristocratic. Next to

a bear-baiting, what can surpass a good noisy, brawling game of football upon the green? The ball is a blackened bladder cased in leather; the goal posts are two sticks three or four feet apart at the ends of a field about a hundred yards long. The rules are extremely simple; science is nowhere and if a good field lacks, two impassioned small mobs can rush and contend up and down the village street. Grave persons frown on football and none of the Hollydeans would think of joining. Such Puritans as Stubbes denounce it as "a friendly kind of fight, a bloody and murdering practice" wherein you seek your adversary "to pitch him on the nose, though it be on hard stones." Magistrates scold because it discourages real military sports which help the national safety. It is forbidden at Court, but for once authority is helpless. The game is growing as the joy of the vigorous lower classes, and all the clowns and prentices will run flocking to the scrimmage the minute the work hours are over if the good old cry spreads down the street "all fellows at football."

Somewhat more in favor among "gentle" youth is wrestling, yet it is often very brutal. Rules hardly exist. Broken ribs, fatal internal injuries, even broken necks are direfully common. You catch your opponent, trip him as best you can, throw him, then if he will not yield leap on him and crush in his chest. A "fall" consists in making your adversary's back or one shoulder and the contrary heel touch the ground; a "foil" is when you bring him down but cannot quite force him into this position of utter defeat. Andrew Hollydean is a fair wrestler, for wrestling is of real use in the army. He is a much better fencer, but fencing is best considered when we debate things military (see Chap. XX). By preference both he and his father would put in a bright morning with good horses under them and a good pack baying just ahead.

Considering the times horses are not luxuries, they are necessities. Oxen do all the heavy farm work, but even a fairly poor tenant must keep at least one heavy-paced nag, even though the creature be "hipped with an old mothy saddle," and has "had the glanders, windgalls, spavins, yellows (jaundice), and staggers" and is "shoulder shotten." Being a gentleman of fortune Sir Walter keeps a great stable, though not any greater than many squires of smaller income.

Horse racing is a Scottish sport, popular north of the border, although as yet not very common in England; [1] but for any traveling, not to mention hunting and hawking, horses are indispensable. In the Hollydean stables are beasts for almost every kind of service. The horses of the native English stock are really a superior breed, not very large but "of an easy pace" and "hard to beat." But who is ever content with a home product? Sir Walter has just purchased for his son's use a very good mount indeed—a "Barbary horse," small but extremely swift, with a long slender head and of the most desirable color—bay with a white star in the forehead. For himself, as weight and girth increases, he prefers a "German horse," tall and powerful, of a fine dapple gray; and Mistress Anne for her personal use has a "Spanish jennet," "lusty, young, and proud," of a beautiful black full of silver hairs. However when hounds and horns are in order the male Hollydeans are likely to prefer their little "Galloway nags"—small stocky Scottish horses, of no pretense to beauty, but almost tireless when the hunt grows long and you have to crash through thicket after thicket.

The Hollydeans (like all decent landed folk) are fond of their horses but they are quite as fond of their dogs. The

[1] James I introduced it into England where it speedily became remarkably popular.

creatures are not allowed the run of the mansion quite as much as in those of many country squires, but they are certainly numerous, ubiquitous, and even the private parlors and closets smell not a little doggy. Ringwood, Merriman, Bellman, Sowter, Clowder, Fury, Tyrant, Echo—they are beloved and conspicuous members of the family. When Silver has a new litter it is a public event.

Sir Walter does not indeed carry his passion for dogs to the point that does his neighbor Sir Edwin Hunter; his kennels are carefully filled with harriers, terriers, bloodhounds, gazehounds, lymes, lurchers, greyhounds and the like, carefully selected not merely for their various uses in the chase but on account of the *sweetness and harmony of their cry*. Sir Edwin avows to you there is nothing more delectable than to hear a pack of hounds whose notes of different pitch are meant to harmonize "like a peal of bells." A kennel famous for its cry must be compounded of large dogs "with deep solemn mouths" for basso, twice as many with "roaring loud ringing mouths" for counter tenor, some more with "hollow plain sweet mouths" for middle part, not forgetting a pair of "small singing beagles." Then he soberly tells us, "you shall make your cry perfect and the solemnness and graveness of the noise 'will be delightful to the ears of every beholder.'"

Captain Andrew cynically laughs at this and says he loves his pack for other reasons and that the true hunter takes joy when they are merely sitting on their tails and howling. But what noise, bustle, and joyous excitement when very early on a clear morning the horses are led from the stables, the grooms bring out the yelping dogs from the kennels, the Hollydeans and their guests appear in tight, bright jackets, while Mistress Anne and her maidenly friends often appear in costumes much like their brothers' masculine breeches and large boots. Next the

[247]

'serving men begin swabbing the noses of each leaping, rejoicing hound with a little vinegar to make his scent
keener; and finally the master of the hunt calls out his
jovial, "Switch and spurs! Switch and spurs!" the horns
"ta-ra," and away they go.

With fair skill in the saddle and a good horse under you,
who can deny the saying, "Hunters shall go to heaven
when they die, and live in this world more joyfully than
any other men"? Edward, Duke of York, who was killed
at Agincourt in 1415, long ago described the pleasures of a
well-ordered hunt: "When the hunter seeth a sweet and
fair morning and clear weather and bright, and he heareth
the song of the small fowls, the which sing so sweetly
each in his own melody . . . And when the sun is arisen
the hunter shall see fresh dew upon the small twigs and
grasses and the sun by his virtue shall make them shine—
that is great joy and liking to the hunter's heart."

Hollydean like every fine mansion has its fine deer park,
shut off by high palings cut from the old oaks of the
glades in which the deer browse. The estate is so large that
Sir Walter takes pride in being among those land owners
who never hunt save over their own lands. But if today
a deer is to be sacrificed all the neighboring squires have
been invited in, some of the better yeomen know they can
join if the farm work is not too heavy, and many strangers
from a distance will probably follow in the rear—unques-
tioned if they have good horses and fine jackets.

So the poor scared beast (that has been peacefully secure
for months) suddenly finds itself driven beyond the palings,
allowed to wander at will, then hunted down. The fattest
stags or a tall "hart of ten" are most desirable, because
such huge creatures are most easily tired to death. The deer
has to be found in his lair by a very keen scented but voice-
less dog, a "lyme hound," held on leash. Then he breaks

QUEEN ELIZABETH HAWKING.
Turberville, "Booke of Faulconrie," 1575.

out from thicket to thicket, the whole pack of regular hounds is released, the horns blow their best, and the "hunt in force" tears over the country.

If today the dogs are baffled and often they can be, Charley Scenter, the Hollydean chief gamekeeper, knows all the signs for tracking and discovering the deer. The footprints of the animal of course betray its weight and size, its *entries* are the marks such as bent grass or broken twigs made by the deer breaking covert, the *port* is the token left by the breadth of his horns as he breaks through the trees; lastly, there are the all-important *fewmets,* his droppings, from which an experienced woodsman claims to discover almost everything. There is a familiar picture of the Queen's Majesty, while out on the hunt, halting to inspect a quantity of fewmets spread out on green leaves and held up for her royal scrutiny by the chief huntsman.

Very melodious are the horns as the horses scamper through the woodlands, especially the long clear *recheat* summoning back the hounds that have drifted from the scent. Each rider flourishes a "hunting cudgel," a stout truncheon to keep back the boughs, as they dash in his face in the dense woods and thickets. There is the constant "Hey! Hey!" or *"Via! Via!"* when the horses are encouraged to a leap, or "So boy! So boy!" when they get a little out of hand. At last the deer is exhausted and the dogs close in. "To him! To him!" calls the foremost hunter to the hounds and all the riders behind him join the encouraging "Hyke! Hyke! Hyke!" Then the horns all give out the triumphant mort—two notes, a long and a short, while the last brutal work is done with the riders' crossbows at close range.

The minute the deer is dead the dogs are flogged aside and Sir Walter, as Master of the hunt, leaps down to "break up the deer." He ceremoniously cuts a slit along the

[251]

brisket "to see the goodness of the flesh," and carefully cuts off the head. The regular gamekeepers then butcher the animal and reward the dogs with certain portions. After this, as if the company has not already feasted sufficiently at the "hunt breakfast," while the deer was being discovered and "harbored" by the gamekeepers, all the invited guests gallop back to Hollydean for an incredibly hearty collation in which figure such items as

Gambones of hog—
Then sausages and savory knacks to set men's minds agog.

Deer hunting is the most fashionable and of course expensive fun of "venerie." Not even Sir Walter can afford it often, and his poorer neighbors very seldom; but if all you want is an excuse for a brisk morning with the horses, there is always a hare to test the speed and agility of the dogs.[1]

In some respects a hare can give better sport than a deer. "Poor Wat" is full of "cranks and crosses with a thousand double." He runs among a flock of sheep to spoil the scent of the hounds, will plunge into a herd of deer (that day unhunted), and finally dash into almost impenetrable briars. He knows how to lie low and keep silence while the dogs grope around for scent. In a word hares and their cousins the coneys (rabbits) provide perhaps over half of all the hunting in England.

Deer and rabbit hunting have to contend, nevertheless, with the aristocratic old sport of hawking. Since the early middle ages falconry has been the recreation of feudal lords and princes, and as yet it is not seriously declining. The training of hawks has become a high science with a huge technical jargon. To be able to discuss the problems of hawks has become a kind of test for passing as a gentleman

[1] Fox hunting was not so much in vogue as later, foxes being considered a kind of vermin hardly worthy of the "law" of the chase.

of rank, and almost as many quarrels arise in such discussions as over the fair sex.

Not many years ago Lord Heady and Lord Acreproud, two especially arrogant South English noblemen, after too much wine began to talk of hawks. One praised the haggard, the hawk caught wild and tamed in captivity; the other with an oath was sure nothing could surpass the eyas, the nestling hawk, taken soon after quitting the shell. Words led to taunts, thence to insults, thence to the lie direct, thence to a challenge which luckily cost neither nobleman his life, but which caused a regular blood feud among their grooms, gamekeepers, and huntsmen.

In their private hearts Sir Walter and his heir care much less for hawking than they do for ordinary hunting; hawks kept around a house are very filthy and one can waste an inordinate amount of time over them. To keep fine hawks, however, is almost a necessity if one would pass as a member of the upper gentry. The Hollydeans employ therefore an expert falconer who has learned his high science in France, and Captain Andrew as part of his regular education spent no little time conning that famous and much studied treatise by Tuberville, *Book of Falconry or Hawking*. He is accordingly a fair master of the mystery, talks sagaciously of his tassel-gentle (otherwise his tame male hawk) and of the limitation of the eyas-musket, the male sparrow hawks.

Being such matters of high science we pass over all the subject of the taming of hawks, of fitting them to the jesses (the short straps upon their legs), the varvels (the little rings of silver at the end of the jesses, on which the owner's name is often engraved), and the hood (placed on the hawk's head to blind her and insure complete quiescence).[1] Female hawks are much larger and stronger than male hawks and are consequently more in demand, while sparrow hawks, although smaller and weaker, are extremely smart and tractable creatures very useful in seeking birds like partridges that cannot soar very high. A good well-trained hawk or falcon is very gentle and Mistress Anne has an eyas which she fondles as she might a kitten. Old Skelton, Henry VIII's poet, has his lines praising

> Merry Margaret, as midsummer flower,
> Gentle as falcon or hawk of the tower.

Whatever the pedantry, there is exhilarating sport for Mistress Anne in riding out perhaps near the river with a well-trained hawk upon her wrist. When her brother declares the sport is good, the hood is whipped off and the eyas instantly shoots upward to a great height above the meandering water. Here she remains, flapping about in lazy circles, while Captain Andrew with a couple of dogs beats the rushes by the river marge and suddenly flushes a wild duck that whirs off to apparent safety. Then follows a tingling spectacle. The duck sees its foe but dares not descend to land and struggles desperately to rise above the hawk which puts forth its uttermost speed and swoops around the duck in great rings, while the little bells tied to her legs give forth a melodious tinkling. At last when the two birds are mere dots against the blue, the hawk gains her desired place of vantage. She darts downward like a bullet, and one stroke of her nipping beak on the duck's neck ends the contest in a twinkling. The duck tumbles dead from a great height, and with a rejoicing cry the

---

[1] The lore of falconry was well developed as early as the thirteenth century and a more complete discussion can be found in the author's *Life on a Mediæval Barony*, pp. 57-62.

hawk comes skimming after. The victor is then promptly tolled back to her mistress's hand and the hood by dangling a bit of meat while the dogs retrieve the game.[1]

Falconry thus brings many a good fowl into the larder, but it is too expensive a method when the need is not merely for sport but for abundant food. There are plenty of birds of all kinds in Thorpshire, and in times of the year when fresh beef and mutton are scarce every method is used to capture them. This kind of game is so abundant that there is little effort by the Hollydean gamekeepers to prevent "birding"; the only poachers that concern them much are the deer stalkers.

Barring the little birds good for pies, and numerous water and beach fowl, the main quest is always for partridges and pheasants. These are too large for taking with birdlime, which snares the sparrows and redbreasts; and pitfalls and gins are uncertain reliances. Sometimes several fowlers beat up the thickets and get a good haul of partridges in nets, but it is commoner to trust to the stone-bow or now increasingly to firearms.

The stone-bow is the old military crossbow, shooting not an arrow but a handful of small stones like fine shot. However the Hollydeans are succumbing to the temptations of gunpowder. Until lately firearms have been too cumbrous for sportsmen, but Sir Walter recently brought home from London two very light and handy weapons indeed, called calivers. With their lead shot they certainly work great execution. To creep upon the birds, however, it is often best, whatever the weapon, to employ a stalking horse —a curious affair of stuffed canvas painted like a horse;

[1] Hawking continued in favor with English upper classes until about 1650 when the Puritan Revolution gave a great blow to the prosperity of the nobility. After that it was never able to recover its popularity, owing to its costliness and the increasing efficiency of firearms for fowling.

the fowler puts it in front of him and the ducks swimming
in the pool are never scared at the gradual approach of a
harmless animal; then "crack!" sounds the caliver and you
can pick up the dead birds on the water. "But who that
love sport," quoth Sir Walter, "can find chief joy in gunpowder? Honest gentlemen still prefer their horses, hounds,
and hawks."

ILLUSTRATIONS TO "SHEPHERD'S CALENDAR," 1597. AUGUST.

¶ *Chapter* XVIII: Concerning Festival Days
Sacred and Secular

THE most toilsome folk of Thorpshire thus have
their diversions, and their "Masters" of Worship
have their ascending refinements of sports all the
year round, but at certain seasons and days labor and business drop out of sight altogether. Merry England becomes
"merry" in very truth.

The Reformation has brought a great curtailment in the
old holidays and saints' days which were really so numerous as to be a drag on industry and farming, but a great
many still remain in addition to Sunday, and often prolong
themselves for several days. Certain festivals vary from
reign to reign. As long as Elizabeth rules, the Queen's
Coronation Day (November seventeenth) is celebrated
with loyal enthusiasm through the length and breadth of
England. At Boroughport last year all the cannon along the
walls were shot off, and answered by a thundering salute
from all the guns on the ships in the harbor. This "thundering noise" kept up, salvo after salvo, till the stock of
stale powder was exhausted. Englishmen delight in any
excuse for burning sulphur and saltpeter, as well as for
ringing bells. Even at Hollydean there are two or three
brass "chambers" (very small cannon) which rest harmlessly around the gatehouse and are touched off by the
serving men not merely on secular holidays but also to
welcome or speed some honored guest.

Very lately honest folk just learned the joys of fireworks.
The Queen delights in them, especially if used in the
spectacular bloodless tournaments in such favor at the

[257]

Court. The birthday celebration at Boroughport had its climax in the evening with a great display in which a sham fort was overthrown by a dragon "casting out huge flames and squibs," after a show of plenty of "running rockets, pikes of pleasure, and firewheels."

Few people can provide private fireworks or discharge cannon, but every householder can show his festival mood by festooning his doorways. In the great summer festivals Boroughport streets are a pretty sight. Almost every door is shadowed with green birch, long fennel, St. John's wort, orpin, white lilies or big garlands of flowers, and as soon as the stars peep out they are answered by many oil lamps placed before the houses—often set in tall candelabra, which are allowed to burn all night.

Time must fail us to enumerate all the holidays around Boroughport, for the fair town, like every English town, has plenty of local festivals all its own. The safest thing to do is to speak of a few that are famous throughout the entire kingdom. Since we first descended upon Thorpshire in the early summer let us start our round with the Vigil of St. John the Baptist, otherwise June 24, and often called Midsummer's Eve. This is a very simple holiday. In the evening the lads and maidens all scurry off into the woods, fetch back branches to adorn the house fronts, then give themselves over to dancing of no common violence. Huge bonfires are heaped up in all the markets and crossways. Every possible harper and crowder keeps up his noise until he nigh drops dead. Young and old, gentle and simple gyrate in mad rings around the bonfires. The younger men and boys earn the admiring shrieks of the maids by their reckless leaps across the flames, and ancient custom forbids the City Fathers to stop the revelry and uproar before midnight. "No work in Boroughport next morning!"

[258]

groan the merchants and master craftsmen when they think of their clerks and prentices.

In the autumn are the jolly but very informal harvest festivals. During August, September, and early October days there is too much work in the fields and barns for many junketings barring Sunday, but after the sheaves are bound, the scythes and flails are hung up, and the hogs have been turned loose in the corn stubble, then all of rural Thorpshire draws a long breath. When the last grain is piled into the cart on the Hollydean estates a dozen laughing wenches all crowned with late flowers jump up after it, and beside them is set a kind of huge, crude doll dressed up to represent "Ceres." The lads are there to help the horses, and down the lanes with prodigious shouting goes the cart till they reach the barn. "Up to the manor house!" is then their cry, where a bountiful, jovial feast is spread by the steward in the great hall: vast platters of fat beef, veal, and muttons, but especially plentiful are custards and an enormous "furmenty-pot" of hulled wheat boiled in milk, the time-honored dish for the occasion.

Then a trifle later comes the great and enduring celebration of Hallowe'en. The Church festival of All Saints (November first) comes the next day, but Hallowe'en is really a relic of old Paganism—the night when all supernatural spirits are abroad and it is easiest for mere mortals to see them. All England stands still that afternoon and night; in Boroughport there is a great pageant with elaborate mummery, duly honored by the Mayor in his robes and all the worshipful aldermen. In Hollydean after darkness closes in, there is mad jollity in the Hall; "the pipes and the tabor are now lustily at work, the lad and the lass have no lead on their heels," and there are many special sports such as the hilarious "ducking for apples."

But it is when the days grow very short, when farm work

[259]

slackens to a minimum, and even the trade in the Borough-port shops can be over with in a few hours that Merry England begins to show its true face. Christmas is drawing on; the tight little city and the villages around begin to be agitated with the great public question of arranging the mumming and electing the annual Lord of Misrule.

Every age has its share of mortals who enjoy "dressing up" and disguising themselves as quite different folk than God has made them. This is especially true around Christmas time. As the good song [1] goes cheerily:

> To shorten winter's sadness
> See where the folks with gladness,
> Disguised all are incoming,
> Right wantonly a-mumming:
> Fa la! Fa la! Fa la!

But successful mumming and reveling require a leader, and that leader is particularly my Lord of Misrule. It is no light thing to receive this honor; there is quite as much responsibility as riotous mirth about the office. The election is quite a ceremony. One afternoon the nave of St. Michael's (the better the place the better the deed) is packed with all the "wild heads of the parish"—in other words all the brisk fellows who may have a part in the revels and pageantry. After much vehement discussion they elect their "Grand Captain of All Mischief my Lord of Misrule." The potentate this year is Myles Pranker, by sober calling a ropemaker, but known through Thorpshire for his leadership in every form of lawful fun making. He is very much more than a clown; very likely his Worship the Mayor sees to it that some one is chosen who can keep the mirth within decent limits.

[1] This song seems to be as old as the sixteenth century, but its actual date is uncertain.

A ROYAL PICNIC.
Turberville, "Booke of Hunting," 1575

[261]

Once named, in any case Lord Pranker becomes active: He names some twenty "lusty guts" to serve under him, names a Fool and Jester as his two chief assistants, and issues many sonorous proclamations in the style of the Lord of Misrule at the Queen's Court itself: "the High and Mighty Prince Myles, Prince of Purpoole, Archduke of Stanphia, Duke of High and Nether Boroughport, Court Palatine of Fetterlane," etc. The rich merchants and neighboring squires seldom grudge to add a noble to the fund at his disposal, poorer householders present "ale, cheese, custards, cakes, tarts, and meat," and a few Sundays after his election comes his regular presentation to the community. St. Michael's is packed that morning; no slothful pleads "lawful excuses" for not coming to prayers, but the rector goes through the service as rapidly as possible and with one eye upon the main portal. Suddenly a fearful discord of shrill pipers and rattling drummers can be heard coming nearer and nearer. "Amen!" comes promptly from the chancel just as the door opens wide and my Lord and all his rout swing right into the church.

"Prince Myles" rides in a kind of unsteady litter borne by four reeling and shouting myrmidons. Around him are his chosen twenty. Their leader wears a huge tinsel crown, and he and all the others have donned astonishing robes of yellow green or "other light wanton color." They add to these gold rings, scarves, and ribbon; also colored handkerchiefs are wound around their shoulders "borrowed from their pretty Mapsies and loving Bessies for bussing them in the dark." Around their legs they have numerous small bells, as do Morris dancers, which keep up a prodigious tinkling. About the regular escort of my Lord curvet dozens of wondrously clad hobbyhorses and dragons.

The gaping people "laugh, fleer, and mount the pews," while the revelers with mighty shouting go straight down the central aisle up to the chancel, "their pipers piping, their drummers thundering, their stumps dancing, their bells jingling, their handkerchiefs swinging about their heads like devils incarnate, their hobbyhorses and other monsters skirmishing amongst the rout." Then on the very foot of the chancel they halt, make a mock obeisance to the rector, parade down the side aisles, and so out of the church. If the day is fine they next set up arbors of boughs in the very churchyard among the tombs, spread out food and drink, and so with braying music dance well into the evening—all the maids joining them; and "thus (the outraged Puritans protest) these terrestrial furies spend the Sabbath day."

All this is merely preliminary to the great mummery and mirth of Christmas. The farm work now is at its lowest ebb—old Pagan custom, newer Christian custom, the natural human desire for a long spell of relaxation and jollity—all conspire to provide nearly a fortnight of absolute holiday. This means however a period of frantic energy for all the Hollydean cooks and scullions. If their master should fail to feed all his friends and dependents to surfeit, the whole family would feel the disgrace. As the happy season approaches, suddenly there appear as out of the air whole swarms of beggars who bawl for alms at the gate and know they will not be denied however scant the deserving. Messengers sent from house to house on errands are likely to be plied with hospitable liquors. The season too excuses a deal of ruinous card and dice play. You shout "Good cheer!" and "God be with you!" to perfect strangers. Everybody, no matter how raucous, goes about murdering tunes, and there is considerable exchanging of gifts although most of these are reserved for New Year's.

At last approaches Christmas Eve. The church bells, swung by practiced hands, are pealing melodiously through the frosty air. All the young Hollydeans have been out with the children of the better tenants into the woods. Home they come dragging the great Yule log, across the thin, crunching snow.[1] As the merry throng tugs past, all who meet them courteously raise their caps. The Yule-log is supposed to bring good luck and promise of long feasting. As it is enthroned on the iron dogs in the cavernous fireplace in the hall, there is a general burst of singing led by Sir Walter himself. The song can begin like this:

> When Christ was born of Mary free
> In Bethlehem, in that fair citie,
> Angels sang there with mirth and glee
> *In Excelsis Gloria.*

After that a whole evening of informal feasting, music, and merriment with the Christmas waits drifting out from Boroughport, sure that, after their lusty "God rest you, merry gentlemen" and the equally popular "I saw three ships come sailing in," they will be bidden inside to stow away as much food and drink as will permit them to wander back to the town.

But on Christmas Day itself Hollydean Hall is in its glory. Great columns of smoke rise from the kitchen chimneys. The Hall is one jolly mass of relatives, tenants, and retainers. The excitement is almost too great to wonder who ought to sit above the salt. An enormous feast is served—one ponderous meat course after another, with sack and ale without limit. Amid vast excitement there appears the peacock, skinned, roasted, and sewed up again in all his haughty feathers and with gilded beak; it is borne by Mistress Anne herself, her lawful honor as eldest daughter, who presents it proudly to her parents as being "the food

[1] The Yule-log was really reminiscent of the old pagan feast of Juul, when at the winter solstice great bonfires were burned in honor of Thor.

for lovers and the meat for lords." But the noise increases when a little later, borne shoulder high by nobody less than the gallant Captain Andrew, appears the boar's head upon the broad silver plate. Instantly the whole hall rises and old and young begin to sing:

> The boar's head in hand I bring,
> With garlands gay and rosemary,
> I pray you all sing merrily
> *Qui estis in convivio.*

> The boar's head, I understand,
> Is the chief service in this land:
> Look, wherever it be found
> *Servite cum cantico.* . . .

And so through many verses.

Finally before the last of the great plum puddings has disappeared, lo! a great knocking at the doors. "Room for the High and Mighty Prince Myles, the Lord of Misrule and all his noble company"; and in is swept Myles Pranker and his whole retinue of mummers, dragons, and hobbyhorses. "My Lord's" jester addresses Sir Walter in a long witty oration about his noble ancestry to which the good, hungry knight makes jocular reply. Pranker quits his high litter and leaps upon the table: "Strike up music!" The benches and trestles are dragged aside. Immediately there is vigorous and incessant dancing. Perhaps it stops at curfew, perhaps not till hours later. All manner of people have drifted up from Boroughport to share the Hollydean cakes and ale. At last the viols and rebecs trail off wearily. Some of the uninvited guests will have to snore on the floor until morning; but the majority are still sober enough to clutch one another and reel home, trolling the praise of this carnival when:

> More liquor is spent, and there's better content
> To drive cold winter away!

Christmas is merely the introduction to a long season of feast and riot that lasts into January. New Year's Day is the time alike for wassailing and healths. Once more all the desired tenants and friends flock into Hollydean Hall. The master assembles the company around a huge bowl of spiced ale, curiously called the "lamb's wool," and as it goes from hand to hand each drinker shouts out "Wassail!" being the old Saxon "To your health." Meantime a great crowd of poorer folk are pressing up to the doors displaying big wooden bowls, quite empty but tied with ribbons, which they are sure the steward will fill up for them. Such suppliants sing, on being gratified:

> Wassail! Wassail! over the town,
> Our toast it is white, our ale it is brown:
> Our bowl it is made of the maplin tree
> We be good fellows all, and I drink now to thee!

This is the day for general exchange of gifts, often of large value, a custom that later will be shifted to Christmas. Up at Court every member of her household, however humble, makes some present to the Queen. The lords give her fine jewels and watches, the ladies silk hose, smocks, embroidery, and gewgaws. The royal apothecary gives her a large pot of green ginger; the "sergeant of the pastry" a great pie of quinces and pears.[1] The Queen reciprocates with gifts of gilt plate in some proportion to the giver's own generosity. Down at Hollydean Mistress Anne and Arabella receive no such treasures, but there are little tokens

---

[1] It was entirely proper to present the Queen with gifts of money outright. The bishops usually gave her £10 to £30 apiece each New Year's. Twenty goldpieces in a silken purse made an excellent impression. On New Year's Day, 1578, Elizabeth took in a total of £993, 13sh.

of loyal affection from all the upper young servants, and Arabella rallies her companion upon the gift of an extremely fine tabby from young Master Stockwood: "And why, sis, must you now turn so red?"

The noise and feasting continue furiously up to their climax on "Twelfth Night" (January fifth). In the town the carnival keeps up boisterously, but now especially is the great celebration of the farmers. Huge bonfires are lighted in the grain fields. All the hinds and yeomen of the neighborhood dance around these fires, leap over them, pass around cider, and shout at the top of their lungs. Then they rush back to some prosperous farmhouse where the womenfolk pass out an enormous cake, which however cannot be eaten immediately but must be taken direct to the barn. Healths of strong ale are solemnly drunk to each of the oxen, and then the big cake is set in the horn of the biggest ox. The owner tickles his nose with a straw; he tosses his head and flings off the cake, to be scrambled for by all the lustier boys. Back to the farmhouse then for still another night of song, jollity, and, one must fear, hard toping.

At last Boroughport and Hollydean with all the other parishes in England have slept off the pork pies and the sides of beef, and tankards of spiced sack and the deluge of jolly ale. Lucky the man without an aching head and a queasy stomach. Then the cold gray light of "Plow Monday" summons farmer, tradesman, and prentice back to sober work. All but the worst of them in their heart of hearts are almost glad of it.

As the winter wanes there are some more holidays. On February second (the Feast of the Purification of the Virgin) there was in old Catholic days a solemn procession with candles around Boroughport, and the custom has not been given up yet, although frowned upon by good Protestants. On Shrove Tuesday, just before Lent commences, there is a general carnival, much bell ringing, football playing, masking, cockfighting, an enormous consumption of pancakes—the viand of the day—while bands of boys wander from house to house begging edibles and singing:

> Pray, dame, something:
> An apple or a dumpling.

Good Friday and Easter are of course great festivals although shorn of part of their importance by the Reformation. Easter being the end of the meager diet of Lent, there is grand activity in all the butcher shops the Saturday previous—a sharpening of knives, cleaning of aprons, and then a tremendous marketing preparatory to the great Easter dinners. Equally busy are the tailors, the gown makers, and the drapers and mercers, for Easter is the day when all Boroughport goes to church in its bravest and newest finery, whether gallant, matron, or maid.

By this time the weather again is getting bright, and people are in a mood for another round of outdoor festivals. The sheep-shearing, executed just as soon as the sheep can safely spare their winter coats, is an excuse for a deal of eating and drinking among the farmers and especially for a wholesale devouring of cheesecakes and "Warden" (pear) pies.

But St. George's Day, April twenty-third, in honor of the old patron saint of England, is the real sign that winter is fairly over. Boroughport gives itself to an elaborate procession. Bell ringing, cannon booming, house fronts adorned with young green and with tapestry; then in the column the Master of the grammar school and all his scholars with rosy well-washed faces and neat blue gowns, the clergy of the fair city, the worshipful Mayor and Aldermen in furred scarlet robes and chains of office with the great civic maces

borne before them and after them; inevitably a most valorous St. George on horseback, prancing around with white
plumes and flashing armor; a most horrible and realistic
dragon, the legs of the two boys inside it seldom in unison;
an Egyptian princess (to be rescued from the dragon),
Alderman Strongbox's pretty, self-conscious daughter; and
lastly all the gentry and dames from the estates near by in
silk and satin, velvet and spangles, upon their best barbs
or jennets. Then bear-baiting, field sports, and archery contests to the heart's content. A glorious day for Boroughport.

But the real welcome to the sun and flowers comes just a
week later. Through the days leading up to May first, Mistress Anne goes about with her charming young head in a
whirl and her mother forgets to chide her forgetfulness of
embroidery lessons and even the pious admonitions of
Master Crabtree. What preparations! What incessant coming, going, and joyous conferences! As the great day is at
hand all the houses from stately Hollydean Hall to the
poorest cottage in the village or in Boroughport hide their
doors and windows under great shades of fresh, young
greenery, especially of the beautiful white thorn just burst-
ing from the bud. On the last day of April it is useless to
expect work out of the prentices and farm hands. "Knock
off!" order the most surly masters, knowing any other commands are useless. As the afternoon advances there is a
general shouting "To the woods!" and all the city and villages seem to be streaming off into the forest glades—
whooping, scampering, chasing, plucking, hacking—under
pretense at least of hunting the great Maypole.

Toward evening, Master Crabtree and Lady Catherine
hope and pray the revelers will all return laden with
boughs and spring flowers. Ignorance is the best comfort
when it comes to asking how many of the lads and wenches
will decide not to come back all night; May Day is never

a season for prudish morality. "Thanked be God, Anne
and Arabella are at last in bed without scandal," avows her
Ladyship to Sir Walter when the latter reports the utter
demoralization of the serving men and maids.

The short night is too long for any youngster. At gray
dawn all Thorpshire is stirring. If any family did not send
out its contingent for boughs, ferns, and blossoms, it is
abroad now. Then just as the sun strengthens, "Praises be,
we are to have a fair day"; and the intoxicating odor of
spring arises from all the meadows and greenwood. Lo!
the crashing and dragging, the low of many oxen, the
shouting of hundreds, the delightful discord of uncounted
flutes, lutes, and viols—and out of the depths of the forest
comes the Maypole.

A fallen monarch of the woodland. It takes twenty yoke
of oxen to haul him over the rough ground. The beasts
have great nosegays bound around all their horns. The
uproar as the growing procession sweeps on toward Boroughport is terrific. Every one is trying to murder a song,
with such snatches predominant as:

> O the month of May, the merry month of May!
> So frolic, so gay, and so green, so green, so green!

Near the old North Bar, the landward gate of Boroughport, the great mob stops. My Lord of Misrule takes command and with him are sturdy helpers. They twine brightly
colored ribbons and cords about the Maypole, twist flowers
and boughs into these, then with great pushes and "ahing"
lift it into place. Great banners stream from its top.
The ground underneath has been smoothed for dancing,
and in the level spot around have been erected huge leafy
booths under which are benches for resting and long tables
set out with abundance of food and drink.

After that my Lord Pranker brings a certain order out of the confusion. The mayor, Sir Walter, and Lady Hollydean and other local notables enter a special pavilion set for viewing the pageant. Opposite is another pavilion and in front of it a high throne shrouded in spring flowers. Music at last that is melody and not discord. All the assistants, hobbyhorses, dragons, etc., of the Lord of Misrule prance and parade, but after them the regular dancers. Of course it has to be Robin Hood and his merry men, or May Day would not be May Day. First there are six tall young men clad in leather jerkins, with woodsmen's axes slung over their shoulders; then six girls all in blue with primrose crowns—the sons and daughters of town magnates or country gentlemen; then Robin Hood himself, a long, lithe youth in grass-green tunic trimmed with gold, with hose blue and white, and bearing a magnificent bow with silver bugle slung about his neck; and after him come his archer guard, often all in green with Robin's prime adjutants— Little John, also in green, and fat Friar Tuck in russet with a ponderous quarter-staff on his shoulder. Next amid louder cheering a full dozen of other girls in orange-tinted kirtles; they are throwing white flowers upon the ground as they advance making a carpet, first, for another damsel in brown and green—Robin's beloved Maid Marian, and then for her gracious Majesty the May Queen herself. Her Royal Grace wears a long gown of white linen fringed with silver but draped with a network of gold. Her long brown hair, which falls in curls about her shoulders, is surmounted by a silver garland twined with blue violets. Needless to add she wears all the jewels she can borrow about her bare white throat and on her long white arms.

She takes her throne amid a new burst of cheering. The rest of the procession runs to the ribbons streaming from the Maypole. "Begin!" orders her Majesty, blushing divinely. The music crashes. The dancers fling their limber young bodies into the figures. They will be soundly tired before the ribbons at last are wound, the viols quiet, and the dance breaks up in general rush for the refreshment booths.

Anne Hollydean is not the May Queen—that honor has fallen to the daughter of the Governor of the poor—but she is reasonably content. The May Queen, like other monarchs, enjoys more show than reality of power. She must sit dumbly on her throne and look smiling and beautiful while all her friends are having (most genuinely) "their fling" around the Maypole. But Maid Marian, required to dance her hardest, is Mistress Anne herself, hair streaming, garments flying, with added glow and tingle because Robin, leaping about just next to her, is Master Tom Stockwood himself.

While the dancers whirl in their circle, the dragons and hobbyhorses make a rush into the gaping crowds, with more shouting and screaming when Pranker's minions dash handfuls of meal into the faces of clowns that get too near, or smack their crowns with great puffed-up bladders. There follow long rounds of special dances and mock battles between the hobbyhorses and dragons. The spectators presently rush in and join the whirl; while again and again young and old voices join in some chorus very like this:

> Trip and go, heave and ho,
> Up and down, and to and fro,
> From the town, to the grove
> Two and two let us rove!
> A-Maying, a-playing,
> Love hath no gainsaying,
> So merrily trip and go!

[273]

Mistress Anne sleeps the sleep of tired youth that night. "May Day is over until next year, blessed be God!" Master Crabtree is saying as he retires to his chamber.

ILLUSTRATIONS TO "SHEPHERD'S CALENDAR," 1597. SEPTEMBER.

¶ *Chapter* XIX: Concerning Craftsmen, Tradesmen, and Merchandising

L IFE in Thorpshire is not all dancing and junketing—Heaven forbid! My Lord of Misrule goes back after May Day to his rope yard and works a little harder than ever as honest Myles Pranker. Inasmuch as we have seen somewhat of the yeomen, the tenantry, and the farms, it behooves us to look now about Boroughport and learn a trifle concerning its craftsmen, its shops, and its commerce.

The greater commerce of England, the foreign exports, the great mercantile companies, the growth of that wealth which may some day transform the kingdom, concern us not. We only reckon with what is promptly heard and seen as we move around Boroughport.

The good town is a flourishing trading community and has not lost that number of enterprising men who have drifted from the more decadent cities to swell the great mass of London. The old gilds, however, have become greatly weakened by the Reformation which confiscated their endowments, and are unable to control trade and industry to the extent they did before 1500. Nevertheless all forms of business are closely watched and regulated by the Corporation; strange craftsmen and tradesmen soon find themselves in difficulties; and the result is that many workers and traders have tended to drift out to the open villages where conditions are much less onerous. In Hollydean parish there are at least two smithies that are not suffered to set up in the borough, because their owners will shoe horses and shape iron for decidedly less than the charges for smith-work provided by city ordinance.

Nevertheless Boroughport is a town of busy shopmen and citizens. You hear the clang of a forge or the whir of a loom on about every street, not to mention the constant knock, knock, from the shipyards and the whir of ropes and shouting of sailors along the water front. Only articles of luxury are as a rule imported; roads are so bad that even English wares that cannot come in by coaster often are better made up near the spot of consumption, although the complaint is bitter that imports are increasing so fast that many craftsmen—especially such as the cappers, glovers, and hosiers—are decaying down to mere retailers of alien products.

All economic life in the sixteenth century has undergone a grievous shock, thanks to the influx of precious metals mostly from the Spanish Indies. It will be reckoned that between 1492 and 1545 the supply of silver and gold in Europe doubled. Then in 1545 the very rich Potosí silver mine in South America was discovered. The supply doubles again between 1545 and 1600. All this means a steady rise in prices, ruin for some, wealth for others; but inevitably a complete shaking of old values.

Boroughport contains a few "very rich" merchants. Master Anthony Strongcoffer who lately died left £50,000 for his heirs and their lawyers to jangle over. Few outside of London could equal him, but fortunes of £100,000 are by no means unknown. Sir John Spenser, Lord Mayor of London in 1591, is fabulously wealthy; it is even whispered that he possesses almost £800,000.[1] Not the greatest earl in England can equal such riches.

Nearly all such princelings call themselves "goldsmiths," and their class trails down to very petty jewelers and usurers indeed. Take (as a better example) Master Edmund Fairdeal, who has his stall near Boroughport Market Cross. He

---

[1] That was his estate when he died in 1609.

is a grave and pious man of a Puritanical cast and a great
commender of Master Crabtree's Calvinism. At his establishment you can buy gold and silver plate, costly rings,
sets of christening spoons. But he will also sell you bills
of exchange on Antwerp, Augsburg, or Venice. He trades
in foreign moneys, and accepts deposit of funds which he

COINERS AT WORK.
Holinshed's History, 1577.

puts out on venture for his own chance of profit or loss.
Against good security you can borrow money from him at
ten per cent. It has been a long hard battle to get the right
to collect interest on loans legalized, but at last in 1571
Parliament passed a statute making interest up to this rate
lawful, although the prejudice against "usury" still hangs
on. Popular opinion is always on the side of the borrower,
and plenty of gibes are flung at interest-taking creditors,
such as:

Here lies Ten in the Hundred
In the ground fast rammed;
'Tis a hundred to ten
But his soul is damned.

Master Fairdeal is an honorable man with a keen sense
of mercantile honor and of his obligation to his own de-
positors and creditors. He says truthfully he has never
tricked young heirs into ruinous bargains, that he always
pays in good money, and that when a loan is made he never
tries to evade the usury laws by making the debtor take
part of the loan in semi-worthless articles at an outrageously
high valuation (brown paper, spices, hops, and even hobbyhorses having sometimes figured in such transactions.[1] He
avows he has never had a debtor flung into jail save when
the fellow proved fraudful. For all that Master Fairdeal still
has a very evil name to live down. "Usurer!" all the tavern
loungers fling at him, repeating the old mediæval taunt
"How can money breed money?"

Master Fairdeal privately sighs. He is the victim of the
long iniquities of the clutching money lenders who have
laughed at all law, have wrung the faces of the poor, who
have filled the debtors' prisons, and have been only pawn-
brokers instead of honorable "goldsmiths." But a great
and valid profession and calling is on its way.

Not the least of Master Fairplay's gains (his foes say his
extortions) comes from the exchange of moneys. The sixteenth century is the heyday of the money changer—
Spanish dollars, Venetian ducats, French crowns, Dutch
florins are always thrusting into every money bag.

Under Henry VIII, Edward VI, and Mary, English
coinage was disgracefully based. A shilling came to be

[1] Another article for usurers to thrust off on spendthrifts and other
credulous borrowers was "lute strings," a kind of silk alleged to have
considerable speculative possibilities.

worth really only sixpence. Not the least of Elizabeth's wise deeds was the restoration, early in her reign, of the money of the realm to its proper fineness. Even so, English coins alone present enough perplexities to the simple. There are seven kinds of gold coins, whereof the ryal (15 shillings), angel (10 sh.), and noble (6sh. 8d.) are the most common in circulation; [1] in silver there are not merely the shilling and the sixpence (generally called the "tester") but, wanting a national copper coinage, amazingly small thin and inconvenient silver pieces such as the threepence, the penny, and even the halfpenny. For lack of silver small change, many Boroughport merchants issue brass, tin, lead, and even leather tokens acceptable locally in trade for a halfpenny or a farthing.

All coins, from the "heavy sovereign" of thirty shillings down to the petty silver, are clipped and sweated in a manner scandalous, and it is a common iniquity for usurers to buy up "cracked angels which cannot fly for soldering" and force them off on helpless borrowers.

The shops of Boroughport are very small, but they are certainly very numerous. Go down almost any street and you are incessantly beset by the "What d'ye lack!" bawled by all the watchful prentices. Some of the better shops are really neat establishments with glass in the upper part of their fronts although with the lower part still completely open during the day and closed at night by heavy shutters. The goods are spread outside these open windows; the prentices stand beside them Argus-eyed for any customer.

Smaller dealers simply put up little stalls or stands along the street, and often directly before private house doors. There is an ordinance against this, but the constables

---

[1] The pound sterling was practically only a money of account, although there were a certain number of "light sovereigns" of 20 shillings each struck off.

usually close their eyes as they head toward the ale house. Other inconveniences in getting about shopping are serious. Being only a provincial town Boroughport is not as yet greatly afflicted as London is by the crowding and din of heavy wains and the lumbering new-style coaches, but on stormy wintry days there are troubles enough for honest marketers. Flowerpots are being blown off the window ledges into the very narrow streets, spouts are sending down baths from every house, the great signboards swinging overhead are creaking and threatening to tumble; doors and shutters slam incessantly; fortunate if in addition some woman at an attic window does not scream "look out!" and fling down a bucket of filthy slops on its way to an even filthier gutter.

Manufacturing and retailing are by no means sharply separated. Sir Walter required a new pair of riding boots. a few days ago. He found them in Master Bradawl's shop in considerable variety; but they had all been cobbled for the local trade in the rear of the shop by the proprietor's journeymen and prentices. It was only when he required a fine velvet doublet that he had to go to Master Goldlace's establishment which made up nothing but simply purveyed foreign luxuries.

Small tradesmen have a bad name as shameless prevaricators. "His conscience is a thing that would have lain upon his hands, and he was forced to put it off," is a standing gibe at the retailers. Part of this odium is deserved, and is one of the reasons why retailers are banished socially by all gentle folk. But competition is fierce, and trade is so subject to government regulation that every twist seems desirable for a hard-working tradesman who brings up a family. The price of bread, ale, and other necessities is controlled sharply; any attempt to expand business runs against a whole network of restrictions; taxes are not very heavy but are levied so irregularly and suddenly as often to be a great hardship. If you hire a journeyman helper you must pay him as much as two shillings sixpence per week, and his board comes to a clear six shillings beyond that. His employer must often pinch and screw therefore to make both ends meet!

However, the average small industrialist-retailer is less concerned with his journeymen than with his prentices. Manufacturing and trade alike are founded upon the prentice system. When a town boy is too poor or too stupid to be entrusted to Master Thwacker at the grammar school, there is a great family council upon the decisive question—"Where can he be bound?" If he has a father or an uncle who needs a helper in some recognized calling—well and good. Jack Tanner was the son of a leather worker and the grandson of a leather worker. His eldest son will be trained for the odorous mystery, although the lad has a great love for books and a secret hankering to study Latin.

It is practically impossible to set up for yourself without having literally "served your prenticeship." By the great Statute of Apprentices passed in 1562, no person is suffered to exercise any "trade or mystery" without having been prentice for seven years. One's trade competitors see to the firm enforcement of the statute, although many callings can be learned in much less time. All around Boroughport you see the blue coats and flat woolen caps, recognized uniform of the prentices. Some are fine smart fellows who have little to complain of. Merchants and shopkeepers are forbidden to take as prentice any lad from the country under the rank of yeoman's son—this keeps the run of rustic yokels from intruding into the trades and retains a high human level for the town population. But many of the poorer handicraftsmen have pupil assistants who (whatever their origin) are dirty, hard-pressed drudges indeed. There

[281]

is practically no protection against long hours, hard words, and often harder blows. The master is expected to give his prentice a little pocket money (often most intermittently bestowed) but no regular wages. The prentice shares the family table, but frequently gets only the scraps of bread and drippings (gravy) and little enough at that. When not at the shop or bench he is almost a servant to the household, fetching and carrying, and bearing the lantern when master and mistress go out evenings. Often a boy is bound to a calling for which, after a short trial, he seems hopelessly unfitted—no matter, it is extremely difficult to shift to something else. The City Fathers insist on many restraints to keep the prentices orderly; and that is reasonable for they are often a cubbish lot, addicted to brawling, never far from their famous wooden cudgels, and the battle call "clubs!" will often bring about a desperate combat between two large groups up and down the streets.

In fine, the prentice system squeezes out much of the originality of a lad, by forcing him into harsh discipline and learning his trade in a purely routine manner. It is likely to coarsen if not brutalize him. His master is expected to teach him morality and piety, and many masters have a regular system of mulcts—twopence for absence from family prayers, fourpence for "toying with the maids," fourpence for teaching the master's children "bawdy works," and a penny for "wearing a foul shirt on Sunday." But many a household is no school of virtue, and the prentice will seldom excel his master or mistress.

On the other hand young Jack Tanner is likely to learn his trade thoroughly; the discipline will teach him a certain self-control, and if his master is an efficient, upright man (and many masters are), probably when Jack finishes his seven years he will get more out of life as a prosperous leather worker than if he had gone to Master Thwacker's school and ended as a half-starved schoolmaster himself or an equally undernourished country curate. The prentice life is a constant lesson in the dignity of labor. It is not derogatory for the sons of gentlemen to be articled to the upper merchants.[1] Jack knows that the great Sir William Hollydean himself was a kind of prentice in London, and that his Worship the Mayor once turned the grindstone for a master cutler. "The blue coat is a garb of honor," they all tell the prentices; "work hard; learn; the whole world is before you."

Apart from the small industries ministering to strictly local needs there are a few manufactures around Boroughport on a somewhat larger scale. England is exporting large quantities of excellent woolen cloth. There are certain centers for this industry especially in Norfolkshire and Kent, but it is spreading out in many directions. Up and down Thorpshire go the "wool staplers." They buy the wool from the farmers in the various market towns and often carry it off on their own backs (or in great bulging saddlebags) to distribute among the combers and spinners who often are farmers' wives scattered through the villages. The weaving and dyeing of the better cloth, however, is very likely done in Boroughport; not, of course, in factories but in very small establishments—a master and one or two journeymen and prentices. The finished bolts go to the warehouses of those merchants who are gradually building up the foreign trade of England.

Certain other industries are developing. Up in Staffordshire there is a whole area given over to small smithies and iron workers. Indeed the metal industries might expand very rapidly except for the serious shortage of firewood for

---

[1] The prejudice against "trade" and the narrow pursuits available for a "gentleman" were less hampering in the age of Elizabeth than they unhappily became later.

the smelting in the little iron mills. The fuel problem is becoming serious in parts of England. So many fine forests are being threatened and yet the demands of the smelters seem insatiable. Perhaps some day sea coal, available as yet only in the coast towns, may be really common. After that England can well become the forge-fire for half of the world.

The great influx, too, of skillful and industrious Flemings, fleeing from Spanish oppressions, is also shaping the economic life of England. There are many refugees from Antwerp and Ghent in Boroughport just as there is a greater colony in London. They make superior lace, do superior dyeing, and are better brass workers, tapestry weavers, and glass makers than Englishmen. The native workers do not welcome them, but they make their plodding, faithful way, and such leaders as Sir Walter say they are worth their weight in gold for the new arts and crafts they are introducing into England.

But native or foreign all-English industrial concerns as yet are very small. The number of prentices and journeymen one master may maintain is limited by statute. The needful tools and machinery in almost every trade are cheap and simple. Every prentice dreams of setting up for himself after an intervening period as journeyman wage earner, if he does not marry his master's daughter and become lord of the little workshop himself. Some day conditions may change but as yet there are no "factories" in all Thorpshire.[1]

However articles are made, the Hollydeans are far more interested in how they are sold. There are no regular shops

---

[1] At rare intervals something like "factories" were attempted. The famous Jack of Newbury is alleged to have employed nearly 1000 men, women, and children in a single huge woolen establishment. This was most exceptional and the apprentice system and the absence of costly machinery worked all against it.

open in the village, although there is plenty of intermittent buying and chaffering around the ale house opposite the parish church. To be sure of doing shopping you must ride or walk into Boroughport. As a rule the ladies, when their needs are not pressing, wait for their smallwares until the weekly visit of Frank Vender. Frank is a pedlar of slightly superior cast. He has a horse with big bags and leads a second with a still heavier pack. About every Tuesday he turns up at the Manor, spreads out his stock in the porter's lodge, chucks the porter's oldest girl under the chin, and bids her mother "Call the ladies."

The minute Lady Catherine and her daughters come in sight with a whole bevy of maids behind them, he begins his patter: "Ah! my fair and noble dames, what is't ye lack?—Fine wrought smocks? Perfumed gloves? Fine bone lace or edgings? Silk garters, very neat? Combs or glasses do you need? And pray cast your gentle eyes upon this pocking stick for your backs, and note the silver handle." After a quantity of lace, silk embroidery, thread, and ribbons have been purchased by the ladies, the maids go ohing and ahing through the display. The serving men and farm hands drift in for mere masculine wares. After an hour or two Vender is then off with his packs to the house of some good yeoman.

Trips "to town for shopping" will be frequent as long as honest folk have coins in their purses, but beyond the things that never get into Frank Vender's pack and only Master Draper or Master Haberdasher can supply, a vast amount of purchasing remains for the markets and the fairs.

Merry England rejoices in markets. Petty villages, if far from any town, often have them and on an exceedingly small scale. "Three women and a goose make a market," runs a familiar proverb. Every Friday in Boroughport you can buy many things not so easily obtainable on other days. Many industrialists dispose of their products only at the markets—their business is too insignificant to warrant a regular shop. To sell in the market farmers from the towns around are admitted who would be strictly forbidden to hawk their butter and eggs, corn, and capons around the town. On Friday mornings there is a prodigious clatter and bustle in the streets, with the yeomen and better tenants riding in with their full panniers to sell and purchase, and with housewives turning out to fill their larders for the week. Many little stalls and tables are set out in the area around the Market Cross, but not a chicken or a sack can be bargained away until the Gild Hall bell begins clanging. This is to give every one an equal chance, and to head off "forestalling"—cornering the market by greedy, ready-money wholesalers. There are also certain stalls selling wares manufactured at a distance and not commonly in the shops of Boroughport. All these traders wait for the ding-dong of the bell, after which for a couple of hours the Market Cross seems another Tower of Babel; and enough lies are told during the bargaining to rejoice the heart of Satan. Long before noon, however, the clamor dies down. All the food products are sold off; the dealers in fancy wares collapse their tables and buyer and seller go off to boast or bemoan their fortunes in the ale house.

This is every Friday. In many places Thursday, Saturday, and especially Monday may be the Market Days. But a market however lively is a poor thing beside a fair; and Boroughport, like most English incorporated towns, boasts a grand fair about twice per year.

The greater is frequently imitated by the lesser. Boroughport Fair takes after its more famous rivals. The biggest fair in all England is probably Stourbridge Fair held in a large field near Cambridge. Its best rival is the renowned

Bartholomew Fair near London, which is however better known for its spectacular sideshows and thimble-rigging than for the vastness of its commerce. Small fairs abound and they are frequently a nuisance. Every pretentious place demands one. In Warwickshire in May there are five fairs in as many small towns opening within a space of thirteen days. These fairs often upset orderly trade, unsteady the lads, and do no good to the country, but they meet the fondness of your common Englishman for plenty of riot and noise and an excuse for idling about, wasting his silver, and getting overcharged with ale. Some fairs specialize in certain commodities. Yarmouth Fair is the best place in the realm to buy herring; Ripon and Harborough are among the places for fine horses and colts, and so with many others. But Boroughport Fair is typical in that it becomes what a later age might call an open-air department store with every possible article on sale from "caddises" (worsted ribbons) to the furniture of mansions and even the tackling of ships.

Early in the fall all Thorpshire feels the itch to take the road to Boroughport. He who cannot go plies his friends with commissions. Sir Walter entrusts Master Steward with long directions as to the wine, wax, malt, salt fish, cloths, and napery he is to stock in for the winter. Long before the opening day the town is full of itinerant Morris dancers, jugglers wtih their apes, and minstrels who sing or at least bawl out ballads. At the corners professional story-tellers gather the incoming yokels about them, while repeating their old tales (never threadbare) of "Sir Topas," "Bevis of Southampton," "Guy of Warwick," and many another. The constables of course have to bestir themselves. The "blind harper" who seemed anxious to keep a tavern room roaring for a groat is discovered to be a notorious coney-catcher who has drifted from London seeking his country "gulls" to swindle.

Then the morning of excitement; more bell ringing and cannon inevitably, and a procession to the broad field outside the walls, their Worship the Mayor and Corporation with red robes, gold chains, and mace bearers, all parading this time to inspect and declare open the small city of tents, stalls, and lodges that has sprung up for six days on the greensward.

The year has been prosperous, commercial hopes are high, and rich traders have brought in their wares even from London. By an art magic there has sprung up a Jeweler's Row, a Brazier's Row, a Pewterer's Row, and a veritable cloth exchange. You can buy now many articles of luxury unobtainable in everyday shops anywhere save in the metropolis. Of course every kind of edible and drinkable is on sale. Farmers even from a distance are welcome to come in and sell as they certainly are not at the ordinary markets. True town rivalries cannot be downed. A trader from Portsmouth (one of Boroughport's dearest commercial enemies) is likely to be beaten up suddenly with cudgels, and the local glovers use every means short of murder to keep the Southampton glovers from buying up fine skins at a bargain.

In the main, nevertheless, Boroughport Fair is a legitimate and honest place. The perjuries around the horse traders' stalls are not excessive for the trade. Brawls are promptly suppressed, and a summary court with a jury of merchants is in constant session to settle any money dispute that may arise during the chaffering.[1] The crowd brings together a legion of bakers, butchers, cooks, porters,

---

[1] These courts were called the Courts of Pie-Powders (*pieds-poudreux* —"dusty feet"), because the cases were settled as fast as the dust could fall from the foot.

carters, and general purveyors who add to the hurly-burly. All the nimble lads for miles around have drifted down (if possible with female companions) to learn the London fashions, the latest cut of "gally hosen," and of French hoods. The girls eye the ribbons, the "inkles" (tape), coifs, and stomachers. The gallants pick up the perfume pomanders, not to mention the lace and scented gloves that their dames and sweethearts long for. Almost everybody takes home the new ballad to the tune, "Two Men wooing a Maid"— which is all the rage now in this part of the country.

Yet what would be any fair without its wonders and sideshows? The younger Hollydeans, including the sophisticated Captain Andrew himself, are wholly willing to forget all about the cambric and satin her Ladyship wants to purchase, and the new *Discovery of the Indies* which her good knight sees in the bookstall simply to elbow up to a long array of "wonders." Here are monkeys dancing upon a rope, a horse with hoofs like rams' horns, a goose with four legs, and a cock with three—"Born over in Hampshire, good people, born over in Hampshire." Of more interest to gentle visitors most certainly is the wonderful display of German clockwork—the Salutation of the Virgin, and (on another mechanism) the Ocean, with Venus, Neptune, Orion, and the Dolphins all moving about as true as life!

As for the commoner folk they gape and cheer before a realistic puppet show, presenting a most classical subject— the story of Hero and Leander, but with the Thames substituted for the Hellespont to avoid puzzling the unlearned. When the showmen cease squeaking and pulling the strings, it is time to wander among the stalls of the toy sellers, the gingerbread women, the pie women, or listen to the summons of quack doctors to come into their tents and be cured of most hideous maladies. Most of the hawkers and showmen are sheer rascals—but what of it? Every mortal at certain times enjoys being cozened.

Presently there is an unwonted uproar. A gingerbread woman's table has been upset. While she is delivering a shrill tongue-lashing upon the bumpkin that jostled her, a great crowd gathers. Then a fat squire shouts aloud, "My purse!" "My purse!" shouts a sailor, wedged up against him, clapping his hand to his pocket. Instantly people rush in from every side, and the hubbub is unspeakable when (for the Devil loves to betray his own), by amazing luck, a sheriff's officer sees a weasel-faced fellow wriggling out of the crowd. The thief is nipped with the purses before he can pass them to a confederate just in the background. The gingerbread woman is hustled away too; very likely she had upset her own table as part of the game.—That ends the story until the next grand assize and possibly the fearful rites of Tom Hemprope.

When the fair is over, a great calm settles over Borough-port. The lads are stuffed with "wonders"; their Mopsies and Dorcases have got their ribbons and green kerchiefs, and their money in any case is all spent. The country purchasers load their commodities into great bags which can be slung across the saddles or human backs; Hollydean buttery is stocked for the winter and Captain Andrew is reminding his sisters how incomparably superior are the fairs around London. "Then they would tire my head still more," avows poor little Arabella.

¶ *Chapter* XX: Concerning Matters of War and the Gallant Duello

ELIZABETH'S England is a land of blessed peace. Wars, as we have seen, torment the Continent, great battles are fought upon the seas, but barring a single feeble raid of the Spaniards upon Penzance a foreign foe sets no foot upon the kingdom, save as he comes as a prisoner. Gladly therefore do we exempt ourselves from discussing pitched battles and sieges, the campaigns of his white-plumed Majesty Henry IV of France, of his Spanish adversary the Duke of Parma, and of the scientific modes of warfare being developed by that puissant young Dutchman, the Stadholder Maurice of Nassau.

But if there is no active warfare near Boroughport there is plenty of talk thereof; armed forces are constantly leaving the port for fighting the Queen's enemies in France or the Netherlands, and since 1588 a small body of troops has kept watch and ward at the castle by the harbor mouth ready to welcome any bold Don who may dream of avenging the Armada. We cannot therefore quite omit some words concerning the military system as peaceful Thorpshire sees it, concerning weapons of war and the practice thereof, and lastly concerning that private combat still too frequent betwixt gentlemen—namely, the gallant duello.

The English are a fighting race, and yet the permanent force at the disposal in peace times of their sovereigns has been incredibly small. Before the outbreak of war with Spain her Majesty had about one hundred picturesquely clad "beef eaters" for her personal guard. There were a few armed men at the Tower of London and certain other great

[291]

fortresses like the Castle of Dover and the forts guarding Portsmouth. A somewhat larger force was at Berwick-on-Tweed commanding the Scottish border. Otherwise the Queen was almost wholly dependent upon emergency levies among her loving subjects to meet any sudden crisis.[1]

Things have somewhat altered in war time but there has been no fundamental change in the system. Englishmen hate standing armies, would rather risk a serious invasion than maintain one, and have enormous confidence in the blessed barrier of the sea.

The head of the Queen's militia in Thorpshire is Lord Wellborn, a great nobleman, who is Lord Lieutenant. He appoints the lower officers, assesses the number of men to be supplied from each parish, and commands the whole if the levy is supposed to take the field. For service overseas volunteers are collected, if possible, by the Lord Lieutenant and his deputies. There is no legal requirement to serve in foreign wars, and it is no slight task sometimes to fill up the English contingents serving in the campaigns in France and the Low Countries against the Spaniards. If volunteers do not come forward (and the pay is miserable and other inducements scanty) there are various methods. The Justices close their eyes at illegalities, when it is needful to make up the local contingent. The first resource is always the jails. Last year when a sudden summons came down from her Majesty all the prisoners in Boroughport Jail waiting trial on capital charges were enlisted in Sir John Norris's famous regiments on the continent; their indictments would be dropped against a promise not to return to England without official permission. A dozen highwaymen and other cut-throats thus saved the hangman's fees, and,

---

[1] It is needless to speak of the insufficient and often ragged and disorderly forces which were supposed to uphold the royal authority in Ireland.

it is to be hoped, killed a few Spaniards before being killed themselves.

Roving vagabonds caught by the constables are dealt with in the same way. In 1591 a hundred "loose and masterless men" were thus seized in London and kept locked up until the ship was ready to carry them to the Low Countries. If such means fail another resource is at hand. On Easter Sunday when every man is bound legally to take the Sacrament, a strong press gang can close about the parish church and hold the entire congregation prisoner until the proper number of healthy young fellows have been set aside for the army. Technically illegal? Doubtless, but the Queen's needs silence private right.

Such bezonians [1] are as a rule no loss to the community, but good captains groan when they see them. "The very scum of the earth"; "the worst of everything is thought good enough for this service";—so high officers write home in disgust about their "reinforcements." Bad captains are not sorry to have such carrion killed off rapidly—they can draw the pay for the dead men, and if there is a muster will pick up "shadows" or "fagots" (clowns from the neighborhood) to stand in line to make up the proper number until the inspection is past. The whole army service is penetrated with corruption; a bribe to the recruiting officer's sergeant will let a "pressed man" skulk home again. Lucky if the sergeant does not divide the coins with his superior. After the troops are levied it is a task to get them from their parishes to the spot of military rendezvous. They are entitled to a halfpence per mile "coat and conduct money," but there are more abuses about that. You can never be sure of your contingent until the ships set sail. In 1592 Sir John Norris, while waiting at Southampton, reported that a full hundred of his men had run away. The hue and cry

[1] From the Spanish *bisoño*—*"raw recruit."*

[293]

was raised; the constables made a great noise of pursuing but not a rascal was brought back. Probably they had been received into farmers' houses and thence aided to escape into distant parishes.

Curiously enough these jailbirds when in foreign parts turn out after all to be Englishmen. They fight bravely, if not with the finished discipline of Continental veterans, and have made a gallant showing on many fields; but it is fortunate for her Majesty she can trust her seamen rather than her land forces in the contest with Spain.

For home defense, however, there is the militia. Every gentleman of above £1000 income is required to keep on hand a certain quantity of weapons and armor as well as horses fit for military service. At Hollydean the armory with its supply of bills, bows, and harquebuses is a familiar part of the house. Sir Walter is colonel of the militia for the Boroughport region; his neighbor Sir William Truncheon is second in command of the regiment. Under them there are squires who are captains, lieutenants, and ancients (ensigns), yeomen who are corporals, and every able-bodied man in the region is obliged to come to the annual militia muster under pain of the stiff fine of forty shillings. Their naïve evolutions on that day lead to the scornful remarks of such real soldiers as Captain Andrew who has smelled real powder. Half the line jumps when a culverin is shot off. There is practically no uniform except a big red cross of St. George sewn on the jerkin of each private. It is a great feat if a company can execute such a simple order as "double the files!" "Lucky the Spaniards do not meet them!" Still they are healthy Englishmen. In an emergency they might not run as quickly as professional soldiers would think. But if the military training is deplorable the martial spirit is a thing to be reckoned with. The English are ever a fighting race. The fondness for vigorous sports assists greatly. To be good at wrestling and quarter-staff play is never a harm when it comes to push of pike in the battalia. Singular and unfortunate is the gentleman's or yeoman's son who cannot ride. The art of war is still very simple. It is reckoned that England contains 120,000 forcible men who can be mobilized into some kind of military organization pretty rapidly. Perhaps it was as well for the Duke of Parma that in 1588 he was not able to invade England as the royal Philip ordered him.

The daily weapon of the gentlemen is the sword, and we shall soon speak of fencing. The country folk and the prentices content themselves with the less "gentle" quarter-staff and cudgel and are lawfully required still to become good bowmen. Among the prentices clinched fists are regularly supplemented by heavy clubs. "I'll cudgel that opinion out of ye!" is the normal end to many an argument. Then the disputants smash at one another until one of them collapses with a broken head. Quarter-staff is more scientific. The weapon is a light, tough piece of wood. One contestant grasps it in the middle with one hand while the other keeps a loose hold between the middle and one end. Here again the aim is with a spin and thwack to knock your opponent down and at least give him a bloody pate and nose. Two powerful skillful men are really a sight to behold; if well matched they can clash and fend for an hour and then stop unharmed from sheer lack of breath.

Outside of any town or village, however, on any fine afternoon you can hear the warning "Fast!" followed by the whir of an arrow and the rejoicing "God save the mark!" [1] if the shot has been a good one.

Archery is still very popular and, it is fondly believed, is still a valuable element in the national defense. Every lad

---

[1] Namely, "Let no later arrow displace mine in the target as a better shot." The cry became however a general stock phrase.

knows all about Crécy, Poitiers, and Agincourt. People shake their heads when it is suggested that gunpowder is making the yew-bow useless except for killing crows and rabbits. As late as 1572 the Queen, when negotiating to send Charles IX of France six thousand men, promised "half of them should be archers." Around London the annual parade of the city's archers three thousand strong and led by their captain general the "Duke of Shoreditch" is a great civic ceremony culminating in elaborate shooting matches at Smithfield. A prodigious store of bows and arrows is in the royal armory at the Tower; and in 1588 when nearly all the militia were called out, from one-fifth to one-half were armed with bows although the remainder had firearms, pikes, or bills (hook-shaped pole-axes).

The law does all it can to promote archery. Every merchant trading with countries producing good bow staves is required to import four such for every ton of merchandise and ten for every tun of wine. The letter of the statute requires compulsory archery practice every Sunday morning in every parish, just after church. The act of Henry VIII forbids any person over twenty-four to shoot at a mark set under two hundred and twenty yards—effective military distance; and very lately in 1591 a royal proclamation warns the Queen's subjects that archery is not merely a "good recreation" but "of great use in the defense of the realm"; therefore all games prohibited by law—especially "bowls, dicing, cards, and such like"—are forthwith forbidden afresh and archery ordered "revived and practiced."

This proclamation is as well observed as other royal proclamations—and no better. But whatever its military value archery is certainly a noble sport and very popular. Fine gentlemen never disdain to show their retainers how they can outshoot them. In the great hall at Hollydean hangs a whole sheaf of silver arrows, prizes won by the lords of the Manor from generation to generation in archery contests, although probably none of Sir Walter's ancestors could "cleave the wand at four hundred yards," as the ballads tell of Robin Hood.

At a little distance from Hollydean are set out the archery butts for long-range shooting. Here there are covered booths where the Hall and village people can watch the contests on sunny afternoons, and plenty of honest folk will drift up from Boroughport if the report goes that Dick Greenjacket the head gamekeeper and Harry Keen the town champion will shoot off a round. The range is two hundred and forty yards across the close-clipped greensward at the end of which is set the "clout," [1] resting upon a bank of turf. To "hit the clout" at this range calls not for point-blank accuracy, but skill in sending the arrow to a great elevation—a pretty undertaking.

Whatever the military value, archery is a fair sport to look upon. Dick Greenjacket stands firm and upright, his left foot a stride before his right, both his arms stiff, his left holding the bow at arm's length, his right with the first three fingers and thumb drawing the string up to his right ear. When he is ready to shoot his whole body goes into bringing the arrow close up to the head, and immediately he lets fly without hanging on the string. The shaft quivers on the edge of the clout; a great shout arises and Greenjacket at amazingly short intervals sends three more arrows (two of them nearer the center) after his first. Then he steps back to give the turn to the town champion.

Such practiced archers use yew-bows about six feet long and with a "weight" (pull) of nearly ninety pounds. These bows are beautifully polished, rubbed with wax and tallow, and kept from frost and damp in fine waxed cloth. The

[1] A canvas target eighteen inches across, stuffed with straw and with a white circle in the center.

arrows, about thirty-three inches long, are made of ash or oak and feathered from the wing of a gray goose. To handle such a powerful weapon demands not merely strength but truly scientific skill—every fiber in the archer's body entering into the exertion of bringing the arrow up to the head and then releasing it the instant the eye sights the point as bearing on the target.

Some twenty arrows are shot by each contestant, with much betting among the witnesses, and many cheers of "aim!" whenever a particularly lucky shaft is sped. The boys and younger men shoot during the rest intervals with lighter bows at nearer targets at point-blank range. Finally amid Hollydean rejoicings, Dick Greenjacket wins by a shaft in the very middle of "the white" and kneels to receive the silver arrow from his devoted admirer, Mistress Anne herself. Harry Keen takes his defeat like a sportsman, and merely says something jocularly about revenge; and then the whole contest has to be waged over again at the ale house. If archery wanes as a sport something will be lacking in Merry England.

Has the bowman still a place in warfare? The question is fought out ten times per day wherever old-style and new-style soldiers gather. Firearms are still so clumsy and experimental that a strong case can be built up for the good old trusty yew. The harquebus, the standard infantry firearm, has an accurate range of barely a hundred yards. Wet weather can spoil its powder and extinguish its match. In the excitement of battle a soldier forgets how to load it, crams down the bullet first, and disables his weapon. Then too the bow is infinitely lighter than the harquebus, and does not weary out a man merely by carrying it; and finally —best argument of all—a bowman can shoot off half a sheaf of arrows while your harquebus man fires once and reloads his unwieldy weapon.

Plausibly said; but the most experienced captains think otherwise. The celebrated Sir Roger Williams says he would rather go to battle with five hundred good match-locks than fifteen hundred bowmen. In bad weather bow-strings slack and arrow feathers flake off—as bad a trouble as dampness on powder. Firearms are constantly improving in range. Archers in battle get nervous and shoot wildly— especially if their opponents have noisy firearms; and (very important) a bowman to shoot efficiently must be well fed and untired; the man with firearms may be half starved and dog weary. If still he can load and aim properly he can kill the enemy just the same. Finally a trained harque-bus man can now fire actually forty good shots per hour; his ammunition is much more portable than the clumsy sheafs of arrows. He will be blazing away accurately when your bowman is standing helpless.

The real argument is this, however—even a good bowman cannot kill a foe in armor except at extremely short range; firearms are deadly at much longer ranges, and although there are "bullet proof" cuirasses on sale they are so heavy that their wearers are almost useless for any military exertion.

So the bow is disappearing from its long primacy among weapons, and when a force goes into battle about one-third is likely to be "shot." The ordinary arm of the harquebus man is the musket. This piece including the stock is about five and a half feet long and weighs so much that a forked rest is almost indispensable. There is the lighter caliver but this is more a sporting piece and not for battle service. Cavalry men, travelers, and the like however find dags or the smaller tacks—both kinds of clumsy pistols—much more useful. To discharge all these the main reliance is still on the very simple matchlock, a bit of slow match touched into the priming by a trigger. Officers and fine gentlemen sometimes display petronels, in which an elabo-

[299]

rate mechanism revolves a small wheel against a bit of pyrites, sending off sparks which light the priming. These "wheel-locks," however, are expensive and not very reliable. There is also the snaphance—discharged by something very like the flintlock of later days; but these are still rare and undeveloped. The matchlock is fairly convenient provided your match is still burning. To be sure of a spark soldiers often march with a long piece of tarred rope dangling from one shoulder and lighted at the end. It is a picturesque sight to see an army marching along in the darkness with its hundreds of sparks all moving and twinkling.

Concerning cannon we say very little. Artillery of many sizes from great sixty-pounders down to half-pounders have been known these two hundred years; but they have proved most useful in sieges, both for attack and defense, and on shipboard. Every army takes along a small artillery train for reducing fortresses. If there is a battle the guns are lumbered to that point where presumably they will do the most good. When the foe comes within reach the culverins (eighteen pounders), sakers (six pounders), and falconers (three pounders) play on them to break up their files and scare their horses. The service of the guns is very slow. After a few shots, likely there is a charge. The gunners run back in haste for protection behind the pikemen. After that the cannon are out of commission till the end of the battle when they fall sure prize to the victor.

To send harquebus men into action unsupported by other arms has never been dreamed of by the most competent captains. Many a battle (such as Ivry in 1590) has been settled by the battering charges of great masses of cavalry trusting mainly to the old cavaliers' weapons—the lance and sword. However the backbone of an army often seems to be the pikemen. The pike is "the gentleman's weapon"; it is more honorable to carry it than a musket, and grasped by an efficient soldier it is a terrible implement indeed. In the ordinary English levy the pikes greatly exceed the matchlocks, and a band marching with all its eighteen-foot pikes in the air looks like an enormous moving porcupine. However the pike is too heavy to carry long distances in this manner. On open marches the soldiers hold them close to the steel head and let the long butt trail upon the ground. The result of thus "trailing the pike" is a tremendous clattering as often as the infantry advance across the cobbles of a village street.

English soldiers are partial also to a very ancient native weapon—the bill. This is a staff weapon with a head like a bill hook but furnished with pitiless spikes on the top and back. "Bills and bows!" is still the regular alarm cry in a camp. Bills are especially popular in the militia because they can be used in hedge and other forms of peaceful work. In campaign work the battalia or regiments [1] are likely to have a sprinkling of bill men to help out the pikes, although the bill is so much lighter than the pike that it is likely to be trusted to the weaker men and therefore the least efficient.

When the Thorpshire militia is reviewed, there still appears to be plenty of armor and very beautiful armor too. Nearly all the wealthy country gentlemen have fine corselets, morions (open helmets), and thigh guards while they curvet around on horseback. Similar protection, less decorated and costly, is worn by the more powerful pikemen who parade in the front ranks. But armor, though splendidly inlaid and becoming now a true creation of art, is gradually dropping its importance and becoming merely a glittering show. Full panoplies of mail are seldom worn

---

[1] The regiment at this time was a more or less fluid brigade made up of a number of companies or "bands" and without any very permanent organization.

even by the heaviest cavalry, and are kept mainly for the splendid show warfare of the tournaments. It is gunpowder that is doing it. There is no real protection from musket balls save ever-increasing mobility.

Gunpowder then, despite all anathemas against it,[1] is beginning to transform warfare and thereby a great part of general civilization. It implies more than simply a new method for killing men. The long process is beginning whereby war becomes so complicated and expensive it can be indulged in only by very powerful governments, and there is a gradual clamp being put on these local blood-lettings, which, by their enormous number in unsettled times, produced more real misery than all the world-jarring conflicts which spread themselves in the histories.

However the old feudal traditions die hard. At the Court, where the Queen dotes on stirring spectacles, rich young noblemen still tilt in the ring breaking blunted lances on horseback, and thrust and fend at one another with dulled swords. Tournaments before Gloriana take place about every so often. In 1581, for example, she graciously allowed herself to be "besieged" in the "Fortress of Perfect Beauty." Earl Arundel, Lord Windsor, Sir Philip Sidney, and Foulke Greville, proclaiming themselves the "Four Foster Children of Desire," endeavored to capture it. They had to meet twenty-two high-born "defendants" who took turns in defending the Virgin Queen—an extravagant display of prancing horses, gilded armor, flourishing of steel, flapping pennons and gorgeous surcoats, along with melodious trumpeting. Of course nobody was hurt in the least. Baronial warfare is in its second childhood.[2]

[1] Such protests as those of "a certain lord" in Part I, Henry IV, Act I, Scene III, against "villainous salt-petre digged out of the bowels of the harmless earth," were frequent enough in the age of Shakespeare.

[2] Tournaments practically died the death with the accession of James I, who detested martial displays and in fact almost everything military.

If, nevertheless, the tournament is a mere vestige of the retreating Middle Ages, much longer will survive the tradition that every man of consequence should protect his honor by his own prowess. All but the most peaceful types of gentlemen wear swords, often harmless enough bits of steel in handsome scabbards which they wear as part of their daily dress. Well-born boys of ten are likely to be ordered by their mothers to belt on their little walking swords when they accompany their parents on visits of ceremony or even only to the tradesmens' shops. Merchants can get along with mere penknives, prentices and yeomen with heavy cudgels, but a blade at one's thigh is practically indispensable for one who would pass for a man of family.

That being the case, to know something of fencing is a needful part of a polite education, and the average lad of quality is likely to take far more congenially to his fencing master than to his Latin.

Captain Andrew Hollydean began to study the noble art of the swordsman long before he went to the university. At Cambridge he enjoyed the best of masters and learned to pass as a high practitioner of the "Noble Science of Defense." He began his training just as a great change was coming over English methods of fencing. Until after 1570 the genteel method of personal combat was with sword and buckler. The sword was long and heavy, and on your left arm you carried a buckler—a small light target which had a sharp spike about a foot long projecting from the center. On this spike you could catch your enemy's sword if you were skillful, or stab him outright by dashing the buckler in his face. A duel with bucklers made an outrageous clamor, and the buckler itself often interfered with the full play of its possessor's sword. As a result by 1580, thanks also to foreign influences, the old sword-and-buckler play went out very rapidly. Instead came the rapier-and-dagger, far more scientific, and now sword-and-buckler fighting is left to the brawls of serving men.

The rapier is a keen slim sword with a three-foot blade and the dagger has a twelve-inch blade beside the handle. You hold the dagger in your left hand to parry thrusts against your body, while trying to send the sharp point of the rapier through your antagonist. There are even fencers so advanced that they dispense with the dagger altogether, making the rapier do for both sword and shield, but that style of very developed practice is not common yet.

Captain Andrew like every other good fencer has his collection of fine rapiers—some of which are merely handsome curiosities, others are tested and valued friends. If you are likely to have quarrels thrust upon you, you cannot be too careful of the choice of your weapon. Your life may rest on its balance and keenness. Andrew has a beautiful "Isebrook" from Innsbruck in Tyrol, which by the elaborate gilding inlaid in the blade makes it a magnificent weapon of ceremony; but if he sees a serious passage-at-arms ahead, his choice is probably a steel-gray, wavy-lined Bilbo from Bilbao in Spain, although the famous Toledo blades also from Spain have still plenty of valiant admirers.

Fencing is a science, with its professors, its literature, and its very familiar jargon. Master Crabtree notes with a sigh that when a new package of books came up last from Whitepaper the stationer, the young captain, discarding an excellent homily *Garden of Holy Homilies,* and a fiery *Discomfiture of the Romish Tyrant,* thrust his nose deep into the *Giacomo di Grassi, His True Art of Defence,* an elaborate treatise on fencing just translated from the Italian.

In any gathering of young gallants almost as common as talk of cockfighting and bull-baiting are the cant terms of the fencers' lore—mostly from the Italian—the *stoccata* (thrust), the *pararla* (parry), the *passado,* the *punto re-*

verso, and all the rest. Fencing masters abound. There are several in Boroughport who like to pass for Venetians although probably they are only rascally Frenchmen. They all try to maintain "colleges" and make a great show of elaborate science. The walls of their establishments are hung with blunt rapiers, mailed gloves, and masks, and at popular hours these spots are the great rendezvous of all the holier "gentle bloods" in nearer Thorpshire.

To hear one of these masters-at-arms talk, you would suppose fencing was strictly a question of mathematics of "time, distance, and proportion," and of "one, two, and a third in your breast." The most popular form of fencing is supposedly "Italian," but the "Spanish School" has its worshipful advocates. Here the geometrical or "Euclidian" principle is carried to extremes. The adversaries move round and round in circles, striving never to come uncovered within touch of each other's weapons. There are three different passes to be learned, all based on an attack by movements of the foot geometrically measured, and it is by adroit combination of these passes that you hope for victory. Italian fencing is more natural and really effective, but the Spanish style is fascinating to watch; greatly it resembles a form of grimly vigorous circular dancing.

Fencing like archery is a noble exercise not profitless for the defense of the realm, but (for men's sins!) there is quite another motive behind much of the zeal which fills the fencing schools. Fortunate is the man of family who reaches the calm waters of later life without having to "defend his honor" in at least one duel.

The old mediæval judicial duel [1] when litigants settled

---

[1] A case of a legally allowed judicial duel in England occurred as late as 1571. The lists were cleared and Common Pleas Judges came as umpires; but the challenger took fright and failed to appear. Only in 1818 was the judicial duel abolished by statute.

land titles with battle-axes has actually disappeared, although laws permitting it are still on the statute books. Duels now are strictly private affairs, without more legal standing than common brawls. It is well understood they must not be over matters for lawyers but over personal and private differences. Also they must be conducted between men of the rank of gentlemen, with a show of courtesy, fairness, and honor. It is most disreputable to bandy words, then draw swords, rush out into the street, and cut and thrust like two quarrelsome prentices with their cudgels. Furthermore never must two or more men assail one alone; if he is killed the law shows no mercy. Everything in short must be done to make a duel a "private trial of difference," and if the contest is perfectly fair the law and the pardoning sovereigns are likely to be pretty merciful in event of a tragedy.

All this may sound strange enough to a later age, yet really there is a social advance. Mediæval duels were often cold-blooded assassinations thinly disguised by a few formalities. Great lords could outrage private gentlemen most foully and whistle at any demand for satisfaction. Now it is said again that the haughtiest earl in England cannot proffer an affront to an obscure, country squire, and not have to answer his challenge or suffer such public contempt as even great noblemen must feel.

Dueling is grievously common in England, but it is more common in Spain and Italy and still more common in France. In that nation it is really devastating half the seignioral houses of the kingdom. Any trifle, when young gentlemen get together, is an excuse for a contest. "Who fought yesterday? Who is to fight today?" Paris gallants ask when they meet almost every morning. Worse still two or three friends of both of the parties are expected to join in the fray. A single duel can mean three or more tragedies.

When Captain Andrew served in France he was caught in such an encounter. Two acquaintances quarreled over the color of a ribbon worn by one of their mistresses. "A mere trifle!" "No matter—let's fight!" Andrew was dragged into a contest "from which I could not in honor escape." He got a shrewd wound in the thigh. One of his friends was slain outright. "It could have been far worse."

Wholesale duels of this sort are hardly known in England but ordinary ones are sadly common. Only since we began visiting Hollydean Captain Andrew has been second in a familiar type of combat. One of his old friends, Lieutenant Headstrong, has returned on furlough from Holland. At the Mitre in Boroughport he met a Master Wrangle, also back as gentleman volunteer on a naval cruise. The two began chewing the delicate question: "Did Lord Thomas Howard desert Sir Richard Grenville when the latter was cut off with the Revenge?" Different judgments led to loud speech, harsher words, personalities, and finally Headstrong rose and cried to the astonished taproom, "Thou hast lied—and touched me in my very honor." Wrangle merely clapped his hand on his hilt, and then before a dozen witnesses, deliberately bit his thumb and made a contemptuous gesture toward the lieutenant.

This was the clearest possible invitation to a challenge; but rather than brawl before the tapsters the two gentlemen bowed coldly and each sought his lodgings. An hour later Wrangle by Headstrong's servant received a written defiance stated (per best usage) in plain brief language, "thouing" [1] Wrangle several times and bidding him name a second who could confer with Captain Andrew, Headstrong's second.

Wrangle, foreseeing such a missive, had already asked a

---

[1] "Thouing" was the token either of extreme contempt or of extreme familiarity.

certain naval comrade Master Brackish to aid him in probable eventualities. Brackish and Hollydean conferred immediately. Headstrong and Wrangle had been old friends—could not the matter be patched up? This was not an ordinary quarrel about cards, dice, social standing, or women. Alas! The lie direct had been passed before witnesses. There are many kinds of lies classified carefully in the books on "Honor and Arms." Conditional Lies, Certain Lies, the Lie Special, the Vain Lie and last but not least the Lie Direct. Would not Lieutenant Headstrong qualify his charge with an "if"?—in that case Wrangle might bring himself to some form of apology. But Headstrong would proffer no "if," and Wrangle would make no move toward an apology. There was nothing left but to fight the matter out.

Various young bloods have used dags or other pistol-like firearms, but they are still unreliable and leave few advantages to the braver man. The matter was therefore settled with sword and dagger just at dawn in a pretty meadow outside of Boroughport. The contestants came each with his second and one servant apiece, set as a scout to head off intruders. Andrew had dropped a private hint to Dr. Bleeder. That worthy was not actually present, but was awake and ready to be summoned. The seconds measured the swords and daggers for equality; and chose a smooth bit of turf while the principals, far apart and at a distance, stripped to their shirts; and being each fairly religious men, muttered the Lord's Prayer and other soul-saving petitions. Then they were set some twelve paces away, rapiers in right hands, daggers clinched in left, with Hollydean and Brackish standing a little back on either side, their own swords ready to stop any foul play.

"On guard, gentlemen!" shouted the captain. Headstrong and Wrangle leaped toward each other, their blades dart-

ing in the new sunlight like lightnings. Headstrong shot
his point at his enemy's heart, but the dagger turned it, and
he barely leaped back in time to avoid the counter thrust.
Being both vigorous young men, very angry and quite well
matched as fencers, for a good ten minutes they thus
pleased the Devil by trying to murder each other. They
were red, sweating, panting when at last Wrangle put all
his force into an overbold passado. Headstrong parried and
came back with a clear thrust into his opponent's shoulder.
Wrangle with a harsh groan reeled backward, but the seconds dashed down the lieutenant's rapier before he could
deliver another stroke.

Dr. Bleeder reached the scene in time, and for once
thought his patient had lost blood enough. The blade had
spared Wrangle's lungs and in four weeks he was about
again. If he had perished Headstrong would have been
tried for manslaughter, but could have escaped by reading
his Neck-verse and being branded on the thumb as are
several dashing gentlemen well known in Thorpshire.
"Honor has been fully satisfied"—Wrangle and Headstrong
are now quite friendly and comradely together.

ILLUSTRATIONS TO "SHEPHERD'S CALENDAR," 1597.   OCTOBER.

¶ *Chapter* XXI: Concerning Travelers and Inns

TO Boroughport and Hollydean we come, and near them we remain until we bid Merry England "Godspeed" forever. But Thorpshire is not the whole kingdom much less the whole world. Sir Walter and Captain Andrew have seen much of the Continent and visit London at least twice a year. Other voyagers and travelers are constantly coming and going. Perforce, therefore, we turn our eyes to the roads and the methods of journeying of the Queen's lieges, and to their taverns, inns, and like places of public accommodation.

Already Englishmen of family are beginning to delight in touring the Continent; beautiful cities, the imposing courts of kings and princes, lordly castles, flourishing universities all have great attraction. As soon as a young man has a university degree, if possible he goes across the Channel. Spain is closed to all good Protestants on account of War and the Inquisition, but Italy (right at the Pope's doors) is more tolerant. You can go straight to Rome and catch a glimpse of the Pope himself. Going or coming Paris is sure to be visited for better or worse, and probably the Rhinelands and such stately places as Heidelberg, North Germany, and Holland are constantly visited by soldiers and men of business but have no such attraction as the luxurious South. Above all Venice is the lure for many Englishmen; its splendid luxuries, its canal pageants, its commerce with the Levant—all fascinates them. They talk about it, read about it, write plays about it, and whenever possible visit it.

In the minds of many sober people foreign travel and especially visits to Italy do infinite harm. Italy is denounced by the sensible Roger Ascham as a veritable "Circe's court." Pliable young Englishmen drift to Italy and become "Italianated." They come home not so much Catholics as atheists, learn to meddle in other men's matters, bring back merry books that ruin all morality, and generally delight in vanities and filthy living. "Being mules and horses before they went, they return changed into foxes and wolves." All this is sad enough, but foreign travel is still so much of a romantic adventure that you must search hard for the young gentleman who declines the opportunity to make for Montpellier, Bologna, or Padua under the pretext of "improving his studies"; despite all risk of fetching back "a naughty conscience, an empty purse, and a weak stomach."

Foreign travel in any case is so costly, requiring usually several horses and servants and a well-filled purse, that whatever the harm done it cannot become a widespread evil. On the other hand gadding about England is all in the day's work. Every good merchant is forever going to London on trade or legal business. Every social aspirant is frequently headed for the Court. Oxford and Cambridge students are always coming and going, also the very important students at the Inns of Court. Pack-horse carriers and carters are constantly on the road; and the more local demands of business and the assizes provide plenty of journeys into the county towns.

Truth to tell this domestic travel is not made more easy by the state of the roads. On matters of state, with expense no object, messengers can indeed accomplish considerable feats. Four days after Prince (now King) James was born to Mary, Queen of Scots, in Edinburgh the tidings had spanned the four hundred odd miles to London; but ordinary intercourse can often drag at a snail's pace. The breakdown of the old manorial system and the suppression of the monasteries early in the sixteenth century almost halted the upkeep of the roads for years; bridges became unsafe and ruinous, while holes and ruts perhaps were filled up with a few faggots and brush-wood and became sheer death traps for men and horses. Even now conditions are abominable. Road repairers have no system; each parish is a law unto itself. By law the Queen's highway should be fifty feet wide. Often it is suffered to dwindle to twelve feet, with bushes spreading out into the wheel tracks. In winter such "roads" are mere drains and water courses.

By the statute every parish has to have a surveyor of roads, and the richer inhabitants must supply teams and laborers; the poorer must work four days a year on the roads. Thus a little is done, but no public service is more scanted. Around Thorpshire as elsewhere it is complained that travelers do great harm to the grain by riding inside the fences—the public ways are so intolerable. Inland there are many desolate regions, as between Oxford and Cambridge, where no wheeled vehicle can pass all winter; and in Warwickshire the woods crowd down so thick that travelers always say their prayers against lurking robbers ere entering. "Roads (it will be written) were not made— they happened, because a sufficient number of people and horses trod out a track."

When considering the Queen's justice, we met with Hal Liftpurse who watched the roads. Poor Hal has been hanged, but has left plenty of old comrades who take their toll every day. Certain places not far from London are notoriously the robbers' "happy hunting grounds"; such as Gadshill near Rochester,[1] Shooter's Hill near Black-

[1] The scene of Falstaff's exploit.

heath, also the deserted stretches of Salisbury Plain and Newmarket Heath.

When entering a belt of forest, look to the priming of your firearms and above all try to reach a good inn before nightfall. The penalty for highway robbery is the same as for murder, and a highwayman will not hesitate to shed blood. However as a rule travelers are chicken-hearted people; they would rather surrender their purses than risk being run through or shot down. A successful highwayman cultivates the character of a picturesque ruffian, wears a hideous mask, rides a splendid horse, and enjoys displaying a rough humor. Sometimes robberies are so frequent that they can be used for government purposes. In 1562 Sir William Cecil (later Lord Burghley) employed two young gentlemen to halt and rob near Gravesend the messenger of the Spanish ambassador, whom diplomatic immunity protected from lawful search. His Excellency did not suspect that his correspondence was betrayed until much later.

The sheriffs and better constables scour the country, every hangman does his duty, and gradually the safety of the roads is improving, but matters are still pretty perilous. It is a troublesome matter to send a sum in coin from Boroughport to London to discharge a sizable debt, and be sure the gold reaches your creditor. In any case travelers with valuables had better each man carry his "case of dags," and travel in watchful companies. Then perhaps he is safe—but the strangest mishaps can happen.

The roads being what they are, wheeled vehicles have at best a hard time over them; still skillful carters with stout horses can usually get through in the better seasons of the year. After all even a lightly laden cart can usually carry more than several pack horses.

The carts are ponderous, creaking, two-wheeled affairs,

but they are gradually driving out more primitive means of freightage. Boroughport is a seaport and so most of its trade with London comes and goes by coaster, but the centers usually have each its string of carts which makes a circuit of the nearer market towns and goes on to London at set intervals. Small places are content with one wagon per fortnight to London while sizable places can give trade for three a week. There are always certain inns betwixt which they lumber back and forth.

At Boroughport the courtyard of the Pelican is a scene of great bustle when one wagon fills up for Salisbury, another for Winchester, another clear for Bristol. The carriers are hale, competent men who besides their fees for freightage make an excellent thing by handling private correspondence, in absence of a regular postal service. A letter is thus passed from inn to inn the length of England, and will probably reach its destination—say in two or three weeks, provided the season is fine.

Some carriers also take a few passengers, if there are not too many boxes; but this service is tedious, uncomfortable, and mainly used only by "women and people of inferior condition" who are too weak to walk and too poor to ride. In any case freight by cart is a fairly expensive luxury, putting transportation of heavy bulky articles at a discount. A package from London to Keswick in the Northern Lake Country costs a flat penny per pound, with nearer places pro rata. No wonder that most of the common articles used near Boroughport are made up directly in Thorpshire.

The carts usually manage to crawl over the roads, but long strings of pack horses with their heavy panniers are still everywhere to be met with—especially away from any of the greater lines of travel. Now and then you can meet a horse litter—a litter slung between two steady-paced horses and supposed to be extra comfortable for delicate ladies and for invalids. But very near Boroughport, where the roads are fairly tolerable, and in the radius around London where they are better still, the village children will stop, gape, and perhaps bow or curtsey when a wonderful thing labors by—a great coach!

Coaches are still a novelty in England. It is alleged they were first invented in Hungary in the fifteenth century. More certain it is that in 1564 William Boonen, a Dutchman, began to build them at London. In a short time all the great ladies and rich gentlemen began desiring them. Probably the first reason was that they were more ostentatious and proclaimed the owner's glory; but it was soon found that (for exalted folk) they were really more economical. Even if they needed four or six horses and a coachman and footman, a whole retinue of servants could be tucked away in the "boot," rear seats, roof, etc., without having to provide a separate mount for each.

Lady Catherine has of course her coach with which she makes arrogant display whenever the ruts are not too deep to keep it from trundling into Boroughport. It has four wheels and an elaborately carved roof from which wave brilliant plumes. The sides are quite open, and her Ladyship is not often averse to displaying herself upon the deep cushions upholstered with scarlet velvet and silver lace. If she desires privacy there are heavy curtains ready to be drawn. Clinging to the rear guards or the roof, are always three or four footmen. Three or four maids are always wedged in behind their mistress. The six horses have no sinecure. Only last week, in fairly dry weather, the wheels crashed through the brushwood over a clayey rut on a road near Hollydean, and all the horses and all the swearing and pushing of the four footmen were unavailing until a dozen clowns had run up from the village.

For all that, a well-painted coach is a magnificent thing, proclaiming with every creak and rattle—"I convey greatness." The occupants have to pay the price of vanity by being grievously shaken. There are no springs, not even leathern straps from which to swing the coach-body, only cushions which perhaps break the jolting if the roads are tolerable. Only recently the Queen herself has complained of "her aching pains" from a necessary journey in her coach.

Around Boroughport coaches are still a novelty. To be a "coach family" is a sign of belonging absolutely to the upper gentry. In London they are now decidedly common, and there is the "caroche"—a smaller four-wheeler for town use. The narrow streets, it is complained, are actually becoming dangerous on account of the reckless driving. You can hire a small two-horse coach for ten shillings per day for driving around the metropolis, but long journeys in them are almost out of the question. The roads become so vile that even with many horses you can hardly get thirty miles from St. Paul's and the Tower.

If you need not luxury and pride but speed and service the best thing is to ride post. Along all the roads where the Queen's couriers are likely to be passing, an inn with government post horses can be found about every ten miles. These horses will go at a "false gallop" fully ten miles an hour and not become winded before they reach another posting station. If your body can endure this hard riding you can therefore cover well over one hundred miles a day. Nominally these horses are strictly for government business. Actually if you have any favor with the Queen's ministers or a noble lord, you can get authority to hire a horse on some pretext for fivepence the mile—this including the horse of a guide. If you have no such license you must pay sixpence. The guide must be paid for taking back the horses when you reach the station, but a company of travelers can club together and greatly reduce this charge. With such a system a man who can spend money can tear from one end of England to another in a marvelously short time—if he is not more dead than alive when he reaches his destination.[1]

If you have neither wealth nor pride you must take the road on ordinary horseback or afoot. Every gentleman and all but the poorest yeomen own at least one horse, and many a good tenant has two or three. Sir Francis Walsingham, by no means a very wealthy magnate, at one time stabled almost ninety. City folk, of course, are often horseless, but in London you can hire a tolerable nag for two shillings the first day and eighteenpence for each following day until he is returned, but these are London prices, At Boroughport as in almost any other provincial town a shilling per day is the orthodox charge for horse hire. If you would not hire and are a clever bargainer, it is very usual to buy a horse at the beginning of your journey and sell him off again at its end. This can make an expedition very cheap indeed.

On your own or a hired horse you can make up to fifty miles per day, although plenty of leisurely gentlemen think thirty miles an abundance if the stages lie between comfortable inns. A ride of more than so long always becomes wearisome. Saddles are small, hard, and very uncomfortable especially for bony, heavy riders. If there is a woman to be transported on a pillion behind one of her menfolks the stages have to be shorter still; although plenty of ladies

[1] Queen Elizabeth died in the early hours of March 25, 1603. Sir Robert Carey, riding at uttermost speed, brought the news to Edinburgh on March 27, so late that King James had gone to bed.

of quality can be met riding astride on a masculine saddle and keeping up with the best.

However there is little shame in depending on shank's mare. Foot-passengers are less hindered by the abominable roads and can take innumerable paths and short cuts closed to horsemen. Well-born students regularly walk long distances to and from the universities, as Hooker walked from Oxford to Exeter in 1570. Companies of actors literally "stroll" from town to town with their baggage piled in a wagon. Small merchants and respectable pedlars can be met with their scrips and packs at any hour of daylight, preferably of course in little companies for fear of robbers. Your Elizabethan has good legs; twenty-five miles per day is a fair average, and less than two weeks will get you from end to end of England.

Whether on shank's mare or gray mare the constant thought of every traveler unable to command hospitality turns upon an important subject—his inn.

Inns for the accommodation of travelers are by no means always the same thing as taverns or ordinaries, which are mainly for providing simply meat and drink, and which another age may call restaurants, although many ordinaries will have a few chambers where guests can spend the night. Ale houses are of still lower order—mere purveyors of drinkables, although doubtless you can get a simple dinner at most of them. In London the difference between these classes of public resorts is sharply drawn; in Boroughport and still more in the villages along the highways it often grows much fainter.

Boroughport, with its ocean commerce, fair, and many shops, gives business for at least a dozen regular inns and a dozen more ale houses. Their names are much the same as you will find in any town in England—indeed there seems to be a certain Act of Parliament about the names of inns which makes a hanging matter of any originality. There is the Pelican whence the carts and wagons start, the Mitre which commands the best trade of the army and naval officers, the White Hart where the country gentlemen foregather, the Mermaid that is the grand rendezvous for the justices and lawyers in assize season, the Greyhound, the Bell, and Golden Lion frequented by various classes of land merchants, the Swan and the Angel where you can meet all the sea traders and merchant captains, the Garter always sought by visiting yeomen, the Three Tuns where clerical gentlemen like Master Crabtree always go to discuss predestination and whether the living over at Tithington will soon fall vacant, and finally the cheap, disreputable Golden Lamb and Prince's Arms frequented "by people of the vulgar sort."

The best of these inns are very good indeed. Englishmen never fail to boast of their hostelries when it comes to bragging about the good things of their country. When Sir William Prosper, an old London friend of Sir Walter's, rode into Boroughport, uncertain lest an unwarned arrival at Hollydean might inconvenience the family, he spent his first night at the White Hart. A magnificently carved and painted sign, a "white hart" elegantly executed and a real work of art, projected seven feet over the entrance. Master Welcome the host had paid thirty pounds for the sign and was justly proud of it—for a fine sign is the outer token of cheery comfort within. The moment Sir William and his servant clattered up to the horse blocks, the warning whistle of the boy on guard brought out instantly Master Welcome with four or five blue-gowned waiters. The host took in his new guest's quality with one glance, and made his best bow as he stood in a spotless apron while the boys helped the visitor alight. At once Sir William found himself apparently in the hands of devoted friends. Inside the portal all was pleasing and cordial—the oak panels, the deep bays and cavernous fireplaces on which great wood fires crackled joyously; all said at once "Hard traveling is over."

The horses were being led off into the wide and busy stable yard, while the host himself conducted "his Worship" into a fine lavender-scented chamber with its enormous bed. Through the latticed windows came the glimpses of a small but well-stocked fruit garden. There was a faint and pleasant smell of excellent cooking coming up from the kitchen. Master Welcome, more like an old acquaintance than a servant, drew off Sir William's muddy boots, inquired about the road, and then what his guest would enjoy for supper. Being a gentleman of consequence the knight preferred to dine privately. Before long an excellent meal was being served on the portable table, but himself a genial experienced traveler, Sir William promptly asked Master Welcome to join him at the end over a bottle of good Malmsey; and the two talked at length in a friendly rambling manner, without condescension or overfamiliarity until Jane the trim chambermaid appeared with the warming pan (for the evenings are chilly) to run between the fine linen sheets.

The White Hart, in brief, is an inn of the best class. Welcome avows that on grand occasions he can lodge and feed two hundred persons with their horses. He is confident (if you press him) that he has the finest hostelry in Thorpshire and that outside of London few inns can surpass his in elegant bedrooms, furniture, bedding, fine cooking and wines, and even in costly plate. A delightful homelikeness and freedom pervades such a place, so that it can be well written in Master Harrison's book, "Every man may use his inn as his own house in England." Down in the public room (if you would not commune with your

own greatness more privately) there is a friendly elbowing
and bustling at the common table where hot capons and
warm sack are followed by great clouds of tobacco, inter-
mitted with more wine, while two boys sing madrigals to a
lute very sweetly.

Not all guests can command the "best chamber" as can
Sir William, but all can have separate bedrooms with their
own keys, and always clean sheets and no fear of nocturnal
enemies. Master Welcome will charge such a visitor as Sir
William six shillings for his supper, breakfast, bed, and
servant's accommodation, with another shilling for each
horse, but ordinary guests can get off for two shillings.
These charges, of course, are high enough to insure for the
White Hart as a rule only desirably gentle company.

Nearer the water front in Boroughport the Golden Lion
caters mainly to trading folk dealing along the wharves.
It makes no such pretentions as the White Hart, but Mistress Spry, its presiding genius, has a wide fame for hospitality. A pert, bustling, comely woman whose husband vanished on a sea voyage, her house is a congenial spot for a
certain type of company. As old Skelton, Henry VIII's
poet, said of a similar hostess:

> She breweth nappy ale,
> And maketh thereof fast sale,
> To travelers, to tinkers,
> To sweaters, to swinkers
> And all good ale-drinkers.

To be sure if you go to the Golden Lion you cannot
always be sure of clean sheets and a peaceful night. Also
if, too trustingly, you give your horse to the ostler, and
say "rub him down and feed him well till morning," you
had better visit him in the stable and make sure of his
treatment, otherwise the next morning you may find him

neglected and half-starved, although "oats and hay" are sure to appear on the bill.

For sixpence, however, you can sit down at the general table and have plenty of hearty fare. This the more welcome in the evening because very many of the poorer travelers after breakfast will ride all day with no more dinner than a little bread and cheese from their pockets. Mistress Spry, however, makes quite as much gain from her ordinary and ale house which are frequented at all times of day by townspeople seeking drink more often than food. As you enter the door a frowsy-headed boy in a blue coat begins his rattle: "Welcome, welcome, gentles; what wine will you drink? Claret, metheglin, or muscadine? Canary or a charnico? But by your nose, sir, you at least would love a cup of our best Malmsey. Or do you prefer the Frenchman to the Spaniard—we've just tapped a pipe of splendid Bordeaux?"

Such a place always tries to sell wine instead of the less expensive ale, but Mistress Spry is not above the latter trade as is indicated by the big red lattice on one side of her door—the regular sign for an ale house.[1]

Inside you enter a big "parlor" reeking of late years with tobacco smoke, and full of small groups of men with their elbows on small tables, while the blue coats and dirty white aprons bustle about bringing glasses, tankards, dice, playing cards, tobacco and pipes, or food, and always answering the impatient guests with "Anon, anon, sir!"— "At once, at once!"—usually the sign for another long expectant interval.

In such a place high words, brawls, or even challenges to duels are daily commonplaces. Mistress Spry has a pair of brawny arms very useful for thrusting drunkards out the door. On the walls are blackened boards on which

---

[1] Sometimes the lattice was painted green instead of red.

regular customers have their scores chalked up from flagon
to flagon. The hostess professes to keep a very moral house.
Bona Robas and Doll Tearsheets are strictly excluded, although every now and then there is the rustle of farthingales; and members of the fair sex, discreetly protected by
vizards, are admitted to certain private dining rooms where
one must hope all conduct is sedate and orderly. In the
great parlor there is incessant "music"—viols, lutes, citterns,
and nondescript fellows braying out popular songs—by no
means of a godly character. However the Golden Lion is
outwardly a far more reputable place than such a den as
the Prince's Arms, where you can bunk for twopence, and
for twopence more get a meal that will at least stave off
hunger.

The cheaper kinds of ordinaries and ale houses earn of
course the anathemas of the Puritans. Master Stubbes
speaks for many when he denounces these resorts where,
so long as a man has any money left, he may sit in company swilling, gulling, and carousing from one to another,
till never one of them can speak a ready word, and "in
short become worse than beasts."

At present, however, Mistress Spry studies good morals
and honest service more than formerly. A great scandal
has nearly ruined the Golden Lion. When Hal Liftpurse's
exploits were sifted at the assize, it was discovered how he
chanced to hit on so many travelers worth the robbing.
Mistress Spry had a head chamberlain, one Simon Fetcher,
an obliging, handsome fellow, who made a point of assisting every newcomer with his bags, mails, and coffers up
to his room. There was no danger of being robbed in the
Golden Lion; the law makes every innkeeper strictly
responsible for the safety of his guests' property, but
Fetcher cast an apprising eye over every article that entered
the inn. He had a very cunning hand, and by merely lifting

and rattling a parcel could guess shrewdly if there was value inside of it. If a traveler carried a case or bag to his chamber himself, Simon promptly shifted it about as if to set it in a better position; and he never failed to note if a guest kept weapons handy (as if guarding some valuables) or seemed watchful and nervous; and of course a few tactful questions usually brought out where he was going and by what road. Finally if a guest entrusted any wallet to the hostess for especial safekeeping, Fetcher promptly pricked up his ears.

All this was common enough in the small, sordid inns where belated wayfarers had to halt in the lesser villages, where it could be said there was never a robbery without an inn servant behind it; but Boroughport had been proud of the honesty of its hostelries. Judge then the clatter of tongues when it came in at the assize that Simon Fetcher had regularly collected firm tidings of travelers worth plundering and sent them by a confederate horseboy to the audacious Hal Liftpurse watching the roads a few miles away! Fetcher and the boy of course were promptly double-fettered in jail, and might well have followed Liftpurse to the gallows had not they saved their necks by being allowed to enlist in a company off for Flanders. Betwixt Spanish bullets and camp fever they will scarcely see Boroughport again; the only question now concerns Mistress Spry—had she any inkling of her myrmidons' proceedings? "Before God an innocent widow!" she swore to the magistrates, and they let her off. For all that, on any second suspicion his Worship the Mayor will promptly close the Golden Lion.

¶ *Chapter* XXII: CONCERNING SHIPS AND SEA-
FARING

BOROUGHPORT is a harbor town, and though we
may not quit the dry land it behooves us to wander
along its quays and docks and inquire about those
"that go down to the sea in ships, that do business in great
waters," and especially about the craft they navigate.

The good town does not boast of a royal dockyard, but
some of the Queen's men-of-war are constantly warping
into or out of the inner harbor, and of the various merchant
craft there is sometimes almost as large a forest of masts as
in any English port barring London. The knock of the
ship carpenters' axes is rising all day from the shipyards,
and for broad reaches along the shore you can catch the
clean pleasant smell of the timber chips where pinnaces
and barks have been constructed. If the ships, to the eye
of another age, must seem small, their modest size makes
them very numerous in order to meet the needs of even
sixteenth-century commerce. Any mild sunny day along
the water front, therefore, can give you an imposing marine
spectacle.

English seamen, long content with modest ventures to
Spain or Scandinavia, are coming into their own. The
Cross of St. George has flaunted itself in the mighty river
Plata, has passed and repassed the Straits of Magellan, has
ranged the western shores of the Americas, crossed the
Pacific, trafficked in the doubled Good Hope, visited St.
Helena, and come home with safety and glory.[1]

[1] Thomas Cavendish, following in Drake's track, came back from the
second English circumnavigation of the globe in 1588.

[325]

Such voyagers have returned "with their sailors clothed in silk, their sails of damask and their topmast covered with cloth of gold," and while less is said about the numerous expeditions which tragically failed there has been profit and success enough to put all the adventurous blood of Englishmen atingle.

Not merely have Drake, Cavendish, Frobisher, Gilbert, and Raleigh battered in the doors of the West, but Willowby and Burroughs have sought the Northeast Passage, Chancellor has opened the White Sea route to Russia, and plenty of English captains have fought the Barbary Corsairs and the Spaniard while riding the trade routes to the Levant. English travelers have crossed Russia and sailed the Caspian, others have made the overland journey to India and made known the Great Mogul's court to the Queen's lieges.

Even apart from the great plundering voyages, such as Drake's to the Spanish Americas, many of these ventures have been highly profitable. A tall merchantman in which Sir Walter Hollydean has a large interest has lately come back from the East Indies. She was beset by two great Portuguese carracks but beat them off gallantly. The spices, silk, and indigo which she brought back have paid over two hundred and fifty pounds for every hundred placed in the venture—an astonishing profit, but justified by enormous risk of total loss from wreck, pirates, and public enemy, not to speak of the heavy expenses of any distant voyaging. A second venture to the Levant, slightly less perilous, has paid almost equally. The good ship carried out a full cargo of kerseys, cottons, and other staple English cloths, also many calfskins which sell very well in Sicily. She brought back silks, camlets (camel's-hair cloth), rhubarb, malmsey, muscadel, and other wines, sweet oils, raw cotton, fine woods, Turkey carpets, gall, pepper, and a great supply of Arabian spices. When she unloaded, her wharf looked like a huge Oriental bazaar.

Any day in Boroughport Harbor can be heard the clanking of the capstan bars, as the anchor rises for some far-voyaging argosy, and the deep-throated chant of the seamen:

Lustily, lustily let us sail forth.
The wind trim doth serve us, it blows from the North.

and so through many uncouth stanzas until the concluding:

Make them good cheer
And hold all together, as friends linked in love,
The cans shall be filled with wine, ale and beer.

Along the wharves are any number of weather-beaten fellows, with marvelously unkempt beards, wolfish teeth, heavy earrings, and garments from every coast under Heaven's canopy. Their talk is all of florins, ducats, dollars, reals, moidores, and sequins, or of seeing mermaids, cannibals, venomous trees, huge snakes, and treasure houses crammed with diamonds. Greasy fingers point at wondrously colored maps.

A merchant captain is trying to pick up hands for his voyage to Virginia and is dilating to a knot of gaping youths, banging his big scabbard to emphasize each assertion, "Why will not every brisk lad in Boroughport take ship for a country where the beauteous Indian maids are languishing away for love of tidy Englishmen? Gold is more plentiful than copper with us. Why, man, all their dripping pans and chamber pots are pure gold, all the prisoners are fettered in gold; and as for rubies and diamonds, they gather them in by the seashore to hang on their children's coats and stick in their caps. If you will but settle in Virginia you may be an alderman and never a scavenger. You may be a nobleman and never be a slave. You shall live freely there without sergeants, or courtiers, or lawyers." [1]

History will never record how many of the lads caught by this oratory will live to return with a true report of the extent of "Virginia riches," but the actual facts about the new Wonderlands opening beyond the seas are so astonishing that every kind of adventure can be believed. The grave Sir John Hawkins's companions were sure they saw crocodiles "as big as a boat" which would "cry and sob like a Christian body" to induce their victims to come within reach. It is a bad sailor indeed who cannot return with his yarns about Cipango, the cities of Atlantis, and exhibit very likely "a piece of the horn broken from the unicorn in battle with a dragon, before he was poisoned by the dragon's deadly tail."

Many a glib fellow can be more convincing still. Very lately a burly Captain Mendax called for a bottle at the Golden Lion and then kept the public room breathless for half the evening. He had been on a voyage around Africa. Off Teneriffe he was so near the moon it was "marvelously hot"; there he came on a harmless giant "with a great beard in which a bird did breed." At one point he found so much gold in shallow water that divers brought up thirty hogsheads of it in three days. On the isle of Madagascar were met men without heads and eyes in their breasts, and grapes as big as loaves of bread. At Zanzibar emeralds and rubies were purchaseable for their weight in iron; and the sailors gathered up diamonds with rakes under the spice trees. But unfortunately all this enormous cargo was lost when the ship got too near the "adaman-

---

[1] Of course this is precisely the praise of "Virginia riches" in *Jonson* and Chapman's *Eastward Ho!* produced in 1605.

tine stones or loadstone rocks, and so were cast away the greatest riches in Heathenness or Christendom."

If the wind is bearing fair out into the Channel after a prolonged sea breeze which has kept vessels locked in port, Boroughport Harbor is almost alive with huge square sails—white, blackened gray, and brown. The anchors are going up to the jovial capstan songs, blocks are rattling, boatswains' whistles are shrieking, small boats are pulling about with the last passengers, parcels, or messages. It is a sight to make the most cautious landsman sorry he cannot join in the lusty "Eastward" or "Westward ho!"

Practically all sails, except in the largest vessels, are square and hoisted upon long yards, but there are many types of merchantmen. For mere coastal freight service to London one way, or to Plymouth or Bristol the other, there are the small crayers—one-masted cargo boats that crawl along when the breeze favors and tie up in one little harbor after another. Pinnaces are more the smallest type of men-of-war and are swifter and capable of longer voyages. Then somewhat larger are the hoys. These are flat-bottomed craft sometimes with one square-rigged mast, sometimes with two. Their light draft enables them to make very shallow harbors, and by aid of a ponderous lee-board they can risk voyages to France, the Low Countries, or even to Spain, but they are unwieldy, slow-creeping things at the very best. For really distant voyages your wise merchant adventurer trusts to the caravels and the hulks.

The caravels are of Portuguese origin, and are comparatively long and deep, although seldom completely decked over. A good caravel carries four masts, some with square sails, some with lateen. Caravels were the ships in which the Spaniards made their first voyages to America, and although they are essentially a Southern type of ship a good

[329]

many can be found flying the Cross of St. George. Nevertheless the ordinary and most reliable large merchantman is the hulk.

Sir Walter Hollydean has put a few hundred pounds into the staunch trader *Porpoise*. She has been on a short and relatively safe voyage to Hamburg, and is now back and unloading her cargo of bulky "Easterling" wares at one of the quays. One glance at her proportions shows her a "hulk" in very truth; for being built entirely for cargo and not for speed she is only "two beams long"; that is, her length is only twice as much as her breadth and it takes the stiffest kind of breeze to give her better than a very solemn progress across the water.

The *Porpoise* is a fairly large ship—about one hundred feet long and well over two hundred tons. Greater merchantmen can be built—up to three hundred and fifty tons; larger than this they are too expensive and unmanageable except for very long voyages, although good shipbuilders say they can give you a seaworthy six-hundred-ton ship if you will pay the price.[1]

The *Porpoise* has four masts on which are spread only a few very large sails—a "sprit-sail" slung under the great high bowsprit (to be replaced in another day by the jibs), the foresail and fore topstail, the mainsail and main-topsail, and finally on each of the two mizzen masts a large lateen sail which sailors of a later age will divide into the fore and aft staysail and mizzen of a square-rigged bark. Short as the *Porpoise* is her enormous stern cabin, rising deck above deck and brilliantly painted, and her forecastle— almost equally lofty—give her a very imposing appearance. She is no man-of-war, but pirates of every description

---

[1] After the East India Company (chartered in 1600) gained its stride vessels of 500 tons became fairly common, and vessels of 1000 tons were built, although not always counted profitable.

are on all the seas, and in the low "waist" between the towering cabins are mounted six good culverins, plus various lighter pieces set on the upper works with especial view to sweeping down boarders.

Captain Wanderer is ashore at the Angel conferring with his owners, but the unlading is in charge of his chief officer, Boatswain Heavyfist, who is stalking about thundering out oaths and inspiring all his crew with abounding energy. The boatswain, who has especially to do with the handling of the sails, is next in command under the captain; he has a "boatswain's" mate who is practically second officer, a gunner, gunner's mate, and other dignitaries; but you can know the boatswain by the big silver whistle which dangles ostentatiously from a cord about his neck. Such a ship as the *Porpoise* carries fully fifty men —and would need more for a voyage to the Indies; but the tackling is so heavy and sailors are so cheap that it is best to take a full company. Some of the *Porpoise's* crew are seasoned and competent seamen, but Heavyfist will tell you that a good proportion who made their mark for the voyage are masterless yokels, ale-house runagates, and fellows who found a forecastle pleasanter than a jail. Nothing but the roughest words and the fear of the rope's end will make them reasonably diligent.

Sailors' fare is notoriously abominable, their quarters nasty, the unsanitary drainage from the entire ship is suffered to seep down into the ballast rocks or sand next to the keel timbers, and it is the mercy of God if even a short voyage does not take off a quarter of the company by some pestilence. The constant use of salt provisions makes scurvy almost as common on a voyage as hard weather. Near to the *Porpoise* is tied up the *Mary and Joan*. She came back lately from an African voyage, which we fear had something to do with black ivories. For all their fine boasts several of her surviving sailors stumped ashore with wooden legs, and had to tell tales of "nothing to eat but tallow and young blackamores and of five and five to a rat in every mess, and the ship's boy to the tail." They had to hold their noses as they drank "the stinking water" and at one time were reduced to "cutting up a greasy buff jerkin into tripes and boiling it for their dinners."

Gradually the need of better supplies is being understood. Captain Wanderer is telling his owners that if they desire a voyage to the Indies they must not grudge him plenty of lemons, rice, prunes, and cinnamon, ginger, and sugar to mix with the water, and instead of so much cheap salt beef a fair supply of "legs of mutton, minced and close packed up with butter in earthen pots" or "roast beef packed up in vinegar." Then he can hope to keep his crew in tolerable condition.

The *Porpoise* is a typical merchantman of the larger class; but there is laid up at Boroughport an enormous vessel which landsmen admire but seamen shake their heads about. She is a Portuguese carrack, coming back from the East Indies with a fabulously precious lading, when English cruisers took her off Madeira a few years ago. She is a hundred and sixty-five feet over all, forty-seven feet beam, and *mirabile dictu* fully fifteen hundred tons. But like other monstrosities she is almost unmanageable. Her huge sails make her barely creep across the water with the most favorable breeze. Once safe in an English harbor and fully rifled she has proved quite useless. No one will risk a venture with her. So she lies on the mud bank slowly rotting away; and the water-front wiseacres gravely assure one another "Heaven never intended man to sail ships of such bigness."

But not all the shipping in the busy little harbor is thus

[332]

safe and peaceful. Boroughport is proud of her naval men and their valor upon the seas. The glory of England upon the seas is already an article of religion. Writes prudent Master Harrison: "No prince in Europe hath a more beautiful and gallant sort of ships than the Queen's Majesty—for strength, assurance, nimbleness, and swiftness of sailing there are no vessels in the world to be compared with ours"; and he affirms "that two well-found English vessels never refuse to fight any three or four foreigners."

The Royal Navy has been growing in strength ever since the days of Henry VIII, who, with all his sins, knew the value of sea power. In 1515 he saw completed the *Henri Grace à Dieu,* the most pretentious warship of its day, of 1500 tons, and mounting 186 pieces of ordnance great and small, with a complement of about seven hundred men. This "Great Harry," as she was popularly named, was more for vainglory than for action, although in 1544 she gave a good account of herself against the French. Under Edward VI and Mary the navy retrograded as did almost every other government service, but Queen Elizabeth soon showed herself her father's daughter. Not that an enormous fleet was built; there were only twenty-two royal men-of-war of over one hundred tons when she came to the throne; there will be only twenty-nine of that size when the reign will be ended. But the model of the fighting ships will be vastly improved, their artillery will be equally improved, and above all a force of men-of-war's men from admiral down to powder boy will be enlisted, trained, and fused with disciplined courage, probably constituting then the best body of seamen the world will witness until sails cease to take ships into battle.

There is no such distinction between warships and merchantmen as may come in a later age. The *Porpoise* no doubt is too broad and sluggish to make an efficient fighting vessel, but at another near-by quay lies the *Trident,* of about her size but rather sharper and speedier. The *Trident* is now unloading a cargo of lumber from Norway, but in 1588 her waist, stern cabin, and forecastle were garnished with as many cannon as she could bear with safety; and with a gallant crew of Boroughport volunteers she sailed out to join Lord Howard when the Royal ships faced the Grand Armada. To fight this great force of the Spaniards the English admirals used no less than 197 ships. Only thirty-four of these belonged to the Crown. The remainder were armed merchantmen, many indeed small affairs useful only as scouts and dispatch boats, but some of them able, heavy ships that gave and took the hardest blows. The *Trident* played her full part in that final death-duel off Calais, when all day long Englishmen and Spaniards poured in broadsides at a hundred yards' range, and Philip's great fleet received what proved its death wound.

Englishmen won the day certainly not because they were braver than the Spaniards, not solely because they were better cannoniers, but because they had evolved a superior type of warship, and understood handling those ships to perfection. Although the Spaniards had long built and sailed ships that made the great voyages to the Indies, they had never shaken the idea that a warship must be essentially a Mediterranean galley adapted for Atlantic purposes. The astonishing victory of Don Juan over the Turks at Lepanto in 1571, when 208 Spanish and Venetian galleys practically annihilated 273 Turkish galleys, seemed to prove what oar-driven craft could accomplish.[1]

The galleys and the galliases (larger galleys with auxiliary sail power) no doubt have advantages in calm Medi-

---

[1] The battle of Lepanto was of course the last great galley battle in history. The crumbling of Turkish naval power insured that nearly all sea fighting should henceforth be on the open ocean.

terranean waters, especially when the wind falls. Twenty-two ponderous oars on the side, each pushed by four or five naked fettered slaves, flogged on by the whip masters running up and down the gangways, can send their long slim craft flying into action. They have beaks for ramming that sometimes are quite formidable; but their only cannon are in the forecastle or stern, useful only when ramming or retreating. When they dash home the strong company of brave Spanish soldiers posted on the forecastle is expected to rush aboard the enemy and carry him with pike and sword—an excellent method if all goes well.

English captains have experimented with galleys and will have none of them. England has no thousands of wretched Moslem prisoners or victims of the Inquisition that can be manacled to the oars. Besides in stormy northern waters a low, narrow galley quickly comes to grief—as did nearly all the oar-driven craft with the Armada before the English could attack them. In the 1570's and 1580's English sea captains and naval architects made a discovery that would affect the entire world—that a good warship should trust to sails alone; that it was better to crush the enemy with heavy cannon than to run alongside and try boarding; that the best naval vessel should carry as many great guns as possible mounted in its broadside; and that the acme of seamanship was to keep that broadside bearing constantly on the enemy until he was sunk or surrendering.

Philip II's admirals never took in this fact before their tragic lesson in 1588. Most of the Spanish ships were sailing vessels indeed; but they were built up to an inordinately great height to overshadow the enemy's decks when it came to grappling. Their cannon were relatively fewer than the English and much lighter—mainly for shooting away spars and rigging, before the actual boarding. Some of them were very large vessels, but all were sluggish sailors very clumsy in handling. When Medina Sidonia advanced up the Channel the English sailed round and round his vast fleet pouring in broadsides, but steadily refusing what the Spaniards vainly longed for—a chance to grapple and have it out with desperate cutlass fighting. Finally, in the great engagement off Calais the English artillery fire was so terrible that the Spaniards became hopelessly demoralized and fled to the North. Those were the tactics that shattered the Armada and made England terrible upon the seas. It is the broadside sailing ship fighting with heavy artillery that will make the British Empire.

Small as the Queen's navy is, it contains ships of various ascending types. There are the scouting pinnaces, from forty to a hundred tons, depending on sail and bearing light cannon, but not so large as to be unable to get out oars in a dead calm. Then there are the various "tall ships"— "middling ships," "great ships," and last but not least "ships royal." Barks are not regular naval vessels; they are the merchant craft hired or impressed into the battle fleet in an emergency. The term "armada" usually means a powerful fleet, but sometimes it is used for a single formidable man-of-war, and there are a good many other Spanish, Portuguese, and Italian nautical expressions in common English use, reminding one that until very lately Cadiz, Lisbon, and Venice have boasted that they ruled the seas.

The greatest fighting ships are often called galleons. It is a mistake to imagine that this is a special name confined to towering Spaniards. It simply means a high *long* warship depending on sails as against the low *round* merchantman. A galleon has a keel about three times her beam, as against a merchantman's twice, and gains thereby greatly in speed and seaworthiness. Since 1565 the Spaniards have used galleons to guard their "flotas" of slow merchant ships bringing treasure from America; then it seemed simpler to have the galleons carry the gold dust and ingots themselves. Hence the name is coming often to signify one of King Philip's armed treasure ships, but there are a number of stately galleons in Elizabeth's own navy; only the English galleons were of swifter build and better armed than the Spanish in the great duel of 1588.

The largest galleon in the English fleet is the mighty *Triumph* of 1100 tons and sixty-eight guns which in the fight with the Armada flew the flag of the redoubtable Martin Frobisher, but she is hardly counted the most efficient vessel in the Queen's navy. It happens there has just dropped into Boroughport to recruit her crew a very famous and gallant ship indeed whose history is writ large in many books besides this—the *Ark Royal,* that in 1588 flaunted the flag of none less than my Lord Charles Howard of Effingham, High Admiral of England; and now she rides at anchor near the quays a stately bulk above all the merchant barks, hoys, and pinnaces.

The *Ark Royal* was completed in 1587 on plans approved by that prince of seamen, Sir John Hawkins, for no less a personage than Sir Walter Raleigh. She was probably built on the Thames in the famous shipyards of the Petts family which for many years will turn out some of the most famous vessels in the English navy. Raleigh (cunning speculator) seems to have built her on his private account, and then sold her to the Queen for five thousand pounds.[1]

She is a warship of the highest class and embodies many improvements which have spelled victory for England. She is of eight hundred tons, and carries fifty-five pieces of

[1] Twentieth-century readers will be interested to contrast this price for a battleship of the highest rating with the $50,000,000 or £10,000,000 which a similar vessel costs when these words are written. Possibly the £5000 did not include artillery, tackling, etc.

ordnance and four hundred and twenty-five men in her crew. As she rides in the harbor her four masts lift themselves arrogantly; the two forward masts display a considerable innovation—topgallant yards and sails making a third great square of canvas above the lower sail and topsail. Along the wharves they tell you that she is fitted to navigate tropical waters. In the hot Indies there is a worm that in a few months will bore right through the heaviest timbers, but the *Ark Royal* has all her keel and bottom sheathed with lead, an almost complete protection. As for her hull it rises to a majestic height fore and aft, the effect increased by painting the whole structure in long stripes—green and white, the Tudor house colors. A great royal lion splendidly gilded rears itself on the beakhead under the bowsprit; the royal arms in full blazonry spread themselves also in gold across the broad stern. The ship is made to seem even larger because, to dry them after wet weather, the "fights" are spread out—long strips of red cloth extended above the bulwarks to conceal the men on the decks from the enemy's fire.

Such a vessel as the *Ark Royal* carries her main battery in two tiers running from stem to stern; there are lighter guns in the high forecastle, more light guns in the "half-deck," the stern cabin, and a few very light pieces on the "quarter-deck"—the very high admiral's cabin superposed upon the half-deck. Few ship afloat support more terrible artillery. The flagship carries in her lower deck four enormous sixty-pounders, the heaviest cannon in regular service; four thirty-three pounders, "demi cannon"; and eight eighteen-pounders—"culverins." On the main deck there are four more culverins, twelve "demi-culverins" (9-pounders), and two 2½-pounders. The other twenty-one guns are not heavier than five-pounders and are set on the forecastle and cabins mainly for sweeping off boarders. The whole broadside of the *Ark Royal* weighs 377 pounds, heavier than that of any Spanish ship in the Armada, although that unwieldy fleet contained at least seven vessels much larger than the English flagship.

English gunnery is the best in the world. Imperfect as methods of aiming may seem, an enormous amount of skill can go into them. Without that cool courage that aimed the culverins while death danced through all the air, the best of seamanship would have profited nothing. Yet the *Ark Royal* looks peaceful enough now. Her people have been given liberty and are pulling ashore in their cocks, jolly boats, and longboats which have just been lowered along the waist. The seamen appear a nondescript lot, clothed in any odd fashion, for naval uniforms are still in the future, although the officers make a fine show with their silvered cuirasses, velvet surcoats, and like braveries. The "sailors" are a special clan of elderly men for responsible but not too active tasks; the "mariners" are the regular able-bodied seamen; under them are the "younkers," the ordinary seamen, the despised *"grommets"* still mere junior, and then the luckless butts of all their superiors, the oppressed "boys."

If the letter of the law is complied with the lot of this ship's company is in no wise evil. Mariners are paid ten shillings per month—fair wages compared with many landsmen—and draw daily as victuals a gallon of beer and a pound of biscuit, with two pounds of beef or "pork and peas" on four days of the week and a good mess of fish on others. But, as usual, paydays come very slowly, supplies are usually bad with standing complaints of putrid beef and biscuit walking with weevils, while fortunate is the voyage in which provisions do not run short and the whole crew put "six upon four"—six men on four men's allowance—to enable the ship to keep the seas longer.

Discipline as yet has not standardized and hardened;

much laxity can make later martinets grieve, and between officers and men there is a hale and hearty familiarity that sometimes is fair comradeship—yet which sometimes breeds disorder. Harsh punishments, of course, are common enough. They begin with making the offenders "swabbers" —to do all the filthy work about the ship; the next stage is whipping with the boatswain's rod—a regular ceremony every Monday morning, and so frequent that old sailors swear they will never have a fair wind unless the ship's boys are on that day "brought to the chest" (soundly whipped), be they ever so innocent. Harsher justice can take the form of ducking at the yardarm and the fearful "keel-raking" (the later "keel-hauling") when the dead-or-alive victim is dragged down one side of the keel under the ship and up the other.

All this makes a Queen's ship a severe enough schoolroom indeed, but because of it or in spite of it is bred an order of fighting seamen the betters of which the world has yet to see. Of not a few of them can be written what Sir Walter Raleigh has lately recorded of Sir Richard Grenville, after he perished in his fight of the *Revenge* against the three-and-fifty Spaniards: "What became of his body, whether it were buried in the sea, or on the land, we know not; the comfort that remaineth to his friends is that he ended his life honorably in respect to the reputation won to his nation and country, and of the same to his posterity, and that being dead he hath not outlived his own honor."

NOW it came to pass that on a fine late August
afternoon Captain Andrew came back from Boroughport with his horse in a canter. He went up
into the great gallery smiling with news which made Mistresses Anne and Arabella clap their hands, but which put
Master Crabtree into his best clerical frown—"Bills were
put up that my Lord Chamberlain's men would be at the
Swan all next week."

Master Crabtree continued in his dumps all through supper. He failed not, when the younger people were aside, to
marvel to his gentle patrons that his Worship the Mayor
permitted such things as stage plays to come hither from
London, and quoted with implied approval the old Master Gosson's denunciation of the theaters as "the inventions
of the devil, the offerings of idolatry, the pomp of worldlings, and the food of iniquity, riot, and adultery," while
the players were "masters of vice, teachers of wantonness,
spurs of impurity, and sons of idleness." To these generalities Lady Catherine gave a certain formal assent; but Sir
Walter promptly told the chaplain: "We must not be too
great Precisians"; and the lady added with a sigh, " 'Tis
useless to forbid the girls, but I shall command that they
both wear vizards."

The truth was that the plague being serious in London,

---

[1] In writing this chapter the author is keenly aware that he is preparing the most contentious and technical section of the book. The
effort is always to deal with safe generalities, although various things
must be affirmed as facts when they may be only strong probabilities.

Master Burbage's famous company, finding its fine play-house, "The Theater," closed by the careful authorities, was fain to make a circuit of the provincial towns. Master Crab-tree at length consoled himself by reflecting that at least the visitors would not be of the lewdest of players, were not clowns and jesters presenting coarse jigs and drolls, and that my Lord Hunsdon, the Chamberlain, was a kinsman to the Queen herself and not likely to give his noble countenance to a mere band of wandering mountebanks, as too often strolling players were.

The profession is still subject to many official bans. "Fencers, bearwards, common players, and minstrels" are still yoked together by the statute as ordinary vagabonds and sturdy beggars liable to be dragged before any justice and whipped, stocked, burned through the ear, and packed out of the parish. The lawful way to avoid this fate is to become a "servant" of some exalted personage entitled to keep players for his own noble entertainment and to divert her Majesty. At odd intervals (runs the fiction) they may perhaps exhibit before the populace. My Lord Hunsdon, we conclude, seldom has to pay a shilling of wages to these "his men," but he gives them his sanction, and similar companies are licensed by other noble lords such as the Earl of Hertford and the Lord Admiral.

Boroughport saw plenty of dramatics in the departed Catholic days. These "Miracle Plays" were strictly amateur performances presented during the holiday seasons by the ancient trade gilds and were much of the nature of very animated pageants. Old people still remember the season when two companies, the Shearers and Tailors, united to present "The Nativity" and the "Flight into Egypt"; the Smiths gave "The Crucifixion," and the Cappers "The Resurrection."

These crude affairs rapidly disappeared after England

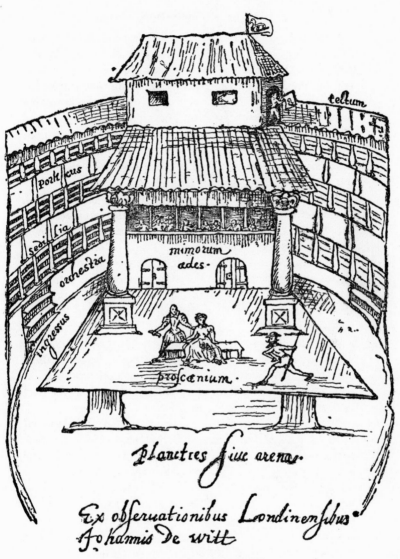

tectum

porticus

sedilia

orchestra

ingressus

mimorum ædes

proscænium

planities sive arena.

Ex observationibus Londinensibus Johannis De witt

THE SWAN THEATRE, LONDON, 1596.
Drawing in University Library, Utrecht.
Gaedertz, " Zur Kenntniss der Alt-Englischen Bühne."

[343]

turned Protestant. Their rivals the "Morality Plays," not based on the Bible but on the impersonal virtues, survived considerably longer. Barely twenty years ago the Corporation itself regaled all Boroughport with a free presentation of "The Cradle of Security." In it the good folk saw a king impersonating "The Wicked of the World," three beautiful ladies ("Pride," "Covetousness," and "Luxury"), and two very solemn old men ("The End of the World" and "Judgment"). After many entertaining adventures and chances for repentance most impiously put by, the wicked, luxury-sodden king ended his sensual life by being carried off to Hell by a swarm of most picturesque Devils—to the great satisfaction and edification of all the beholders.

But the "Moralities" have waned before the incoming of plays dealing usually with flesh-and-blood human life written not by local amateurs, but professional writers of ever-increasing skill and presented by professional actors with powers far exceeding any provincial talent.

Perhaps they will tell us that the first comedy in English of this new kind was Nicholas Udall's rollicking farce "Ralph Roister Doister," written about 1540, and the first tragedy written in blank verse and with great literary pretentions was "Gorboduc," given to the world in 1561 by two young barristers, Sackville and Norton. Doubtless we shall learn too that Udall borrowed heavily from Plautus's "Miles Gloriosus," and that "Gorboduc" has plenty of echoes from Seneca. No matter. The new-style plays speedily won great acceptance and nowhere more than at the royal court, and a whole procession of able playwrights gradually worked loose from the old classical models and developed admirable new models for themselves.

Masters Lyly, Greene, Peele, Kyd, and Marlowe have done this experimental work well; and now their ranks are being joined by Master Ben Jonson and (already praised

[345]

through England) Master William Shakespeare. The result is that the audiences that assemble in the Swan are likely to see something concerning which wise books may be written for years to come.

The Lord Chamberlain's men of course were sorry to close their London theater, but their performance in Boroughport is not likely to be much inferior to those in the Metropolis. The reason is that Elizabethan inn-yards are admirably adapted for stage plays, and until 1576 there have been no permanent playhouses. The square or circular courtyards of many inns, providing an area in the center and galleries for tiers of seats running clear around it, can be made into very sufficient theaters for the average performance. The new playhouses are better in that they admit many minor adjustments and (chief item of all) they save the management from dividing the entrance money with the inn-keeper; but the Burbages have given very many adequate presentations in such London inns as the Cross-Keys in Gracechurch Street and the Belle-Savage on Ludgate Hill; not to mention special performances in the halls of many noble residences and country mansions.

Master James Burbage and his clever son Master Richard are no doubt very able managers and actors, but a large part of their success surely comes from their ability to catch the taste of the public. There is no more idealism about much of the Elizabethan theater than about the theater in other ages. The Burbages are seeking an honorable living; so is Master Shakespeare, who plays rather minor parts for them and devotes most of his time to writing dramas that cram the playhouses. Very many of the productions of the age are the merest hack work—turned out to get the author his fee and the manager his audience. In a few years they will be forgotten. If Master Shakespeare's efforts have a

more lasting quality, that is the glory of his genius; doubtless it does not rise from any conscious design.

He has not come down to Boroughport. When the
London playhouses were closed, we gather he made off to
his native Stratford: to assist shrewdly in untangling his
father's business affairs, to consider investing part of his
recent profits in certain good fields in which he is thriftily
interested, and (we dare guess) to sport not a little with
his half-grown daughters Susanna and Judith,[1] although
he promised the Burbages, ere they parted, to haste along
the copy for a historical play about King Henry IV in
which there is to be a certain comical knight called Falstaff.

Strolling players of the better sort are no innovation in
Boroughport. Apart from interruptions by the plague, few
regular companies remain all of the summer and autumn
in London. Every country town of two thousand or more is
fairly certain of a brief visit annually. But this is the first
time the famous Burbages have invaded Thorpshire. They
are come on from Winchester with rather more than a
dozen people. The chief actors ride horseback; the remainder pile into the creaking wagons which bring on the
fairly elaborate properties. They stop at my Lord Welborn's
noble mansion to give a private performance of Master
Marlowe's "The Jew of Malta." When at last they progress
through Hockley Bar a good part of the idle maids and
prentices in the city are lining the house walls to gape at
them.

The Swan is not the finest inn in Boroughport, but it has
the largest available courtyard. The host has chased out
most of his regular guests, and (against a profitable bargain) surrenders to the troupe complete possession, and the
actors working with skillful energy soon transform the

[1] Hamnet Shakespeare, Judith's twin brother, died in August, 1596, at
the age of eleven and a half.

place into a passable imitation of the London theaters. Before long cleverly written bills announcing the plays have been posted all around the town, and a great hammering from the courtyard tells that the stage is going up. The Burbages (father and son) are skillful actors but they are still more clever managers. They must please all tastes. The prentices and clowns from the country soon tire of many fine speeches and much philosophizing; they demand comedy of the broadest, most elemental type, but there must be enough soaring rhetoric and subtle character-drawing to please the cultivated gentlemen and dames who pay for the best seats. The day is not yet when there can be one theater for the masses and another for the classes—lucky Masters Burbage that their playwrights can appeal to both elements and neither be brought to boredom!

After consultation, the managers and leading actors agree that to make an immediate hit with the townsfolk they cannot do better than begin their week with the "Comedy of Errors." True Master Shakespeare has since written better plays than this, "Romeo and Juliet" and "Richard the Third," but the broad farce is sure to delight the "groundlings," and most of their betters have been too long away from London not to be tolerant of very simple theatrical fare. So then the play-bills in a big sprawling hand are issued forth. All Boroughport is aware that on Monday afternoon the most delectable and ingenious comedy will be presented at prices ranging from one penny standing room in the crowded "pit" to one shilling for the commodious seats for the more demanding gentles.

In the morning the town crier goes bawling through the streets, and about two o'clock, when dinner is well over, a huge ensign is hoisted on the staff by the Swan's entrance as signal that the doors are open. During the next hour all the free space in the courtyard becomes packed. A half dozen lutes and viols discourse tolerable music from the upper balcony but can scarcely be heard above the confusion of the jesting, scuffling, and elbowing crowd. Built out from one side of the courtyard and projecting well into it is a staging of rough boards, toward the rear of which is stretched a curtain presumably with a kind of inner stage communicating with dressing rooms behind. In front of this scaffolding are set rude benches on which become wedged a goodly phalanx of honest townsmen, often thriftily holding their young sons upon their knees. Behind them crowd and elbow the "groundlings" of the pit. In the balconies running around the courtyard and commanding the stage from three sides are comparatively private lodges for the most select of the audience; but what impresses the stranger most is the fact that directly upon the stage and consuming quite a piece of it there are set to left and right a row of stools at right angles to the curtain. These are being filled rapidly by young gallants flaunting their bravely colored cloaks and rattling their scabbards and by affected loud speech demanding constant attention.

As the audience gathers boys run in and out selling apples, nuts, and oranges. There is much hooting, stamping, and cat-calling. A partially arrayed actor peeps from behind the curtain; instantly there is a general yell of "Filthy! Filthy!" To pass the time four gallants on the stage openly spread out their cloaks to form a kind of table, produce a pack of cards, and begin a game of primero. It would be nothing unusual if a pickpocket were presently nabbed amid vast uproar while worming his way toward the exit.

Most of the audience are men. For a woman unmasked to sit on the benches, much more to stand in the pit, might lead to flings against her character; but a polite vizard can cover a multitude of audacities. Mistress Anne and Arabella sit in one of the lodges decorously masked, beside their brother. It does not abate the pleasure of Mistress Anne that young Master Stockwood suddenly quits his stool upon the stage and begins thrusting a pillow behind her back.

Tobacco smoke rises from all parts of the audience. The late summer sun beats down brilliantly into the open court-yard; this is pleasant for of course plays cannot well be given by candlelight,[1] and it is dolorous for the actors to have to contend with bad weather.

At last when the closely jammed multitude is thoroughly noisy and impatient, a brilliantly clad trumpeter stalks out upon the stage and blows three sonorous blasts. Instant silence. The four gallants drop their card game. The curtain majestically rises, betraying some very simple scenery of painted canvas, and a handsome youth, the "Chorus," steps to the front of the stage to explain in well-chosen lines the setting of the play.[2]

Once more may Heaven let us pretermit all wise dis-course concerning the nature of the drama and the art of Master Shakespeare. The playwright had probably been paid the standard twenty nobles ($£6$, 13sh. 4d.) from the management for his manuscript; perhaps he will get a trifle more from the stationer if the play is printed, and if he can find a noble patron to whom the pamphlet can be dedicated he can look for at least two pounds as honor-arium. Fortunately Master Shakespeare has an interest in the company itself—his gains are not limited to this very modest reward for his literary services. When the Burbage

---

[1] Certain small "private theaters" in London, catering to very genteel audiences, seem already to have given evening performances by candle light.

[2] There is no regular "Chorus" in our text of "The Comedy of Errors," but some announcement must have been made from the stage to take the place of the latter-day printed programs.

company is commanded to appear before the Queen it gets
£10 for the performance, and probably it is expecting to
take in as much gate money as that per day (plus the inn-
keeper's share), if the visit to Boroughport is to be successful. Of course inferior companies are glad to get out of
town with much less.

Master James Burbage would not be the successful manager that he is if he failed to understand the whims of his
audiences. It matters little (in the average play) if the good
people one moment are told the stage portrays a ship-
wreck, the next a fine dame's flower garden, the next a
cave from which issues a great fire-belching dragon. But
there is a steady demand for brilliant apparel and plenty
of good swordplay. If it is possible to display counterfeit
lightning and rumble big drums behind the scenes to make
thunder, so much the better. The wagons have brought
down from London a whole arsenal of such properties as
"Hell's mouth," a realistic device for representing the last
entrance of the damned, and black draperies wherewith to
hang the entire theater if the play is a tragedy. There are
plenty of canvas properties such as "mossy banks" and "tree
trunks" for woodland scenes; wooden altars to set up to
indicate a church; benches and tables to suggest an ale
house, and the like. Often a change of scene is produced
by no more elaborate device than having the actors walk
from one side of the stage—which may contain a bedstead
to indicate a chamber—across to the other where a small
forge shows it is a blacksmith's shop. There are also
"clouds" of drapery worked up and down or steered about
by pulleys, and other mechanisms that produce a certain
verisimilitude.

If, however, the scenery is usually the crudest kind of
painted canvas, if the stage properties are simple, if at one
point a change of scene is announced by no more elaborate

device than having a boy appear and hang out a large placard "A Public Place in Ephesus," the costumes of the actors are very elaborate, and any number of Boroughport lads are proud and happy to parade around as guards, attendants, and other lay figures perhaps for twopence, perhaps for nothing at all. The effect on the stage is therefore sometimes very imposing.

The settings are elementary, but the acting can be superb. The younger Burbage, who takes the chief male part, "Antipholus of Ephesus," has all the voice, gait, personality of a magnificent actor. He is supported by a company carefully and intelligently trained. Bad acting of course infects bad companies. Such characters as "King Herod" in the old religious plays rage about with their swords and scepters, bluster and rant, until "out-heroding Herod" becomes a byword. In some play there can be almost an excess of realism. In one bloody melodrama up in London three persons have to be slaughtered upon the stage—for each performance three vials of blood and a sheep's "gather" (heart, liver, and lungs) have to be provided, making the scene altogether too gory.

The women's parts are far less numerous than the men's, and needless to say have to be taken by slender lads. English opinion would be hideously shocked to see actual women upon the stage. Travelers to Venice who visit the theater write home about the Italian actresses with sheer astonishment.[1]

Burbage is supported for the sadly perplexed "Adriana" and the beauteous "Luciana" by cleverly made-up boys, who have been well trained to their parts, and who get just the right high pitch to their voices and know how to "speak small." It adds to the piquancy, perhaps, of certain of the

[1] No women appeared on the English stage until Charles II's time in the 1660's.

love scenes to know that the recipient of amorous confidences is really a fine swinging lad. Between the acts the two comical characters "Dromio of Ephesus" and "Dromio of Syracuse" come out upon the stage and sing improvised songs with shrewd hits at certain people in the audience and perform comical dances. In London one of their places might be taken by William Kempe, the ablest successor to the famous Tarleton, who so often clowns it before the Queen.

The Chorus has told us the play is all in "Ephesus." It might just as well be Boroughport; all the properties and scenery suggest Merry England. The two Antipholuses are dressed as extreme court gallants, the two Dromios look amazingly like rich gentlemen's serving men; Adriana and Luciana display enormous farthingales, and the Duke of Ephesus parades across the stage in all the stiff magnificence of a Spanish adelantado. What matter? Boroughport is delighted.

And so the "Comedy of Errors" proceeds through its five acts until poor Ægeon is happily reunited with his sons, the two sets of twin brothers are reunited, romance is promised Luciana, and the two Dromios go off the stage merrily wrangling. Once or twice the speeches have been interrupted by the pop and hiss of beer bottles being opened in the audience. Another time two prentices got into a brawl scrambling for "bitten apples." Otherwise there was general delight. If it does not rain, the Swan will be packed again tomorrow when Master Richard Burbage will crouch down his back as "King Richard the Third," and thrill all Boroughport by his magnificent wickedness and his incomparable acting!

"A horse! a horse! my kingdom for a horse!"

The younger Hollydeans ride home to the Manor very merrily, small Arabella full of plots to make her mother

give permission for tomorrow, and Mistress Anne bliss-
fully conscious that Master Stockwood's jennet is at her
elbow; but as they reach the Hall they all draw rein—a
fine gentleman, indeed, with her Majesty's very arms sewn
upon his sleeves, is dismounting at the horse block.

ILLUSTRATIONS TO "SHEPHERD'S CALENDAR," 1597. NOVEMBER

THE visitor with royal arms is a gentleman pensioner from Court, an old friend of Sir Walter's, charged to convey the delicate intimation that her Majesty being about to set forth on progress, as usual in the early autumn, would not take it amiss if the worshipful knight "showed his loyalty" by begging to entertain the Queen and her retinue for some two or three days.

Such a suggestion is of course a command. " 'Twill cost two thousand pounds," was the first thought to flash across Sir Walter's prudent mind—but think of the honor! The Queen loves perambulations through England and frequently plants herself not merely upon great nobles but upon wealthy country gentlemen as well; nevertheless it has been years since she has visited Thorpshire. What glory for Hollydean Hall! Its Master sits up late this night with the Court visitor consuming much sack and going over details. In the morning the gentleman departs leaving his host with an aching head and many cares.

Queen Elizabeth enjoys progresses for several reasons. First of all, she has a very human liking for new scenes and excitements; next she seizes every chance to show herself affable and gracious to the multitude of her subjects; thirdly, with true Tudor thrift, she enjoys being lodged, feasted, and fêted at other peoples' expense rather than her own. Just now she is at Greenwich. She is about to set forth with her whole retinue first for a customary visit to my Lord Burghley's residence at Theobalds; then she will work deliberately toward Thorpshire, delighting and dis-

[355]

tracting several other high-born hosts upon the way. She will reach Hollydean during the pleasant dry season about the middle of September. "Little enough time—God preserve us!" laments Lady Catherine.

The day following, Captain Andrew rides off to London as fast as his best horse will carry him. In his absence all the Hollydean people develop a frantic energy. This energy increases when the captain returns with a score of clever scene painters, upholsterers, and a foppish dictatorial personage who has been "Master of the Revels" for various great noblemen. All the carpenters and mechanics in Boroughport are conscripted for the Manor; his Worship the Mayor has a long conference with the aldermen, and all the inns lay in extra pipes of canary and engage a vast supply of capons.

The Queen usually makes about two progresses per year, extending sometimes well over a hundred miles. Gifted with a healthy, vigorous body she seldom minds hard journeyings and will travel in storm and cold that make purgatory for her attendant ladies. Like her masterful father she is always ready to watch pageants and processions; and never yawns at tedious displays which her courtiers find utterly boring. When she travels all the countryside knows it. Her purveyors have to requisition four hundred great carts drawn by six horses apiece. These piled with heavy trunks and coffers, make of themselves an astonishing sight as they lumber from village to village. The military escort is very small, but the great cortège of mounted ladies and gentlemen equals many troops of cavalry. It is, therefore, no inexpensive matter when her Majesty (as she often does) changes her royal mind and puts off her day of departure. Only last year the Queen proposed removing from Windsor to Westminster. The master carter was ordered to come for the wardrobe with his wagon train. Three days in succession he was bidden "Wait." The third time (he was standing under a palace window) he smote his big hand to his thigh and burst out, "Now I see that the Queen is a woman as well as my wife!" Suddenly a voice angry yet laughing from the window, "What a villain is this!" The Queen had overheard him, and at once sent down a gentleman with three gold angels and orders for the carter to "Take that and stop his mouth!" [1]

It is therefore with sober thankfulness that Sir Walter before long hears that her Majesty has started on progress at the time assigned, and will reach Hollydean immediately after the Master of the Revels can report "All is ready."

At length the great day is at hand. Early in the morning crowds of all sorts and conditions of people are taking their stand along the highway, many coming in from remote farms and villages. The lads with the port fires are just on the point of touching off the "chambers" by the gatehouse when the head of the procession comes in sight— but it is only the first of the great train of carts. Then ride in any quantity of pert, bustling, overdressed folk, male and female, whom the honest Hollydean servitors take for earls and countesses or little less, but who are only the grooms and waiting maids of the real attendants upon the Queen. Then at last trumpets shouting, "Uncap, knaves!" and a constantly increasing and approaching roar—Gloriana herself!

Queen Elizabeth seems happiest when there is a joyous clamor about her. Doubtless it will be very true, as Sir Walter Raleigh will write when her great reign is ended: "She led a life of unbroken loneliness in the single-minded pursuit of her duty to her people"; but no other "fair vestal throned by the west" ever will pass her days further from

[1] The original episode is recounted in Birch's *Memoirs*, I. 155.

convent seclusion. Human intercourse is the Queen's life.
Never was there a more accessible monarch, never one
more eager for popularity. As she has written to one of
her ambassadors, "My mortal foe can in no wise wish me
greater harm than England's hate."

The clamorous church bell in the next parish has already
heralded the approach of the royal procession to Hollydean,
when suddenly the whole train is stopped. As the big gilded

QUEEN ELIZABETH'S COACH.
Braun, "Civitates Orbis Terrarum," 1572.

coach-and-six, surrounded by the tall gentlemen pensioners
and their gilt halberds, creaks along, suddenly thrusting in
between the escort comes a red-cheeked hearty young yeoman, doubtless from some farm hidden within the greenwood. His jerkin is of leather, he carries a big cudgel, behind him follows a frightened wife dragging by each hand
a still more frightened little girl; but the countryman
pushes right on and calls out to the resplendent coachman, "Stay thy cart, good fellow, stay thy cart—that I may
speak to the Queen."

"Hold!" comes a command from behind the silken cur-

[358]

tains. The six horses are jerked in. All the gentles and gentlewomen of the escort rein suddenly. The curtains are thrust back. "And what would you say, my honest man?" says a voice clear but deep for a woman's. The yeoman drops on both knees, frightened now by his own boldness, but plucking up courage to answer, "May it please your Majesty; I have the two likeliest little wenches in all Thorpshire, and all their lives it will pleasure them if they but see the Queen and hear a gracious word from her." "God's wounds, but see her they shall right willingly. Come, little maids." A firm white hand is extended from the coach and strokes the two curly heads tenderly. The father and mother press very awkward kisses on the royal fingers. "God bless you both, my maids, you and your worthy parents, and all the good folk like you"; and the coach rattles on, leaving the yeoman staring at two perfumed gloves, embroidered in goldthread, left with each one of the scared little girls.[1]

"Crafty Walt Hollydean," mutters one escorting gentleman to another, "of course he arranged all this." "It seems too natural, but the Queen will come to his house in admirable humor."

Now time must fail us not at least "to speak of Gideon and Barak and of Samson"; and of all the notable pageants, processions, sports, and other high diversions wherewith the Master of Hollydean and the Corporation of Boroughport give pleasure to her Royal Majesty.

Of course Hollydean Hall itself is surrendered to the use of the Queen, and its owners rejoice if they creep late to bed in the hay-mows; but in the neighborhood of the mansion there has arisen a whole small village of buildings for the use of the noble ladies, gentlemen, grooms, yeomen of

[1] An episode precisely like this occurred on one of the Queen's progresses through Huntingdonshire.

the guard, and all the other attendants, great and less, upon royalty. The outside of these structures is covered with leafy boughs and clusters of ripe hazelnuts; the inside is hung with all the fine arras that can be bought or borrowed in the region; the roofs are great masses of ivy leaves; the floors are strewn with sweet herbs and sweet rushes. Out in the park there has been made and flooded a sizable pond the shape of a half moon, and on the water there float many gay skiffs and boats, but above all is a stately pinnace with all its masts, sails, and tackling and brilliant flags and streamers innumerable. Here each night there are magnificent fireworks sent down by post from London.

As for the Queen, the day after her arrival she goes over in solemn state to Boroughport. Outside of Hockley Bar the mayor and all the Corporation, in gold chains, fur tippets, and scarlet robes, are drawn up to meet her, as well as all the Thorpshire country gentlemen, the town burgesses, and the better yeomen.

They dutifully permit themselves to lift their eyes now to a litter wherein sits a woman above sixty, but with a face "very majestic, oblong, fair but wrinkled; her eyes small, yet black and pleasant; her nose a little hooked, her teeth blacked (from too great eating of sugar). She has in her ears two pearls with very rich drops; her hair is of auburn color, but false; upon her head she has a small gold crown; her bosom is uncovered, as all English ladies have it till they marry. She has on a necklace of exceedingly fine jewels, her hands are slender, her fingers rather long, her air stately, her manner of speaking mild and obliging. This day she is dressed in white silk, bordered with pearls the size of beans, and over it a mantle of black silk shot with silver threads. [When she descends and walks] her train is very long and borne by a noblewoman, and instead of a chain she has a collar of gold and jewels." [1]

To the incessant shouts, "God save Queen Elizabeth!" she bows constantly and answers with clear voice, "I thank you, my good people." When his Worship the Mayor kneels before her to proffer his welcome to the town, she graciously pulls off her right glove and offers to be kissed—a hand sparkling with rings and jewels. At the Gild Hall she listens with apparent pleasure and satisfaction to an interminable Latin oration by Master Thwacker, interrupting only once to order a venerable and feeble old nobleman in her escort to cease standing beside her and to take a stool. Then with "You drive me to furbish up my old Latin, Master Orator," she answers "wholly impromptu" with a few Latin sentences not ill chosen—the Corporation having been shrewdly advised that the Queen loves an excuse for displaying her prowess in the Classics.

The next day she condescends to ride out with a crossbow and shoot a fat buck that the prickers send across her way in the park. That afternoon Master Burbage's company, still in the region, gives Kyd's "Spanish Tragedy" in the great gallery. Master Burbage has often exhibited at Court, and the Queen is pleased again to commend him. In the evening there is a spectacle and grand illumination on the pond. Elizabeth seated under a canopy of green satin, watches Nereus, Oceanus, and sundry Tritons sport and splash about in the water. Sylvanus the woodland's god appears making rough advances to a water nymph. He is upset, dragged into the "ocean," and made rollicking sport of by the whole company of sea gods who rush to the

---

[1] This account of Elizabeth is directly from the German traveler, Paul Hentzner, *Travels in England* (1598), and may be taken as accurate and unvarnished. Most English descriptions are too courtly and rapturous.

nymph's assistance. Then the floating pinnace and other craft send up wonderful fireworks. The Empress Titania and all her troop of gauzy fairies dance fantastically upon the greensward, while the squibs and candles cast their unearthly light; and at climax the whole assemblage of gods, nymphs, and fairies gather before the throne, bow with devotion, and sing to sweet harps and rebecs:

> Eliza is the fairest Queen
> That ever trod upon this green.
> Eliza's eyes are blessed stars
> Inducing peace, subduing wars;
> Eliza's hand is crystal bright;
> Her words are balm, her looks are light;
> Eliza's breast is that fair hill
> Where virtue dwells and sacred skill.
> O blessed be each day and hour
> Where sweet Eliza builds her bower. . . .

And so through many stanzas.[1]

Of course on the third day comes the grand climax, and the Master of the Revels is in his glory; no Turkish bashaw more imperious. Ten of the best Boroughport lads divert the Court in the morning by an hour and a half of notable tennis, on which the Queen gazes with fondest interest, although the white-clad maids of honor who sit on stools beside her presently yawn excessively. Then in the afternoon (among other things) Sir Walter craves that his guest honor him again in the gallery, and after the monarch and all her nobles and gentle folk are settled, there begins what at first seems serious business.

A gentleman dressed to life as the usher to her Majesty's principal secretary takes his station by the door, and then

---

[1] These selfsame lines were sung when Elizabeth visited Lord Montague at his Sussex estate in 1591.

comes up a dust-covered, panting fellow in some most astonishing foreign garb, whose clothes hang in tatters about him as if he were a poet ending long and desperate traveling; whereupon the dialog is very like this: [1]

Post: Is Master Secretary here? Did you see Master Secretary? Gentlemen, can you bring me to Master Secretary?

Gentleman Usher: Mr. Secretary is not here. What business have you with him?

Post: Marry, sir, I have letters that import her Majesty's service.

Usher: If the letters concern the Queen, why should you not deliver them to the Queen? You see she is present, and you cannot have a better opportunity.—And he adds many high-flown compliments as to the perfections of her Majesty.

..*Post:* Well, I am persuaded to deliver the letters into her hand; but, sir, they come from the Emperor of China, in a language that she understandeth not.

Usher: Why, then, you are very simple, Post. Though it be that these princes, as the Great Turk and the rest, do always send a translation in Italian, French, Spanish, or Latin, and then it's all one to her.

Post: Doth she understand all these languages and hath never crossed the seas?

Usher: Art thou a Post and hast ridden so many miles and hast not heard what all the world knows—that she speaks and understands all languages in the world that are worthy to be spoken or understood?

Post: It may be that she understands them as a sort, well enough for a lady, but not as well as secretaries should do.

Usher: Tush! what talkest thou of secretaries.—Go on, therefore; deliver thy letters. I warrant she will read them.

[1] The following scene is identical with the one with which Sir Robert Cecil flattered his mistress on one of her visits to Burghley House.

Post: But is it possible that a lady born and bred in her own isle, having but seen the confines of her own kingdom, should be able without interpreters to give audience and answers still to all foreign ambassadors?

Usher: Yea, Post, we have seen that so often tried, that it is here no wonder. But, to make an end, look upon her (with a gesture toward the throne)—how thinkest thou—dost thou see her? Say, truly, sawest thou ever more majesty or more perfection met together in one body? Believe me, Post, for wisdom and policy she is as inwardly suitable as externally admirable.

Post: Oh, sir, why now I stand back; for first you say she hath majesty, and that never likes audacity. Next you say she is full of policy. Now what do I know, if policy may not think to hang up a Post if he be too saucy?

Usher: Oh, simple Post! Thou art the wilfullest creature that liveth. Dost thou not know that, beside all her perfections, the world hath not such a prince for affability? Come, gentleman; come, plowman—the hour is yet to come that ever she refused a petition. Will she then refuse a letter that comes from so great an emperor?—No, no; do as I bid thee. Draw near her, kneel down, kiss thy letters and deliver them; while she is reading them and if ever thou have worse words than "God have mercy, fellow" and "Give him a reward!" never trust me while thou livest.

Whereat the "messenger from China," with irresistibly comical and outlandish genuflections (it is young Burbage himself), does precisely as he is bid and kneels presenting his packet at the throne. The Queen laughs (of a lesser dame we could write—she giggles), thrusts her handkerchief into her mouth, accepts the packet—a silver box of sugared ginger—and answers merrily, "God have mercy, fellow"; and then to the superb Captain of the Bodyguard standing by, "Give him a reward, Raleigh."

So the afternoon is a great success. In the evening is the inevitable banquet—hundreds of magnificent costumes, masculine and feminine, seated at the long tables up and down the great gallery, the vast apartment partly lighted by the "firewheels," and "balls of wildfire" being sent off on the pond for the benefit of the throngs outside, and scores of the best youth of Thorpshire bearing in the innumerable dishes "all glass and silver." Her Majesty of course sits on a dais under a silken canopy, and Captain Andrew on bended knee does the honors of service for the mansion. After all is over Master Thwacker will embalm the list of certain dishes among his antiquarian portfolios: [1]

Her Majesty's Arms in sugar work.
The Several Arms of the greater Thorpshire families.
Castles, forts, ordnance, drummers, trumpeters, and soldiers of all sorts in sugar work.
Lions, unicorns, bears, horses, camels, bulls, rams, tigers, elephants, and other beasts in sugar work.
Eagles, falcons, cranes, bitterns, pheasants, partridges, cocks, owls, and all that fly in sugar work.
Snakes, adders, vipers, frogs, toads and all kinds of worms in sugar work, likewise all manner of fishes.

Finally after the prodigious supply of hearty meats:

Marchpanes, grapes, oysters, mussels, cockles, crabs and lobsters.
Apples, pears, plums, preserves, suckets, jellies, marmalades, pastes, and comfits of all sorts.

At last the feast ends. Sir Walter is aware he has entertained right royally—but the cost has run beyond all expectation. "Three thousand pounds at the least" when all

[1] Very like were the state dishes when the Queen visited the Earl of Hertford's seat at Elvetham.

[365]

the entertainers and artificers are paid. In any case all ends the next morning when the great coach is at the door, the escort is all mounted, and from the wilting foliage of one of the bowers a band of musicians sings a melodious farewell:

> O come again, fair nature's treasure,
> Whose looks yield joy's exceeding measure.
> O come again, Heaven's chief delight,
> Thine absence makes eternal night;
> O come again, world's star—bright eye,
> Whose presence doth adorn the sky;
> O come again, sweet beauty's son;
> When thou art gone our joys are done.

"Nature's Treaure" (as per custom) keeps all her retinue waiting while she stops to beam radiance upon her bending host and her deeply curtseying hostess. Surely it is an impious rumor that two of the maids of honor look so white and weepy, because last night in the last Toilet mysteries, the royal lady lost her temper and used the flat of her mirror upon them as they assisted in the perilous honor of removing her stomacher!

She passes a richly broidered scarf to little Arabella, and with a "Wear this, sweet minion" hands a bracelet of price to the adoring Mistress Anne. (The scarf and the bracelet will be treasured by the receivers' grandchildren.) To Sir Walter and his lady she "protests that the beginning, process, and end of her entertainment has been so honorable they shall hereafter find reward thereof in her special favor." Then after a step toward the coach she turns, as with some afterthought:

"But that tall son of thine, my good Walter. Fair report has come to us of his valor in France, and that last pageant deserves more than the breath of thanks.—Come hither,

Captain. Your sword, Harry Hunsdon." (To the Lord Chamberlain.) "Kneel down quickly, sirrah; they all wait for us." Two light taps on the shoulder and then, "Rise up, Sir Andrew Hollydean."

Boom! boom! boom! go the ordnance as the royal company canters or lumbers up the road to the north. But who of the delighted Hollydeans is hearing anything? Sir Walter has forgotten all about the three thousand pounds.

ILLUSTRATIONS TO "SHEPHERD'S CALENDAR," 1597. DECEMBER.

¶ Index

INDEX